SPORT IN AOTEAROA NEW ZEALAND

This fascinating book investigates the sporting traditions, successes, systems, "terrains" and contemporary issues that underpin sport in New Zealand, also known by its Māori name of Aotearoa.

The book unpacks some of the "cliches" around the place, prominence and impact of sport and recreation in Aotearoa New Zealand in order to better understand the country's sporting history, cultures, institutions and systems, as well as the relationship between sport and different sections of society in the country. Exploring traditional sports such as rugby and cricket, indigenous Māori sport, outdoor recreation and contemporary lifestyle and adventure sports such as marching and parkour, the book examines the contested and conflicting societal, geographical and managerial issues facing contemporary Aotearoa New Zealand sport.

Essential reading for anybody with a particular interest in sport in Aotearoa New Zealand, this book is also illuminating reading for anybody working in the sociology of sport, sport development, sport management, sport history or the wider history, politics and culture of Aotearoa New Zealand or the South Pacific.

Damion Sturm is Senior Lecturer in Sport Management at Massey University, New Zealand.

Roslyn Kerr is Professor of Sociology of Sport and Dean of the Faculty of Environment, Society and Design, at Lincoln University, New Zealand.

SPORT IN AOTEAROA NEW ZEALAND

Contested Terrain

Edited by
Damion Sturm and Roslyn Kerr

LONDON AND NEW YORK

Cover image: Sydenham Junior Rugby Club at the New Zealand Junior Rugby Festival, Queenstown, 2015 (Photo Credit: Emma J. Stewart/ Breitmeyer).

First published 2022
by Routledge
2 Park Square, Milton Park, Abingdon, Oxon OX14 4RN

and by Routledge
605 Third Avenue, New York, NY 10158

Routledge is an imprint of the Taylor & Francis Group, an informa business

© 2022 selection and editorial matter, Damion Sturm and Roslyn Kerr; individual chapters, the contributors

The right of Damion Sturm and Roslyn Kerr to be identified as the authors of the editorial material, and of the authors for their individual chapters, has been asserted in accordance with sections 77 and 78 of the Copyright, Designs and Patents Act 1988.

All rights reserved. No part of this book may be reprinted or reproduced or utilised in any form or by any electronic, mechanical, or other means, now known or hereafter invented, including photocopying and recording, or in any information storage or retrieval system, without permission in writing from the publishers.

Trademark notice: Product or corporate names may be trademarks or registered trademarks, and are used only for identification and explanation without intent to infringe.

British Library Cataloguing-in-Publication Data
A catalogue record for this book is available from the British Library

Library of Congress Cataloging-in-Publication Data
Names: Sturm, Damion, editor. | Kerr, Roslyn, editor.
Title: Sport in Aotearoa New Zealand : contested terrain / edited by Damion Sturm and Roslyn Kerr.
Description: New York : Routledge, 2022. | Includes bibliographical references and index.
Identifiers: LCCN 2021037541 | ISBN 9780367472580 (Hardback) | ISBN 9780367472566 (Paperback) | ISBN 9781003034445 (eBook)
Subjects: LCSH: Sports—New Zealand. | Outdoor recreation—New Zealand. | Sports—Social aspects—New Zealand. | Outdoor recreation—Social aspects—New Zealand. | Maori (New Zealand people)—Sports.
Classification: LCC GV679 .S6 2022 | DDC 796.0993—dc23
LC record available at https://lccn.loc.gov/2021037541

ISBN: 978-0-367-47258-0 (hbk)
ISBN: 978-0-367-47256-6 (pbk)
ISBN: 978-1-003-03444-5 (ebk)

DOI: 10.4324/9781003034445

Typeset in Bembo
by codeMantra

CONTENTS

List of contributors	*vii*
Preface	*xi*
Acknowledgments	*xiii*

1 Introduction   1
Roslyn Kerr and Damion Sturm

2 The neoliberal context and conditions of New Zealand sport   7
Thomas Kavanagh and Robert E. Rinehart

3 Advertising, branding and corporate nationalism: the
contested terrain of the Aotearoa New Zealand All Blacks   19
Steve Jackson and Damion Sturm

4 British traditions and new frontiers for New Zealand cricket   31
Greg Ryan

5 Netball and the (re)production of a dominant femininity:
the good game for kiwi girls   42
Amy Marfell

6 Māori (indigenous) knowledge in sport and wellbeing
contexts: "Tūturu whakamaua kia tina!"   53
Farah Palmer, Bevan Erueti, Angelique Reweti,
Chrissy Severinsen and Jeremy Hapeta

vi Contents

7　Policy, modernisation and the politics of sport integrity　69
Michael P. Sam and Timothy M. Dawbin

8　Symbolic equality in Aotearoa New Zealand
sports organisations　81
Alida Shanks, Sarah Leberman, Sally Shaw and Geoff Watson

9　Sports coaching, education and development: a continually
contested terrain　95
Tania Cassidy

10　The sporting mythscapes of Aotearoa New Zealand　107
Mark Falcous and Sebastian Potgieter

11　Global/local celebrity and national sport stardom:
examining Sonny Bill Williams, Brendon McCullum
and Lydia Ko　119
Damion Sturm and Koji Kobayashi

12　Outdoor recreation in an age of disruption: change,
challenge and opportunity　133
Stephen Espiner, Emma J. Stewart and Megan Apse

13　Masculinities in alternative sports: ultimate Frisbee[TM]
and parkour　146
Hamish Crocket, Richard Pringle and Damien Puddle

14　The contribution of positive relationships to girls wellbeing
in a New Zealand school basketball team　159
Ricardo Milheiro Pimenta and Richard L. Light

15　The health and wellbeing benefits of active ageing
through participation in an annual sports event: marching
out of the margins　171
Trudie Walters and Richard Keith Wright

Index　*183*

CONTRIBUTORS

Megan Apse is a Social Researcher working independently and for a Christchurch-based consultancy in New Zealand.

Tania Cassidy is Associate Professor in Sport Pedagogy and Coaching in the School of Physical Education, Sport and Exercise Sciences, University of Otago, New Zealand.

Hamish Crocket is Senior Lecturer in Health, Sport and Human Performance and Deputy Dean of Te Huataki Waiora School of Health at the University of Waikato, New Zealand.

Timothy M. Dawbin is a PhD candidate in the School of Physical Education, Sport and Exercise Sciences, University of Otago, New Zealand.

Bevan Erueti (Taranaki, Te Ati Haunui-ā-Papārangi, Ngāti Tūwharetoa) is Associate Dean Māori, College of Health, and a Senior Lecturer in the School of Health Science, College of Health, Massey University, New Zealand.

Stephen Espiner is Associate Professor in Parks, Recreation and Tourism, Co-Head of the Department of Tourism, Sport and Society and the Head of Centre – Sustainable Tourism for Regions, Landscapes and Communities, at Lincoln University, New Zealand.

Mark Falcous is Associate Professor in Sociology of Sport at Otago University, New Zealand.

viii Contributors

Jeremy Hapeta (Ngāti Kuia, Rangitāne, Ngāti Raukawa, Ngāti Huia, Ngāti Toa) is Māori Advisor Research Impact and Innovation Team (Office of Research and Enterprise) and Lecturer in the School of Sport, Exercise and Nutrition, Massey University, New Zealand.

Steve Jackson is Professor in Sociology of Sport in the School of Physical Education, Sport and Exercise Sciences at the University of Otago, New Zealand.

Thomas Kavanagh is a Teaching Fellow in Sociology of Sport at the University of Waikato, New Zealand.

Koji Kobayashi is Associate Professor in the Centre for Global Strategy at the University of Otaru, Japan.

Sarah Leberman is Professor of Leadership in the School of Management at Massey University, New Zealand.

Richard L. Light is Professor Emeritus at the University of Canterbury, New Zealand, and Adjunct Professor at Southern Cross University and the University of Technology Sydney, Australia.

Amy Marfell is an independent researcher and General Manager – Sport and Community at Sport Waikato, one of New Zealand's 14 Regional Sports Trusts.

Farah Palmer (Waikato; Ngāti Maniapoto) is Associate Dean Māori for the Massey Business School and Senior Lecturer in the School of Management, Massey University. She is also New Zealand Rugby and Sport NZ Board member and current Chair of the NZ Māori Rugby Board.

Ricardo Milheiro Pimenta is Research Fellow for the Japanese Society for the Promotion of Science at Waseda University, Japan.

Sebastian Potgieter is a Socio-Cultural Teaching Fellow at the University of Otago, New Zealand.

Richard Pringle is Professor of Sport Sociology and Associate Dean of Graduate Research within the Faculty of Education at Monash University, Melbourne, Australia.

Damien Puddle works for Sport Waikato and Hamilton City Council in New Zealand as their Local Play Advocate. He volunteers as the CEO for both Parkour NZ and the international federation Parkour Earth.

Angelique Reweti (Ngāpuhi) is a doctoral candidate in the School of Health Sciences and teaches within Te Pūtahi a Toi/the School of Māori Knowledge, Massey University, New Zealand.

Robert E. Rinehart is an Adjunct Associate Professor at Lincoln University, New Zealand.

Greg Ryan is Professor and Social Historian of Sport at Lincoln University, New Zealand.

Michael P. Sam is Associate Professor in Sport Development and Management at the University of Otago, New Zealand.

Chrissy Severinsen is Senior Lecturer in Public Health in the School of Health Sciences, College of Health at Massey University, New Zealand.

Alida Shanks is a doctoral candidate in sport management in the School of Management at Massey University, New Zealand.

Sally Shaw is Associate Professor in Sport Management at Otago University, New Zealand.

Emma J. Stewart is Associate Professor in Parks and Tourism and Co-Head of the Department of Tourism, Sport and Society at Lincoln University, New Zealand.

Trudie Walters was a Senior Lecturer in the Department of Tourism at the University of Otago, New Zealand, at the time of writing this chapter.

Geoff Watson is Associate Professor in History in the School of Humanities Media and Creative Communications at Massey University, New Zealand.

Richard Keith Wright is Senior Lecturer within the Department of Sport Leadership and Management at Auckland University of Technology, New Zealand.

PREFACE

Early in their careers, both of the editors drew substantially on *Sport in Aotearoa New Zealand Society*, edited by Chris Collins and Steve Jackson, first published in 2003 and later in 2007. Some of these chapters became well-worn from the regular photocopying and scanning to use in various classes. When it became apparent that there were no plans for a third edition, we decided to take up the challenge of creating a new, but similarly structured, text ourselves. When we contacted any authors we could think of who were working in the sociocultural aspects of sport and recreation in New Zealand, we were delighted with the response, and similarly with that from Routledge who were supportive from our first suggestion of the book.

As these chapters were written during 2020, during the peak of the pandemic in New Zealand, we are deeply grateful to all the authors for producing such high-quality work under such difficult circumstances. It was a pleasure to work with so many amazing New Zealand sport and recreation scholars who work across so many domains. Specifically, we are delighted that the book includes work authored right through from postgraduate students to internationally renowned professors.

ACKNOWLEDGMENTS

Damion would like to thank Yi Wei for her love, patience and support along our life journey. It's never easy balancing two careers and raising two children, so thank you for all that you do and provide for us, and for allowing me the space to pursue such endeavours.

I especially want to acknowledge my two bundles of joy – Mikaela and Isaac. I love and am eternally grateful for all the time that we play, grow and develop together. You put everything into perspective and make everything better. And, yes, this is what daddy does when you are sleeping! This book is dedicated to you both.

To my parents, Karen and Bryce, thank you so much for everything you do for us and for helping to make what is often a hectic life more manageable. Much love from our little family.

Roslyn would like to thank her husband Richard for all his immense support, and also her daughter Charlotte who finds it tremendously exciting to have books at home with her mother's name on the front. I am also very grateful to so many amazing colleagues at Lincoln University who are a never-ending source of inspiration.

Damion and Roslyn would also like to extend a heartfelt thank you to all of our contributing authors. Thank you for your willingness to be part of the project and for investing your time and efforts during the challenges and disruptions of a global pandemic. We are also really chuffed with the buy-in across the majority of New Zealand's universities (and beyond), as well as with the spectrum of postgraduate students through to internationally renowned professors that have contributed to the book. Again, thank you all for making this an invaluable critical collection on sport in Aotearoa New Zealand.

1

INTRODUCTION

Roslyn Kerr and Damion Sturm

It is easy to fall back on well-worn clichés that celebrate, lionise, and elevate Aotearoa New Zealand as some form of sporting paradise that is somehow unique, exceptional or distinctive. Indeed, clichés around the nation's ability, in a sporting sense, to "punch above its weight" in terms of global recognition and sporting success for a small nation with limited resources compared to most are often touted, hailed and lauded. In its most obvious guises, New Zealand has recently or regularly achieved in the well-known or increasingly global sporting fields of rugby, cricket, netball, sailing, golf and rugby league, not to mention across other codes including motorsport, combat sports, cycling and rowing. Often "Kiwi" athletes are also prominent, if not successful, in some of the lesser known or less globally celebrated sports such as kayaking, canoe slalom, shot put, equestrian and snowboarding. Additionally, New Zealand's landscape, abundance of natural resources and "clean, green" environmental stereotypes lend themselves to further assumptions of endless opportunities and healthy, active lifestyles being availed and adopted by *most* New Zealanders. Hence, again, no matter how clichéd or problematic the assertion may be, there remains an underlining assumption that sport and recreation operates as a central and celebrated focal point in the daily lives for many in this geographically remote South Pacific nation of approximately 5 million people.

However, in reality, an array of ruptures, undercurrents and contestations distort this initial, idyllic, sporting narrative. Hence, when the appointment of Sport New Zealand's (SNZ) first female CEO, Raelene Castle, was announced in November 2020, she was billed by SNZ chairperson, Bill Moran, as "the ideal person to lead our organisation forward as we continue our important work in addressing declining participation among young people and protecting the strength and integrity of our sector" (Clark 2020, para. 4). Thus, these comments

DOI: 10.4324/9781003034445-1

(and appointment) signpost that, in fact, a range of major issues are confronting sport and recreation while being revealing about New Zealand's current sporting position. Of course, it should also be noted that many of these issues are not "unique" to New Zealand, further disrupting any misplaced notion of sporting "exceptionalism".

The decline of participation of young people is perhaps unsurprising when the wider landscape is considered. As Tania Cassidy's chapter on coaching points out, there has been a decided lack of clear national athlete development pathways for young people to progress in sport. As she notes, the recent creation of the "*Balance is Better*" programme is a bid to address these concerns by focusing on addressing the long-standing problem of an emphasis on winning at an early age, rather than development. Relatedly, Pimenta and Light's chapter points to participation being dependent on young people enjoying sport, including experiencing positive relationships, which requires considerable work from coaches and others involved in sport to facilitate. Moreover, as the range of chapters in this book illustrates, there are a range of other influential factors that contribute to the varied opportunities and experiences that individuals have in sport and recreation in Aotearoa New Zealand.

Several of the chapters included here point to the continuation of historical narratives around gender, ethnicity and age that persist in New Zealand. For example, Greg Ryan highlights the dominance of white males in cricket, Amy Marfell explores the continued emphasis on idealised female appearance in netball, while Walters and Wright demonstrate the significance of the New Zealand-based sport of marching for older women's wellbeing. While a history of sport as a white male enterprise is not unique to Aotearoa New Zealand, the difficulty New Zealand sport organisations face in growing sporting opportunities for a wider and constantly changing demographic indicates that much work is still needed. Indeed, reflecting how far there is still to go, Shanks et al.'s chapter points to the lack of progress that has been made for female representation in sport leadership, notably with seemingly repetitive discourses, statements and a broader lack of action being strong features of New Zealand sport policy over the previous decades.

Referring back to the SNZ announcement, Moran also identified integrity as another issue affecting the sport and recreation sector. Sam and Dawbin explore Aotearoa New Zealand sport policy in depth, arguing that a striking recent change has been the intense emphasis on integrity which often operates as a "catch-all" term to describe a wide array of problematic situations. Sam and Dawbin also suggest that policies are hampered by a modernist emphasis that assumes that best practice can be found through modelling the corporate sector, while in fact reviewing the effects of sporting policies in Aotearoa New Zealand shows that a commercialised focus can encourage less integrity.

Of course, the influence of commercialisation is not just confined to sporting reviews, with the increasing formalisation and professionalisation of many aspects of sport and recreation in New Zealand being significant. Jackson and Sturm's tracing of the All Blacks as a commercial franchise since rugby's professionalisation in the 1990s clearly shows the tensions between preserving the amateur game with its emphasis on national identity and the attraction of global sponsorship and income. These tensions also come through in Sturm and Kobayashi's chapter on three New Zealand sporting celebrities who balance national and global sporting success, as well as opportunities and expectations in very different ways. Yet as Falcous and Potgieter also demonstrate, our understanding of what national identity means for New Zealand sport stems from the way particular narratives of certain events have become part of New Zealand's "mythscape". Thus, as a reflection of the global "great sport myth" coined by Jay Coakley (2014), such narratives, events and mythscapes work to confirm the understanding of sport as inherently "good".

None of these tensions are surprising when considered within the wider context of New Zealand's political history. As Kavanagh and Rinehart point out, the enthusiastic embracing of neoliberalism and "Rogernomics" in the 1980s was a profound political and economic shift that arguably brought increased individual freedoms along with greater inequality. Within sport, it meant the rise of corporate ventures such as professional rugby, privatised facilities and the opportunistic hosting of major and mega-events.

However, long before the advent of neoliberalism was the signing of the founding document of Aotearoa New Zealand legislation: *Te Tiriti o Waitangi* ("The Treaty of Waitangi"). Despite its pretext of guaranteeing a partnership between Māori as *Tangata Whenua* ("people of the land") that were indigenous to New Zealand, and the British Crown, physically represented by Pakeha (white/European) settlers, the inclusion and integration of Māori in sport and recreation has been mixed. As Ryan's chapter points out, while Māori have been over-represented in some sporting codes, primarily rugby, there has been very little inclusion of Māori in sports such as cricket, with similar trends also pervasive for Pasifika populations. The key here is applying the principles of the Treaty itself, which as Erueti et al.'s chapter highlights, means the necessity of ensuring Māori indigenous knowledge is integrated into New Zealand sporting practices. Erueti et al. illustrate how this has occurred in the traditional Māori activity of waka ama, alongside positive developments within rugby due to its large representation of Māori as well as more recently within the New Zealand Olympic team.

The growth of waka ama is one way that indigenous knowledge has become more widely disseminated while also being illustrative of Aotearoa New Zealand's close connections with the land. As Espiner et al.'s chapter also notes, outdoor recreational pursuits have long been assumed to be a part of the New Zealand psyche. Therefore, despite facing challenges in the form of environmental, social and technological change, outdoor leisure pursuits still remain a significant facet of Aotearoa New Zealand's recreational and tourism landscape. Where recreation differs from sport is of course in the absence of competition, a trait also shared by many "alternative" or "lifestyle" sports. Crocket, Pringle and Puddle's chapter focuses on ultimate frisbee and parkour, exploring

4 Roslyn Kerr and Damion Sturm

how these "alternative" activities have undergone processes of sportisation to become institutionalised competitive sports, while also probing the contestable versions of masculinities at play that have characterised sport more broadly since its inception.

As the range of issues raised above indicates, the aim of this book is to highlight and investigate the sporting traditions, successes, systems, "terrains" and contemporary issues that underpin the small nation of Aotearoa New Zealand. Hence, rather than the all too familiar celebratory tropes often underpinning New Zealand sport (e.g., see Falcous and Potgieter's critique of various acclaimed New Zealand sport writers' treatment of key sporting moments in their chapter), the premise of this book is to unpack some of these traditions, successes, systems and "clichés" around the place, prominence and impact of sport and recreation in Aotearoa New Zealand. By doing so, the book brings together a range of issues and themes that help to better understand some of the elements that arguably can be asserted to make certain sport and recreation practices unique or distinct in a New Zealand context, while also readily acknowledging some of the global, commercial, historical, racial and gendered forces at play that have directly impacted upon and influenced sport in Aotearoa New Zealand. Therefore, throughout the book, careful attention is paid to highlighting and unravelling some of the contested, challenging and conflicting societal, geographical and managerial issues facing New Zealand sport and recreation and its alleged "distinctive" features. In order to do so, the book has been thematically organised as follows:

Sport in Aotearoa New Zealand: Contested Terrain opens with a chapter outlining Aotearoa New Zealand's political context, describing several ways in which a neoliberal orientation has played out through sport and recreation. While neoliberalism is certainly not unique to New Zealand, the small size of the nation and the enthusiastic embracing of its philosophies in the 1980s mean that its effects have been exposed in a remarkably transparent and easily discernible manner.

Chapters 3–5 examine the "big three" sports in Aotearoa New Zealand: rugby union, cricket and netball. These three sports have formed the cornerstone of New Zealand's sporting practice and are often perceived to be central to the country's sporting identity. Rugby union and cricket were of course adopted soon after colonisation, with both sports epitomising white male colonial attitudes, while netball was encouraged from the early 1900s as a sport appropriate for women (Ryan & Watson 2018). All three sports dominate the New Zealand media, with the popularity of netball as *the* sport for females, meaning that New Zealand has an unusually high level of coverage of women's sport (Bruce 2008). The chapters here focus on varying aspects of each sport, with Jackson and Sturm tracing rugby union's professionalism and overt commercialisation of the All Blacks, Ryan focusing on the domination of "whiteness" in cricket and Marfell highlighting the continued emphasis placed on traditional feminine ideals in netball.

Chapter 6 explicitly addresses the most important and unique aspect of Aotearoa New Zealand's political and legal landscape: *Te Tiriti o Waitangi*. With colonisation meaning that British sporting traditions dominated from the arrival of British settlers, indigenous Māori games did not feature strongly for a long time. However, as Ereuti et al.'s chapter demonstrates, there are a number of recent contexts in which Māori philosophies are now gaining greater prominence and acceptance.

With the structure of sport in Aotearoa New Zealand being directed by policies from SNZ, these policies have a profound impact on the way participants experience sport in the country. Chapters 7–9 explicitly examine the contemporary landscape in three very different ways. Chapters 7 and 8 focus on the recent phenomonen of sporting reviews, with Sam and Dawbin (Chapter 7) examining the emphasis on "integrity" issues within contemporary sporting reviews that attempt to publicly manage the way policy is both written and implemented through corporate and modernist apparatuses. In a similar vein, in Chapter 8 Shanks et al. also hone in on sport reviews to highlight the lack of progress in gender policies, particularly via the sustained under-representation of female leadership. Related to a lack of progress, Cassidy follows the struggles faced by coaching and athlete development policies in Chapter 9, noting that national frameworks have either proved difficult to implement or remain non-existent.

In line with the prominence of sport within the country and the strong interest in national heroes and successes, Chapters 10 and 11 focus on representations, milestones and memories that undergird New Zealand sport history, traditions and stardom. In Chapter 10, Falcous and Potgeiter analyse the way several events in Aotearoa New Zealand's sporting history have been memorialised around particular discourses that selectively celebrate (and ignore) key facets to reinforce notions of a collective national identity for New Zealand forged through sport. Meanwhile, in Chapter 11, Sturm and Kobayashi also note the contested terrain of sporting achievements through the context of sport stardom, examining how globally successful star athletes are represented in relation to New Zealand national identity.

A shift to outdoor activities underpins the next chapters, with Espiner et al. summarising the immense importance outdoor recreation plays in the recreational lives of New Zealanders (Chapter 12), while also demonstrating that these popular activities are severely impacted upon by natural and human-created disrupters. Taking outdoor activity in a slightly different direction, in Chapter 13 Crocket et al. examine the way two outdoor activities which were not designed as traditional competitive sports are now undergoing processes of sportisation. Underpinning their analysis is also the contestable assertions, embodiments and performances of different masculine ideals in these "alternative" sport realms.

Finally, a focus on wellbeing underscores the remaining chapters. In Chapter 14, Pimenta and Light illustrate how the social relationships facilitated by an athlete-centred coach gave teenage girls a heightened sense of wellbeing while participating in basketball. Examining a completely different age group, in Chapter 15 Walters and Wright note the health benefits and sense of collective

6 Roslyn Kerr and Damion Sturm

belonging for older women engaged in the participant-driven and uniquely New Zealand sport of leisure marching.

As a collection, *Sport in Aotearoa New Zealand: Contested Terrain* affords intriguing insights into and examinations of a variety of salient New Zealand sport topics and areas. This collection metaphorically and symbolically criss-crosses the New Zealand sport terrain to unearth some of the issues and tensions, both large and small, that undergird the contemporary sporting landscape. Ideally such explorations and examinations serve to both resonate with practices and pressures globally, while also highlighting some of the more localised concerns and contestations that are being experienced, navigated and negotiated. By assembling such a strong collection of both authors and topics, the book's intention is to showcase the vibrancy, diversity and intensity of the contemporary sportscape in Aotearoa New Zealand that makes it so ripe for analysis as *contested terrain*.

References

Bruce T. 2008, 'Women, sport and the media', in Thompson S., Obel C., Bruce T. (eds.), *Outstanding: Research about women and sport in New Zealand*, Wilf Malcolm Institute for Educational Research Hamilton, New Zealand, pp. 55–71.

Clark, P. 2020, *Raelene castle appointed CEO of sport NZ*, Sport New Zealand, viewed 20 June 2021, https://sportnz.org.nz/about/news-and-media/media-centre/raelene-castle-appointed-ceo-of-sport-nz/

Coakley, J. 2014, 'Assessing the sociology of sport: on cultural sensibilities and the great sport myth', *International Review for the Sociology of Sport*, Vol. 50, no. 4–5, pp. 402–406.

Ryan, G. & Watson, G., 2018. *Sport and the New Zealanders: A history.* Auckland University Press, Auckland.

2

THE NEOLIBERAL CONTEXT AND CONDITIONS OF NEW ZEALAND SPORT

Thomas Kavanagh and Robert E. Rinehart

Laying the groundwork for New Zealand neoliberalism

Neoliberalism, a set of competitive market-oriented policies that extend into the economy, politics and society (Springer et al. 2016), has had a significant impact on the New Zealand sporting landscape. While the neoliberalisation of the New Zealand economy reinforced colonial economic discrepancies, sport featured heavily in the nation's positioning as an independent, prosperous state (Falcous & Newman 2016; Sam 2015). Neoliberal values were exemplified in the New Zealand sport context in at least three ways: there was a heightening of profession-alisation, as exemplified by the All Blacks; there was a move towards private sector takeover – or sharing – of interventionist, social-based models, as demonstrated by an increase in public-private partnerships; and there grew a greater emphasis on attracting so-called sporting "mega-events" associated with New Zealand.

Contemporary neoliberalism's foundational precepts trace back to the decade of the 1980s. Ronald Reagan and Margaret Thatcher, leaders of the United States and the United Kingdom respectively, disembowelled Keynesian economic social democratic policies, propelling their countries' – and the world's – economies towards heavy reliance upon a free market ethos. In the wake of the Great Depression of the 1930s, John Maynard Keynes propounded an "interventionist" approach, where the government should provide public welfare services and a social safety net for the population (Conway & Heynen 2017). In the perfect storm of late 1970s OPEC nations' oil crisis, Reagan and Thatcher's ascensions to power and a virulent late capitalism, the thirst for free market takeover of much of the Keynesian social infrastructure drove many western nations to the model termed "neoliberalism". In short, the neoliberal agenda demonstrated that private investors were eager, not loath, to enter markets they had formerly eschewed. These included, of course, public media venues, education, health, prisons and sport.

DOI: 10.4324/9781003034445-2

During this period, Aotearoa New Zealand's OECD ranking had slipped from ninth to 19th (Falcous & Newman 2016). Most observers lay this slippage on the twin facts that New Zealand lost its guaranteed export market when Britain joined the European Economic Union and was significantly impacted by the 1973 oil crisis (Te Papa 2020). In response, the New Zealand Treasury argued for a new structure which valued efficiency, growth, competition and private ownership above equality, security and public ownership (Nagel 1998). Labour Prime Minister David Lange agreed with Finance Minister Roger Douglas, and radical free market reforms were introduced, highlighting a dramatic switch from a decades-old democratic socialist economy to a globalised, market-based economy.

This switch towards neoliberalism affected New Zealand citizens along the socio-economic scale in different ways. "For people who do not want the government in their lives ... this [Rogernomics] has been a bonanza", Lange said in 1996. "For people who are disabled, limited, resourceless, uneducated, it has been a tragedy" (cited in Long 2017, para. 25). This admission, after the 1987 Stock Market Crash and his firing of Douglas in 1988, seems to have Lange expressing regret over having let the proverbial genie out of the bottle: by 1986, neoliberalism had arrived in New Zealand.

The rhetorics of "freedom" within "free markets" have instilled in citizens the assumption that individual freedoms are guaranteed by freedom of the market (Harvey 2005). On the contrary, increased surveillance and lack of social safety nets hardly support heightened "freedom". Instead, it has led to increased social inequity, greater economic disparity, larger concentration of resources in smaller numbers of individuals, and, in essence, "interfering with another's freedom" (Neill 1966, p. 7). This "rugged individualist" model, rampant in the United States and Britain, found a welcome home in New Zealand sporting culture. We now turn our attention to neoliberalism and New Zealand sport; specifically, the advent of a hegemonic professional model, public–private synergies and mega-events.

The advent of a hegemonic professional model in New Zealand rugby

Rugby union was forged by financial tensions from its origins, and the move towards a hegemonic professional model in New Zealand rugby union largely mirrored the advent of neoliberal reforms in New Zealand. The three factors that are most significant to this process are the following: (1) the amateur ethos of rugby union, (2) the emphasis on centralisation and (3) the monopolisation of pay TV.

The sport of rugby was divided in 1895, after the middle-class southern clubs clashed with the predominantly working-class clubs of the north of England over monetary reward (Donnelly & Young 1985; White 2004). Thereafter, rugby union codified amateurism as a defining ideology, while rugby league formed as a professional entity (Collins 2008). In Aotearoa New Zealand, rugby union embodied all the characteristics the colonial New Zealander valued – "rural, healthy, egalitarian, dominated by men possessed of admirable physique, natural athleticism, dexterity, adaptability and initiative" (Ryan 2008, p. 43). It was subsequently utilised by the middle classes as a vehicle to keep alive, yet contain, the muscular virtues of the colonial pioneer spirit and established a privileged position as the "national sport" (Phillips 1996).

Rugby union is thus commonly considered a positive social force that unites New Zealanders and a defining feature of regional identity and New Zealand national consciousness (Hope 2002). Successful local and national competitions, a strong national team and a centrally controlled national administration were established, creating an "exceptional" amateur rugby system in New Zealand (Obel 2010). These elements, together with the success of national teams on tours to Britain in the early twentieth century (particularly the All Blacks tours of 1905 and 1924), the introduction of radio broadcasts in the 1930s and free-to-air television coverage in the 1970s became significant in establishing the popularity of rugby union and developing a national identity (Falcous & Newman 2016; Palenski 2012).

Yet these popular, gendered, nostalgic mythologies typically obscured historical tensions and enduring neoliberal and post-colonial structural divisions (Scherer & Jackson 2010). The New Zealand Rugby Union (NZRU) also continued to follow the lead of the English Rugby Football Union (RFU) and maintained its loyalty to the amateur ethos in the face of a widely different context (Ryan 2008). These discourses remained central to rugby union's ideology, trumpeted as a sign of purity and moral superiority over sports that had succumbed to professionalism (Collins 2008). Gradually, however, coaches adopted increasingly professional coaching systems (Donnelly & Young 1985), and administrators began to introduce more competitive playing leagues until financial reward remained the last bastion of amateurism (Phillpots 2000). Demands on elite players' time increased until it was almost impossible for them to develop careers outside rugby (O'Brien & Slack 1999). Amateurism in rugby union came under increasing threat as players began to embrace neoliberal, money-orientated values, and direct (though disguised) payments to players became institutionalised (Sheard et al. 2005).

By the late twentieth century, increasing numbers of players were offered, and began to indicate interest in playing for explicitly commercial enterprises such as Rupert Murdoch's Super League and Kerry Packer's World Rugby Corporation (Collins 2009; O'Brien & Slack 1999). The South African, New Zealand and Australian rugby unions, who were the most vulnerable to losing their star players, formed an alliance (SANZAR) and signed a deal with Rupert Murdoch's News Corporation for the broadcasting rights to the Super 12 and Tri-Nations series for ten years (Pringle 2004; see also Chapter 3). Rugby union's world governing body at the time, the International Rugby Football Board (IRFB), was left with the prospect of losing the southern hemisphere unions (Rayner 2018). On 27 August 1995, rugby union relinquished its central ideological pillar, amateurism, and became an open sport (Collins 2008). The collapse of amateur rugby union coincided with the emergence of neoliberalism. Following Reagan and Thatcher's terms in power, and the establishment of financial deregulation of the "free market", rugby's governing bodies increasingly embraced the ideology of the marketplace and lamented the constraints of amateurism (Collins 2009).

New Zealand rugby's centralised strategies ensured that the All Blacks remained strong as the sport shifted into a professional system (Obel 2010). The NZRU implemented a Council restructure which shifted from a provincial democracy towards a more centralised corporate structure which placed more priority on professional business acumen (Ryan 2008). Players were contracted to the NZRU, as opposed to clubs (O'Leary 2017). Yet unlike most professional sporting models, the NZRU placed heavy emphasis on the international success of the All Blacks, restricting, to some degree, free market outcomes in the rest of New Zealand rugby (Owen & Weatherston 2002). The New Zealand Super rugby teams were not free to maximise profits; they had to work within a structure where the main aim was to maximise the success of the national team. However, this model is not replicated across the globe, and national unions are increasingly vulnerable to northern hemisphere clubs backed by wealthy owners. The greater financial opportunities offered by these unregulated clubs have led to considerable migration of players and coaches to the northern hemisphere (Obel 2010). These tensions are indicative of the ever-increasing professionalisation of rugby union; however, it is important to note "the emergence of a global elite who are well positioned to prosper under a neo-liberal policy culture that opens up countries, and their sporting resources and traditions" (Scherer & Jackson 2010, p. 4).

During the early 1990s, the deregulation of television, in accordance with neoliberalism, had led to considerable increases in rugby union coverage on New Zealand television (Pringle 2004). However, upon purchasing rights to the southern hemisphere competition, NewsCorp on-sold television rights to SKY TV, limiting access to Super 12 and All Blacks tests to paying subscribers. Broadcasting revenue became central to maintaining a professional All Black team and organising New Zealand rugby competitions. By 1997, SKY enjoyed a monopoly position in both pay and digital television, and a lack of anti-siphoning legislation meant that free-to-air networks had virtually no access to telecast live rugby union (Scherer & Jackson 2010). Politicians who urged similar protective legislation were accused of hypocrisy after spending decades insisting on free market philosophies (Ryan 2008). Yet placing rugby broadcasting rights behind a paywall created a conflict; the commercial value of New Zealand rugby union had been established and sustained by allowing the public free television coverage (Hope 2002). By restricting public access SKY was also restricting rugby union's position as "New Zealand's game". As the Rogernomics model led to less government intervention in social programs and more free market opportunities, it meant more resources and income to an elite class of individual athletes, while reducing the social and healthcare impacts for many citizens.

Holding such a dominant position in the national sporting landscape, rugby union's professionalised model has also become the hegemonic structure within New Zealand sport. However, while almost all New Zealand sport has adopted elements of professionalism, most sport continues to operate on an amateur basis. Consequently, many sporting organisations function within a state of tension – in many ways being forced towards professionalisation, while still operating within sporting structures that remain amateur.

Public–private synergies

The second way that neoliberalism had a significant effect on the changing terrain of New Zealand sport was the move towards privileging elite sport as a national aspirational value and concomitant synergies between public monies and private profits. Social democracies, stressing equivalent opportunities and chances, encourage mass participatory practices: practices that enhance public health through exercise and sport. Elite sport in neoliberal times moves tax monies towards limited participation of a select few and drives society's "sport participation" towards sport spectatorship, resulting in higher private gains. While sport elitism flourished under neoliberalism in New Zealand, it did not result in an increase in the quality or quantity of mass participation rates in sport *per se* during the decades of the 1990s and 2000s (Sport New Zealand 2015; Sturm & Rinehart 2018; Walker & Leberman 2012).

In July 2010, the bidding process for a world-class, "tier one" velodrome in New Zealand was initiated by Murray McCully, Minister for Sport and Recreation, and Prime Minister John Key. With the objective of catering to both elite sport and the community, the aims of the proposed Centre of Excellence were to "expand high performance cycling outcomes; increase awareness of and participation in cycling disciplines within the community; and nurture increased levels of high performance cycling talent" (Avantidrome 2020, para. 2). The emphasis, it must be noted, was on "excellence". While the Avantidrome admits that there are "accessible community facilities" (which are the Gallagher Bike Skills Park, Perry Playground, and Te Awa River Ride, arguably utilised by up to "1600 visitors per week" [Avantidrome 2020]), the primary purpose of this velodrome is to "build on the success of Bike NZ's high performance programme" (Blackpear 2019, para. 1).

In fact, the "recreation" aspect of then-Minister of Sport and Recreation Murray McCully's portfolio – delivering mass recreation opportunities for the New Zealand public – was not realised by the construction of the Avantidrome (Sturm & Rinehart 2018). Instead, junior and under-23 cyclists find more apropos – living costs, less media pressure – at the world class, but "second tier", SIT Zero Fees Velodrome in Invercargill (opened in 2006), where development of budding elites is regaining hold (Bonthuys 2018; Southland NZ 2018).

When private corporations agree to the public–private enterprise, they expect something in return for their contributions. In the case of the Avantidrome,

12 Thomas Kavanagh and Robert E. Rinehart

the branding for Avanti Bikes is quite clear. As a New Zealand company since 1985, Avanti have gone the route of many "non-mainstream" sporting or sport-related companies: they sponsor events to a niche market; they design and produce equipment and product from an insider's point of view; and they aspire to have their names (and logos when appropriate) splashed everywhere (Goldman & Papson 2000; Rinehart 1999). The primary sponsor of the Zero Fees Velodrome in Invercargill, on the other hand, is the Southern Institute of Technology. In the late 1990s, SIT's unique no fees policy was initially subsidised by the Community Trust of Southland, Invercargill Licensing Trust, Invercargill City Council, Southland District Council and local businesses (Crayton-Brown 2012). It became a self-perpetuating scheme, resulting in a "financial surplus of $1m in the first year" (Crayton-Brown 2012, para.12).

Just as stadia for some sport codes seek corporate sponsorship and "brand" their sites – for example, Wellington's Westpac Stadium becoming "Sky" Stadium in 2020 (Wenman 2019); FMG (Farmers' Mutual Group) Stadium in Hamilton – or certain "events" – for example, the Mitre 10 Cup (rugby) or the ANZ Premiership (netball) – alternative and non-mainstream sport companies follow a similar pattern. But the infusion of a pre-Rogernomics' type of social democratic funding like the SIT-sponsored Invercargill Velodrome demonstrates that other models may be feasible as well.

Sporting mega-events

As an isolated island nation with a small population, and without the billions of dollars required for infrastructure, New Zealand is unlikely to ever host an Olympic Games (Sturm & Lealand 2012). However, New Zealand has hosted a number of significant global sporting events (Commonwealth Games, America's Cup, Rugby and Cricket World Cups) that could broadly be described, using Roche's (2000, p. 1) definition, as mega-events:

> "Mega-events" are largescale cultural (including commercial and sporting) events which have a dramatic character, mass popular appeal and international significance. They are typically organised by variable combinations of national governmental and international non-governmental organisations and thus can be said to be important elements in "official" versions of public culture.

These are events which hold significant social, political, economic and ideological consequences for the host and attract considerable media coverage (Horne 2007, 2015). Hosting of sports mega-events is often promoted as a valuable opportunity to increase tourism, stimulate inward investment and promote the host venue as a global presence among the world's populations (Gruneau & Horne 2015; Horne 2015; Roche 2000). Yet, sports mega-events have also been associated with large-scale public expenditure, construction of infrastructure and urban redevelopment which provide significant short-term gains for corporate interests but long-term issues for public stakeholders (Hall 2006). Over the past 60 years, every Olympic Games has seen cost overruns, with an average cost overrun of 179% (Flyvbjerg & Stewart 2012). Despite this poor record of significant overspending, cities and countries continue to bid for sporting mega-events because event promoters, property developers and construction firms profit the most while the public sector provides a deficit guarantee (Müller 2015). Additionally, in many cases the sport-related legacies so proudly claimed have not been realised, and instead "white elephant" stadiums are left behind that receive little to no public use and continue to lose value awaiting investment or demolition (Roche 2017). As such, critics question their value, impact and legacy, arguing that hosting such events are more likely to be an indication of greater integration of neoliberal policy, exacerbating the gap between rich and poor and ceding local authority to organisations that lack political accountability (Horne 2015).

Clearly, in New Zealand, the simultaneous moves towards professionalisation of sporting structures and for-profit, public–private synergies made bidding for sporting mega-events a natural effect and result of neoliberalism. Sporting mega-events in New Zealand exploded during the 2010s, with successful bids for the Rugby World Cup (2011), co-hosting of the Cricket World Cup (2015, with Australia) and the Women's Rugby World Cup (2021, delayed to 2022 due to COVID-19). The Rugby World Cup (RWC) 2011, for example, was bid for with the promise that the tournament would generate significant tourism and economic benefits, adding $408 million to GDP and tax revenue; however, more recent RWC estimates suggest a deficit of $200 million on top of the $555 million of public spending on stadium requirements (Jackson 2013). Characteristically for sporting mega-events, the RWC underestimated the costs and overestimated the benefits to the local economy, society and culture (Whitson & Horne 2006).

New Zealand and Australia's successful joint bid for the 2023 FIFA Women's World Cup represents the opportunity to host the largest sporting mega-event to take place on New Zealand shores. The rhetoric surrounding the event is typical of sporting mega-events that occur within a neoliberal framework. Phil Twyford, the minister of economic development, was effusive in his enthusiasm:

> The women's game has grown exponentially across the planet, so this is a fantastic time for us to be hosting the event … We know the eyes of the world will be on New Zealand and Australia while the tournament is running.
>
> *(Rollo 2020, para. 14)*

While he attempted to dampen expectations on a return from the government investment due to COVID-19, Sport and Recreation Minister Grant Robertson insisted, "Regardless of that, the exposure for New Zealand from a tournament like this is massive", while NZ Football chief executive Andrew Pragnell speculated, "the economic impact's really big – around the $180 million vicinity" (Chan-Greene & O'Keefe 2020, para. 5). Links were drawn to the 2019 edition, which was held in France, and was broadcast to more than 1.12 billion viewers (Publicis Sport & Entertainment 2019), and projections that estimate 1.5 million spectators will attend in 2023 (Football Federation Australia and New Zealand Football 2019). Thus, promoting the FIFA World Cup is not just commodifying the built environment but also promoting the dissemination and legitimisation of pro-market values of neoliberalism (Ribeiro & Junior 2017). Discourses of opportunity, economic prosperity and global exposure legitimise the civic, political and economic elites' efforts to capitalise on the commodification of Aotearoa New Zealand, while simultaneously neglecting notions of social inclusion and democratic participation (Ribeiro & Junior 2017).

Subsequently, the New Zealand Government has made the not insignificant contribution of $25 million towards hosting the event. This is especially substantial given the impact of COVID-19 on sporting organisations, with many competitions suspended or cancelled, and $265 million allocated in the government's 2020 Budget towards a Sport Recovery Package (Office of the Minister of Finance 2020).

Contributing to the successful New Zealand/Australia bid was the ability to meet sustainability criteria surrounding infrastructure, namely, being able to run the tournament without the need to build further stadiums. However, several of the New Zealand stadiums would require significant investment before they were ready to host FIFA World Cup matches. In particular, Orangetheory stadium (Christchurch's semi-permanent stadium) would "rely heavily on a significant amount of temporary installations and upgrades to meet several tournament requirements, including those relating to back-up power and other temporary infrastructure" (FIFA 2020, p. 80). This stadium was a temporary solution after the extensive damage to AMI stadium during the Christchurch earthquake in 2011, yet the investment required has been justified in reference to the forecast 28,000 visitors and $23 million the tournament was expected to bring to the Christchurch economy (Hayward 2020). However, the millions of dollars required to upgrade Orangetheory stadium to FIFA World Cup standard will come just 12 months before Christchurch's new $473 million covered stadium is expected to be completed. Orangetheory stadium was only ever supposed to last for five years and has required considerable investment since 2011. The proposal to decommission the stadium and construct a brand-new venue shows an extravagance of taxpayer spending, and little in terms of tangible public benefit. In fact, FIFA's bid evaluation report states,

> A moderate budget for this has been put forward by the bidder, but willingness to invest considerably in the stadium is expected to be dampened if authorities decide to press ahead with proposals to decommission this venue after 2023 and build a completely new stadium for the city.
>
> *(FIFA 2020, p. 80)*

Yet, sporting mega-events are structured in the public discourse as a community good rather than a neoliberal mechanism for attracting mobile capital and a particular type of people (Hall 2006). In the wake of the economic downturn caused by COVID-19, the event is promoted as crucial to furthering tourism recovery and economic development while viewpoints that critique costs to the taxpayer, the elite focus and question the benefits to community well-being are ignored or disregarded.

Conclusion

In this chapter, we have demonstrated that systematic professionalisation within sporting codes has resulted in a concentration of resources away from public needs and wants towards private interests. While pride in one's football or rugby national team may result in a "feel-good" mentality, spectatorial participation does not achieve health aims for most citizens. As well, it is arguable that the gradual move towards professionalisation actually resulted in athletes ceding many of their bargaining powers, powers that may have been fought for (the most evident being rugby players) during a more Keynesian, union-sympathetic, interventionist age.

We have shown that public–private synergies, particularly for stadium (re) builds and legacy projects, resulted in concentration of wealth to a few, while public relations' work argues to the contrary. The befuddled, Orwellian logics of some public–private sports projects demonstrates that sport is, indeed, a world of passionate allegiance and that the passions of a sports-driven public may lead to illogical expenditures that result in great benefits to a few private entrepreneurs with lesser benefits to the majority of citizens.

Finally, and in concert with many of the concentration-of-wealth arguments, we discussed the bids for mega-events. These require massive public monies and private backing. Under a neoliberal system, some of these rationales for a nation state to participate in global sporting mega-events may act as "false flags". As Bourdieu writes, "the nation-state, or better yet the supranational state" (1998, para. 18) is an exercise in "moral Darwinism … [that] institutes the struggle of all against all and *cynicism* as the norm of all action and behaviour" (para. 14, *emphasis in original*).

Thus, the neoliberal economic model has influenced – and is, in turn, influential towards – contemporary Kiwi sporting practices in the twenty-first century. Ensconced in late-capitalist ethos and following much of the rest of the English-speaking world, New Zealand has an opportunity to reject the harmful aspects of the neoliberal model and return to a semblance of Keynesian (and Scandinavian) economics. But will they, when the short-term gratification and profits are so tempting?

References

Avantidrome. 2020, *History of the Avantidrome*, viewed 31 May 2020, https://www.avantidrome.co.nz/about/history.
Blackpear. 2019, Avantidrome, home of cycling, viewed 31 May 2020, https://blackpear.nz/portfolio-item/hoc/

16 Thomas Kavanagh and Robert E. Rinehart

Bonthuys, E. 2018, *A tale of two velodromes*. Stuff, viewed 31 May 2020, https://www.stuff.co.nz/southland-times/102999614/a-tale-of-two-velodromes

Bourdieu, P. 1998, 'The essence of neoliberalism: what is neoliberalism? A programme for destroying collective structures which may impede the pure market logic', trans. J. J. Shapiro, *Le Monde Diplomatique*, viewed 10 July 2020, https://mondediplo.com/1998/12/08bourdieu

Chan-Greene, M. & O'Keefe, M. 2020, *Football: Women's world cup poised to cash in on post-coronavirus tourism boom*. Newshub, viewed 1 July 2020, https://www.newshub.co.nz/home/sport/2020/06/football-women-s-world-cup-poised-to-cash-in-on-post-coronavirus-tourism-boom.html

Collins, T. 2008, '"The first principle of our game": the rise and fall of amateurism: 1886–1995', in G. Ryan (ed.), *The changing face of rugby: The union game and professionalism since 1995*, Cambridge Scholars Publisher, Newcastle upon Tyne, pp. 1–19.

Collins, T. 2009, *A social history of English Rugby Union*, Routledge, London.

Conway, D. & Heynen, N. 2017, 'The ascendancy of neoliberalism and emergence of contemporary globalization', in D. Conway & N. Heynen (eds.), *Globalization's contradictions: Geographies of disciplines, destruction and transformation*, Routledge, Oxon, pp. 17–34.

Crayton-Brown, K. 2012, *Zero Fees a runaway success*. Stuff, viewed 24 December 2020, https://www.stuff.co.nz/southland-times/news/6266832/Zero-Fees-a-runaway-success

Donnelly, P. & Young, K.M. 1985, 'Reproduction and transformation of cultural forms in sport: a contextual analysis of rugby', *International Review for the Sociology of Sport*, Vol. 20, no. 1–2, pp. 19–38, https://doi.org/10.1177/101269028502000103

Falcous, M. & Newman, J. 2016, 'Sporting mythscapes, neoliberal histories, and post-colonial amnesia in Aotearoa/New Zealand', *International Review for the Sociology of Sport*, Vol. 51, no.1, pp. 61–77, https://doi.org/10.1177/1012690213508942

FIFA. 2020, *FIFA women's world cup 2023: Bid evaluation report*, viewed 03 July 2020, retrieved from https://img.fifa.com/image/upload/hygmh1hhjpg30lbd6ppe.pdf

Flyvbjerg, B. & Stewart, A. 2012, *Olympic proportions: Cost and cost overrun at the Olympics 1960–2012*, (Working Paper), University of Oxford Said Business School, Oxford.

Football Federation Australia & New Zealand Football. 2019, *As one: Australia and New Zealand bidding to host the FIFA women's world cup 2023*, viewed 29 June 2020, https://resources.fifa.com/image/upload/bid-book-australia-and-new-zealand.pdf?cloudid=fwtyuwa9pb3encyeqlwc

Goldman, R. & Papson, S. 2000, *Nike culture: The sign of the Swoosh*, Sage, London.

Gruneau, R. & Horne, J. (eds.). 2015, *Mega-events and globalization: Capital and spectacle in a changing world order*, Routledge, London.

Hall, C. 2006, 'Urban entrepreneurship, corporate interests and sports mega-events: the thin policies of competitiveness within the hard outcomes of neoliberalism', *The Sociological Review*, Vol. 54, no. 2, pp. 59–70, https://doi.org/10.1111/j.1467-954X.2006.00653.x

Harvey, D. 2005, *The brief history of neoliberalism*, Oxford University Press, Oxford.

Hayward, M. 2020, *Christchurch stadium needs millions spent before hosting FIFA women's world cup*. Stuff, viewed 29 June 2020, https://www.stuff.co.nz/sport/football/world-game/121952095/christchurch-stadium-needs-millions-spent-before-hosting-fifa-womens-world-cup

Hope, W. 2002, 'Whose All Blacks?' *Media, Culture & Society*, Vol. 24, no. 2, pp. 235–253, https://journals.sagepub.com/doi/10.1177/016344370202400205

Horne, J. 2007, 'The four "knowns" of sports mega-events', *Leisure Studies*, Vol. 26, no.1, pp. 81–96.

Horne, J. 2015, 'Assessing the sociology of sport: on sports mega-events and capitalist modernity', *International Review for the Sociology of Sport*, Vol. 50, no. 4–5, pp. 466–471.

Jackson, S. 2013, 'The 2011 Rugby World Cup: the politics and economics of a sport mega-event', *Movement & Sport Sciences – Science & Motricité*, Vol. 79, pp. 5–10.

Long, J. 2017, *Flashback – The beginning of GST and radical financial changes for Kiwis*. Stuff, viewed 6 March 2020, https://www.stuff.co.nz/national/politics/ 97459362/ flashback--the-beginning-of-gst-and-radical-financial-changes-for-kiwis

Müller, M. 2015, 'The mega-event syndrome: why so much goes wrong in mega-event planning and what to do about it', *Journal of the American Planning Association*, Vol. 81, no.1, pp 6–17, https://doi.org/10.1080/01944363.2015.1038292

Nagel, J. 1998, 'Social change in a pluralitarian democracy: the politics of market liberalization in New Zealand', *British Journal of Political Science,* Vol. 28, no.2, pp. 223–267.

Neill, A. S. 1966, *Freedom – Not license!*, Hart Publishing, New York.

Obel, C. 2010, '"Club versus country" in rugby union: tensions in an exceptional New Zealand system', *Soccer & Society*, Vol. 11, no. 4, pp. 442–460, https://doi. org/10.1080/14660971003780362

O'Brien, D. & Slack, T. 1999, 'Deinstitutionalising the amateur ethic: an empirical examination of change in a rugby union football club', *Sport Management Review*, Vol. 2, no. 1, pp. 24–42, https://doi.org/10.1016/S1441-3523(99)70088-4

Office of the Minister of Finance. 2020, *Cabinet Paper CAB-20-SUB-0219: COVID-19 response and recovery fund foundational package*, viewed 01 July 2020, retrieved from https:// treasury.govt.nz/publications/information-release/budget-2020-information-release

O'Leary, L. 2017, *Employment and labour relations law in the Premier League, NBA and International Rugby Union*, T.M.C. Asser Press, The Hague.

Owen, P. & Weatherston, C. 2002, 'Professionalization of New Zealand rugby union: historical background, structural changes and competitive balance', *University of Otago Economics Discussion Papers,* Vol. 0214, viewed 27 April 2020, https://pennstatelaw. psu.edu/_file/Sports%20Law%20Policy%20and%20Research%20Institute/owen%20 weatherston%20competitive%20balance%20nz%20rugby.pdf

Palenski, R. 2012, *The making of New Zealanders*, Auckland University Press, Auckland.

Phillips, J. 1996, *A man's country? The image of the pakeha male – a history* (Revised), Penguin, Auckland.

Phillpots, K. 2000, 'The professionalisation of rugby union', PhD thesis, University of Warwick, Coventry, UK.

Pringle, R. 2004, 'A social-history of the articulations between rugby union and masculinities within Aotearoa/New Zealand', *New Zealand Sociology*, Vol. 19, no. 1, pp. 102–128.

Publicis Sport and Entertainment. 2019, *FIFA women's world cup France 2019: Global broadcast and audience report*, viewed 30 June 2020, retrieved from https://img.fifa.com/ image/upload/rvgxekduqpeo1ptbgcng.pdf

Rayner, M. 2018, *Rugby union and professionalisation: Elite player perspectives*, Routledge, London.

Ribeiro, LC de Q. & Junior, OA dos S. 2017, 'Neoliberalization and mega-events: the transition of Rio de Janeiro's hybrid urban order', *Journal of Urban Affairs*, Vol. 39, no. 7, pp. 909–923, https://doi.org/10.1080/07352166.2017.1328976

Rinehart, R. 1999, 'Extreme sports – grass roots or electronic sport?' *Business of Sport*, Vol. 4, no.1, pp. 8–9.

Roche, M. 2000, *Megaevents and modernity: Olympics and expos in the growth of global culture*, Routledge, London.

Roche, M. 2017, *Mega-events and social change: Spectacle, legacy and public culture*, Manchester University Press, Manchester.

Rollo, P. 2020, *FIFA women's world cup 2023 "mega-event" dwarfs rugby's global showpiece*, Stuff, viewed 29 June 2020, https://www.stuff.co.nz/sport/football/world-game/121955379/fifa-womens-world-cup-2023-megaevent-dwarfs-rugbys-global-showpiece

Ryan, G. (ed.) 2008, *The changing face of rugby: The union game and professionalism since 1995*, Cambridge Scholars Publisher, Newcastle upon Tyne.

Sam, M. 2015, 'Sport policy and transformation in small states: New Zealand's struggle between vulnerability and resilience', *International Journal of Sport Policy and Politics*, Vol. 7, no. 3, pp. 407–420.

Scherer, J. & Jackson, S. 2010, *Globalization, sport and corporate nationalism: The new cultural economy of the New Zealand All Blacks*, Peter Lang, New York.

Sheard, K., Dunning, E. & Mangan, J. 2005, *Barbarians, gentlemen and players: A sociological study of the development of rugby football*, 2nd edn., Routledge, Florence, SC.

Southland NZ. 2018, *SIT zero fees velodrome*, viewed 31 May 2020, https://southlandnz.com/invercargill/sport-recreation/sit-zero-fees-velodrome

Sport New Zealand. 2015, *Sport and active recreation in the lives of New Zealand adults: 2013/14 active New Zealand survey results*, viewed 21 May 2020, retrieved from http://www.sportnz.org.nz/assets/Uploads/attachments/managing-sport/research/Sport-and-Active-Recreation-in-the-lives-of-New-Zealand-Adults.pdf

Springer, S., Birch, K. & MacLeavy, J. (eds.). 2016, *Handbook of neoliberalism*, Routledge, Oxon.

Sturm, D. & Lealand, G. 2012, 'Evoking "New Zealandness": representations of nationalism during the 2011 (New Zealand) Rugby World Cup', *New Zealand Journal of Media Studies*, Vol. 13, no. 2, pp. 46–65, https://doi.org/10.11157/medianz-vol13iss2id15

Sturm, D. & Rinehart, R. 2018, 'Home of (or *for?*) Champions? The politics of high-performance/elite and community sport at New Zealand's Home of Cycling', *Leisure Sciences*, Vol. 40, no.7, pp. 711–722, https://doi.org/10.1080/01490400.2018.1534628

Te Papa. 2020, *Rogernomics*, viewed 6 March 2020 http://sites.tepapa.govt.nz/sliceof-heaven/web/html/rogernomics.html

Walker, S. & Leberman, S. 2012, 'Structure of sport and its management in New Zealand and Australia', in S. Leberman, C. Collins & L. Trenberth (eds.), *Sport business management in New Zealand and Australia*, 3rd edn., Cengage, South Melbourne, pp. 24–53.

Wenman, E. 2019, *Wellington's Westpac Stadium loses its letters ahead of rebrand*. Stuff, viewed 31 May 2020, https://www.stuff.co.nz/dominion-post/news/117805868/wellingtons-westpac-stadium-loses-its-letters-ahead-of-rebrand

White, A. 2004, 'Rugby union football in England: civilizing processes and the de-institutionalization of amateurism', in E. Dunning, D. Malcolm & I. Waddington (eds.), *Sport histories: Figurational studies in the development of modern sports*, Routledge, London, pp. 53–70.

Whitson, D. & Horne, J. 2006, 'Underestimated costs and overestimated benefits? Comparing the outcomes of sports mega-events in Canada and Japan', *The Sociological Review*, Vol. 54, no 2, pp. 71–89, doi: 10.1111/j.1467–954X.2006.00654.x

3

ADVERTISING, BRANDING AND CORPORATE NATIONALISM

The contested terrain of the Aotearoa New Zealand All Blacks

Steve Jackson and Damion Sturm

Introduction

Although they represent a relatively small nation of 5 million people and compete in a relatively minor global sport, the All Blacks remain one of the most successful and recognised teams and brands in world history. While critics may argue that they have only won three of the nine quadrennial Rugby World Cups since 1987, the fact that the All Blacks have been successful in more than 75% of all games played for over a century and with less funding and resources than larger competitor nations is quite remarkable. Arguably, it is the combination of its size (Sam & Jackson 2015), success and uniqueness that has made the All Blacks both a successful national team and an attractive and valuable global commodity for media broadcasters and corporate sponsors.

This chapter examines the emergence and transformation of the New Zealand All Blacks, one of the most successful sporting franchises in history, following the professionalisation of global rugby in the early 1990s. Tracing the impact of both a global media deal and subsequent attraction of corporate sponsors, the All Blacks are examined as both a national team and a global corporate brand. In particular, the chapter introduces the concept of corporate nationalism (Silk et al. 2005) which has been defined as the process by which corporations use the currency or value of "the nation" – its symbols, images, stereotypes, collective identities and memories as part of their overall branding strategy (Jackson 2004). Drawing on advertisements and promotional campaigns from the early days of professionalism to the contemporary era, this essay highlights the contested terrain of the All Blacks (Jackson & Scherer 2013; Scherer & Jackson 2013) as they try to balance and negotiate the benefits of globalisation with the threat it poses to local/national culture and economies.

DOI: 10.4324/9781003034445-3

The professionalisation and commodification of New Zealand rugby

In the early 1990s when the sport was officially amateur but could more accurately be described as semi-professional, key media interests were beginning to identify the value and unexploited potential of rugby union as a global media commodity (Jackson et al. 2001). Two rival media moguls, Kerry Packer and Rupert Murdoch, who were already in the midst of a battle over television broadcast rights to Australian Rugby League, embarked on what Peter FitzSimons (1996) described as the "Rugby War". In the lead-up to the 1995 Rugby World Cup, there was a frenzy of action with Kerry Packer's World Rugby Corporation (WRC) working aggressively behind closed doors to establish broadcast deals and to offer lucrative contracts to the best rugby players in New Zealand, Australia and South Africa. This bold move forced the New Zealand Rugby Union (NZRU), alongside the other two Unions, to accept that the amateur days of rugby were over. In turn, they quickly signed players to contracts, created new league competitions and identified sources of funding to support the new professional game.

The key to averting the biggest crisis of its century-old existence was NZRU's signing of a ten-year, $800-plus million-dollar broadcast deal with Rupert Murdoch's News Limited (SKY TV) (in conjunction with its Australian and South African counterparts). The deal was a major turning point for the sport of rugby generally and New Zealand's national game in particular. Global media companies need content, and sport has proven to be a valuable form of entertainment that appeals to large, passionate audiences. In turn, media programming that interests large numbers of fans attracts corporate sponsors seeking brand exposure particularly when this can be linked to events, such as sport, that have positive associations with youth, health and nationalism (Jackson 2013).

For New Zealand rugby, the new media and sponsorship deals were essential for survival. However, they were also symbolic of wider changes in both the nation and the national game which were now, more than ever before, located within a wider global economy and subject to foreign interests and control. The nature of New Zealand's global-local dilemma, as well as rugby's centrality within that debate, was noted at the time by former All Black and New Zealand Ambassador, Chris Laidlaw (1999, pp. 177–178):

> There is a real danger that control of the game in New Zealand will steadily be wrested away from New Zealand hands … It is the bottom line of the national personality that is at stake and we are in danger of letting McWorld have it for a few pieces of silver. The massive deals that have been done with major sponsors were the only way of preserving that sovereignty.

These comments capture the double-edged sword of globalisation; that is, to secure enough funding to survive in the future, one might need to negotiate a deal that requires relinquishing some control and ownership to foreign interests. This challenge is a theme that repeats over the next two decades and is evident in the ongoing challenges faced by New Zealand as a nation and the All Blacks as a team operating within the new global economy of sport (Scherer & Jackson 2007; Scherer & Jackson 2010; Scherer & Jackson 2013). The next section outlines why global sportswear company Adidas decided to invest in the sport of rugby and how it negotiated its entry into the New Zealand marketplace and its sponsorship of the All Blacks via the process of corporate nationalism.

The Adidas All Blacks

By the late 1990s, Rupert Murdoch's SKY network had bought the rights to screen a new global sport product – rugby, which included the most successful franchise in history, the All Blacks. Given the power and reach of Murdoch's global media empire, corporate sponsors were quick to seize the opportunity. Thus, when the All Blacks jersey sponsorship came up for renewal in 1997, local brand Canterbury, which had been associated with the team for 75 years, was going to face some stiff competition. Enter Adidas, a sportswear brand with a long history of success, a global network of sports and athletes, and deep pockets.

It was the link between rugby and national identity that attracted Adidas to New Zealand. Adidas CEO Robert Louis-Dreyfus suggested that outside soccer-crazy Brazil, "no other country links with sport as New Zealand does with rugby and the All Blacks" (Lilley 1999, p. 11). That, along with the marketing potential of the All Blacks, led Adidas to enter into one of its biggest team contracts at that time, estimated at more than 100 million dollars over five years. The agreement represented a strategic decision by Adidas (a) to capitalise on a new sport/team that was likely to succeed outside Europe and North America and (b) to harness the major marketing opportunity that media coverage of rugby provided (Adidas thinks big 1999, p. 11). The relationship demonstrates the economic and cultural currency of gaining global exposure through the integrated media technologies of Rupert Murdoch. As a global sporting commodity (and the most powerful within world rugby), the All Blacks became a very attractive "brand". Yet, from a business and public relations standpoint, the relationship with the NZRU presented Adidas with at least two major challenges. First, as a global company they needed to establish a local identity and link their brand with the legendary All Blacks remembering that they were displacing long- standing sponsor, Canterbury. And, second, they needed to find an innovative way of launching and leveraging the "Adidas" All Blacks globally. The solution was to engage in corporate nationalism by, first, aligning the Adidas brand with key aspects of New Zealand culture and identity, and by, second, leveraging the cultural and economic value of the All Blacks to enhance the global profile of the brand.

There were two key themes evident in Adidas' emergence into New Zealand and their sponsorship of the All Blacks. First, there was the emphasis on "Black"

22 Steve Jackson and Damion Sturm

not only in terms of the team's jersey but also in terms of event promotions. The second key theme was the focus on tradition and history which aligned with NZRU's own marketing at the time. Indeed, the NZRU was eager to reinforce the tradition and pride associated with the black jersey perhaps due to concerns associated with emergence of the first generation of fully paid, professional All Blacks.

Adidas used several different strategies to emphasise the two key themes and to construct the image of a long-standing relationship between the brand and the All Blacks. A multifaceted campaign was launched coinciding with the commencement of the sponsorship which included the development of the Rugby Institute in Palmerston North, the release of new product, television and radio advertisements and event promotions. The first and most anticipated initiative was the unveiling of the new All Black jersey on 1 July 1999. The solid black jersey featured the characteristic Silver Fern (the symbol of New Zealand sports teams) on the left breast and the Adidas logo on the right. The key point of difference was a change from the white collar, which had been characteristic of All Black jerseys over the past 75 years, to a new black Chinese-style collar. Notably, this style was reminiscent of the jerseys worn by the legendary 1905 All Black team dubbed "the Originals" (Black collar return 1999). Arguably, this was one of the first attempts by Adidas to engage in the process of corporate nationalism, a strategy to localise and link their brand with the history and symbolic value of All Blacks and New Zealand.

The product launch was accompanied by two television commercials: the "Captains" commercial, which focused primarily on the local market, and the "haka" advertisement which was not only developed primarily for the global market but also screened in New Zealand. The first commercial "Captains" (1999) was a carefully crafted promotional strategy. Directly linked to the launch of the new Adidas All Black jersey, there was a clear attempt to link the past, present and future of the All Blacks. Shot in black and white, the commercial employed numerous nostalgic techniques. In keeping with the theme of history and tradition, the commercial was staged in an old locker room and featured seven New Zealand captains pulling on jerseys that had been "lovingly recreated to the specifications of the All Black uniforms of each era" (Pull up to 1999, p. 30). As each of the captains (Charlie Saxton, 1945–1946; Fred Allen, 1946–1949; Sir Wilson Whineray, 1958–1965; Sir Brian Lochore, 1966–1970; Graham Mourie, 1976–1982; Wayne Shelford, 1987–1990 and Taine Randell, 1999) pulled their jersey over their head, they were reincarnated as the next chronological leader concluding with 1999 captain Taine Randell. Perhaps the most striking and memorable feature of the "Captains" television advertisement was New Zealand singer Fiona McDonald's rendition of the World War II song "Bless Them All". Collectively, the references to boys and battle celebrated and reproduced the idea of a dominant form of masculinity that links valued traits like courage and honour with rugby, physicality and war (Phillips 1987).

Arguably, Adidas employed nostalgic imagery and music in conjunction with sport heroes of the past and present, in order to symbolically manufacture a long-standing relationship with New Zealand rugby. The product launch and television campaign were supported by a variety of other promotions including posters with phrases such as "Black is thicker than blood" and "The legacy you face is more intimidating than any opposition". In combination, these promotional campaigns invoke a sense of the honour and pressure associated with living up to the success and heritage of the All Blacks. Moreover, they represent examples of corporate nationalism to the extent that Adidas, as a global corporate sponsor, was using the cultural and economic value of the All Blacks history and tradition not only to localise by winning over the New Zealand public but also to leverage and elevate its brand within the global economy.

Judging by consumer demand both nationally and internationally, Adidas was very successful in its marketing objectives. Despite the loss of the 1999 Rugby World Cup, Adidas had successfully linked its brand to the All Blacks as evidenced by several advertising and sponsorship awards. However, approximately one year after its brand launch, Adidas was challenged in relation to its second major television advertising campaign titled "Black", which featured the famous Ka Mate haka. This particular case highlights that, despite the power and influence of global corporations, they cannot always do as they please and they do face resistance. The next section examines the contested terrain of the commercialisation of the All Blacks haka, including an intellectual property rights lawsuit.

Adidas, the Ka Mate haka and cultural resistance

In 2000, Adidas released a global advertising campaign titled "Black" (2000) that featured a 60-second television commercial that featured the well-known Ka Mate haka. For those unfamiliar with rugby or the All Blacks, the haka is popularly referred to as a pre-game war challenge that is performed prior to each international test match. Following the respective national anthems, the All Blacks face their opponents near centre field and, in unison, perform a highly aggressive series of chants and body movements. While there are different types of haka for different social occasions, the All Blacks use two official haka, the traditional Ka Mate and Kapo o Pango which was introduced in 2005.

The 2000 Adidas "Black" advertisement was an expensive and highly technical venture that involved an international team of cinematographers. Shot in black and white and slow motion and involving live footage from actual games, the commercial featured intermittent images of moko-faced Māori warriors and the All Blacks performing the Ka Mate haka. According to Howard Greive, from Saatchi advertising, the concept "was always centred around the *haka* and a 'primal' sound design …We always wanted to create a sort of primal scary ad" (Primal Team 1999, p. 22). Furthermore, Greive offers us insights into why

24 Steve Jackson and Damion Sturm

Adidas sponsored the All Blacks and why they specifically wanted to use the haka in their advertising:

> You have to go back to: why did Adidas come in and pay all that money for the All Blacks? It's because the All Blacks can deliver something to their brand that no other team or individual can in sport. Which is they are playing a very, very physical game – it has been called the last warrior sport in the world. Not only that, but they play it with intensity and the easiest way to judge that intensity is through the *haka*. That is exactly what Adidas wanted in terms of what the All Blacks could bring to their brand. It introduced a gutsier, more primal element – as well as the sheer artistry of rugby.
>
> *(Primal Team 1999, p. 22)*

Greive's comments are revealing. First, although he does not explicitly refer to globalisation or corporate nationalism, he does note the unique contribution that the All Blacks can make to the Adidas brand. However, most interesting is Greive's statements about the intensity and physical nature of their style that sets the All Blacks apart, a style characterised by a primal, warrior element that is best expressed through the haka. Notably, despite the fact that Adidas and the NZRU had reportedly consulted with Māori about the use of the haka in the advertisement (Scherer & Jackson 2008), on 11 June 2000, the front page of the *Sunday News* displayed the headline "$1.5m for haka". The accompanying article outlined the position of particular Māori who believed that they "deserve a large slice of the $120 million adidas sponsorship of NZ rugby, because the sportswear giant used Māori imagery in its branding" (Reid 2000, p. 1).

To understand the lawsuit one must understand the history of the Ka Mate haka. This particular haka was composed in the 1820s by Te Rauparaha, a famous Chief of the Ngāti Toa tribe. To this extent Ngāti Toa claimed ownership of the haka and in their view deserved financial compensation from both Adidas and the NZRU. While this particular legal claim failed, in 2011 the NZRU signed a formal agreement with Ngāti Toa allowing the All Blacks to perform Ka Mate at games. Moreover, in 2014 Parliament signed the "Ka mate Attribution Bill" which formally recognised Te Rauparaha as the composer of the haka and acknowledging Ngāti Toa's rights to guardianship of the cultural ritual. This result certainly highlights how groups, in this case a particular Māori tribe, can challenge and resist global corporations. Yet, this story is much more complicated, and while it is beyond the scope of this chapter to provide a full analysis, it is worth noting that the haka itself has been challenged for a range of reasons. For example, the haka has been criticised for giving the All Blacks an unfair psychological advantage, promoting aggression and violence and reproducing stereotypes of Māori warrior culture (Gee & Jackson 2017; Jackson & Hokowhitu 2002). Moreover, the origins of the Ka Mate haka have no connection to sport, and few New Zealanders are aware that Te Rauparaha was responsible for killing members of rival Māori tribes (Revington 1997).

The "Captains" and "Black" advertisements provide two different examples of corporate nationalism associated with the promotional culture of Adidas and their sponsorship of the All Blacks in the early years of professional rugby. Since that time Adidas has remained a loyal sponsor signing a ten-year, $200 million deal in 2009 and renewing this with another $500 million dollar contract from 2021 to 2025. Next, this chapter explores the arrival of another major sponsor of New Zealand rugby: AIG.

AIG, corporate nationalism and the All Blacks

In 2012 Adidas was joined by another major global corporate sponsor, American-based insurance and investment firm, AIG. As a brief background AIG is a company with over 90 years of history which has annual revenue in excess of $US60 billion, 88 million clients in 130 countries and almost 50,000 employees. One might wonder why an American insurance company would be interested in sponsoring a team from a small nation competing in a minor sport, but as this chapter has outlined the All Blacks offer something unique with respect to brands seeking to cut through the clutter of brand sign wars (Goldman & Papson 1996). Yet, it was another major sporting development that likely explains AIG's interest in New Zealand rugby– the 2009 decision by the International Olympic Committee to add Sevens Rugby to the 2016 Olympics. The entry of Sevens rugby into the Olympics was not only going to stimulate the global growth of the sport by nations seeking to win the six new medals on offer (Women's and Men's gold, silver and bronze), as the largest sporting spectacle on earth the event would provide unprecedented brand exposure for corporate sponsors. Thus, AIG signed a nine-year deal (2012–2021) estimated at $20 million per year.

For this large investment AIG made some major demands including prime logo placement in the centre of the All Blacks jersey – something that had been sacred for over 100 years. In addition, they negotiated the sponsorship to include the rebranding of all New Zealand national teams: the All Blacks, the Black Ferns, the Māori All Blacks, Men's and Women's Sevens teams and the Under-20 Men's team. The new sponsorship deal raised immediate concerns from a range of stakeholders. Adidas had concerns about how AIG's brand visibility might clash with theirs. The NZRU had concerns about the potential demands and loyalty of the new American sponsor. However, as if echoing Chris Laidlaw's lament a decade earlier, the former CEO of NZRU, Steve Tew, expresses the challenges of being a small player in the global economy of sport and the need to compromise:

> We have a business that has roughly $100 million turnover a year – it needs to be significantly more than that if we're going to survive, if we're going to grow the game at the community level and if we're going to retain players. It's a challenge for us, and we need some money.
>
> *(Sponsor's logo 2012, para.7)*

The arrival of AIG as a sponsor of the All Blacks was not unlike that of Adidas including a range of promotional strategies that can be broadly described as corporate nationalism. Yet, it is important to note that the context, including the state of New Zealand rugby, had changed over the past two decades. For example, there has been increasing pressure to compete with foreign teams offering more money to players, and, perhaps most frustrating, the international body responsible for developing the sport, World Rugby, continues to be dominated by the interests of UK-based nations resulting in a lack of leadership to make the game safer, more entertaining and more global.

Beyond these challenges New Zealand Rugby (NZR)[1] was facing another crisis linked to the culture of the sport and its governance. Scandals linked to sexist and homophobic behaviour by elite players brought the sports' leadership and its reputation into question (Jackson 2019). In response, NZR established the Respect and Responsibility Review (RRR) which operated from October 2016 until August 2017 and involved a range of high-profile New Zealand athletes and sport administrators, including Kathryn Beck (Chair), Jackie Barron, Lisa Carrington, Kate Daly, Liz Dawson, David Howman, Sir Michael Jones, Keven Mealamu and Dr Deb Robinson and Robyn Cockburn (Author of the Review). Ultimately, six recommendations were made under the following categories: Inclusive Leadership, Better People, Wellbeing, Gender Equality, Engagement and Communications and Accountability and Independence. The aim here is not to examine these recommendations in detail but rather to note how NZR and its sponsors responded to a crisis from a public relations and branding perspective.

Today, we are witnessing a wide range of social movements targeting various forms of oppression and discrimination including #MeToo and #BlackLivesMatter. Notably, many global corporations and their brands have been targeted because of either their historical links with oppression (e.g., slavery) or their role in reproducing stereotypes through their promotional culture. This has led to a wave of corporate social responsibility initiatives that demonstrate a company's commitment to progressive change. Arguably, negative publicity associated with rugby in the late 2010s prompted NZR and its sponsors to want to be seen to be proactive and progressive.

In 2018, NZR, in partnership with sponsor AIG released an advertisement titled: "Diversity is Strength" (2018) which was filmed in Osaka, as part of a broader campaign link to the 2019 Rugby World Cup in Japan. In brief, the two-minute advertisement shows both the All Blacks (Men's) and Black Ferns (Women's) teams arriving at the Osaka stadium. Players are serious and contemplative as they prepare in the dressing room and then enter the playing field. The next images are of the two teams standing together, alternating male and female players who, in unison, put their right hand on their heart (which is notably just under wear the All Blacks silver fern brand logo is located). At the same time we hear the following words from the narrator: "The next battle is truly formidable and deeply devious. It is discrimination. An enemy that cannot be fought alone, it must be defeated together. It will take more than 15, it will takes thousands, millions". As we hear these words we see the players stretching their jersey to reveal the colours of the rainbow with seven military jets flying overhead revealing the same colours. The narrator then states: "Diversity is Strength, Join our Team". It is clear that the advertisement was part of a public relations campaign that was responding to the RRR report, but it was also timely in relation to the New Zealand government's commitment to supporting sport for girls and women. To this extent, the multi-social media campaign enabled NZR and its corporate sponsors (AIG and Adidas) to align their mission statements and brands with key social issues, including homophobia and gender equity, displaying a willingness to be proactive.

In January 2020, AIG announced that it was ending its lucrative sponsorship after 2021. While the departure of AIG will result in a major loss of revenue in the short term, it may be a positive in the long term. This is due, in part, to the fact that the integrity and politics of brands and sponsors are increasingly under the social microscope. Notably, the integrity of AIG has been questioned on numerous occasions including a 2005 financial fraud scandal, the 2008 Global Financial Crisis government bailout which resulted in the company receiving $US192 million of taxpayer funding only to see its executives receive over $US450 million in bonuses, and more recently media reports that AIG has denied an insurance pay out following the death of one of its clients, a police officer, who died of COVID-19. We might ask whether the All Blacks, or any other sport organisation, should risk being associated with such a sponsor as well as what the alternatives might be in a (post) COVID-19 world.

COVID-19 challenges and New Zealand Rugby in "crisis"

The COVID-19 pandemic has impacted on all nations and their sports, including New Zealand. However, in the case of NZR, there were major challenges even prior to the global viral crisis. As previously mentioned rugby was already facing a steady decline in male participation rates, a mounting exodus of players and coaches lured by wealthy foreign teams and a lack of leadership from World Rugby to develop a game that was safer in terms of player welfare but also had a vision for international growth and development.

In many ways, the disruptions caused by COVID-19 to NZR on the field sped up some of its local/global and commercial transformations off the field. With scheduled tours and an array of test matches scrapped, as well as delays to the Rugby Championship (with South Africa notably absent), a more localised focus came to the fore. Indeed, NZR seemingly became increasingly insular and New Zealand-centric in its planning, resulting in public spats between Sanzaar partners Australia and South Africa playing out in the media. For example, Rugby Australia publicly rebuked NZR for its self-interest and bullying tactics, notably in relation to the Rugby Championship schedule, as well as for publicly suggesting that Australian teams would need to submit "expressions of interest" to be considered for a revamped super rugby competition (Knowler 2020). Moreover,

28 Steve Jackson and Damion Sturm

upon confirming its temporary withdrawal from the Rugby Championship and from super rugby permanently, South Africa laid the blame on NZR for its increased domestic and trans-Tasman focus (Kermeen 2020).

In terms of professional competitions, Super rugby was cancelled after eight rounds in mid-March to later be replaced by Super Rugby Aotearoa in June. Comprised only of the five New Zealand franchises, its local success and notable crowd attendances saw the competition retained, with an additional series against Australian teams in 2021 and an enlarged competition, inclusive of a Pasifika franchise, envisaged for 2022 (Hinton 2020).

Intriguingly, despite the promotional campaigns noted earlier around gender equity and diversity, a patriarchal focus on securing the return of men's rugby meant that scant attention was initially paid to women's rugby by NZR. Seven scheduled home test matches for the Black Ferns were cancelled, the domestic "Farah Palmer" Cup a late addition to the calendar alongside the men's Mitre 10 Cup, while improvised trial and "Barbarian" games were added in a piecemeal fashion to give representative players game time prior to the 2021 Rugby World Cup (postponed to 2022 due to COVID-19). Finally, the fact that Pasifika men comprise 40% of super rugby and 50% of All Blacks team compositions has renewed concerns of exploitation by NZR, particularly as assurances of greater inclusion for a Pasifika team continue to be marginalised or delayed (Extra time 2020).

Conclusion

Compared to most countries facing the COVID pandemic, New Zealand has, to date, responded extremely well, and there is much optimism about sport and in particular the hosting of the 2021 Rugby World Cup, the first major gender-neutral named, global sporting event (albeit, subsequently postponed until 2022). Yet, as this chapter has demonstrated, the fate of New Zealand, and its sport, is now inextricably connected to wider global forces. In the post-COVID-19 era NZR will continue to face challenges. Commercially, short term without the All Blacks brand as readily available for global commodification, dissemination and consumption on the field, NZR is reliant upon making its current localised focus sustainable and economically viable. In November 2020, NZR acknowledged a projected loss of $45m which, alongside further cost-cutting measures, may necessitate new commercial endeavours orientated around "revenue growth" opportunities and private equity investors (Hinton 2020). Such transformations have the potential to further dilute or on-sell the All Blacks brand. As such the challenges of securing long-term media broadcasting and sponsorship deals required to operate elite, professional sport will remain for the foreseeable future.

Note

1 The New Zealand Rugby Union name was shortened to New Zealand Rugby in 2013.

References

'Adidas thinks big over All Blacks'. 1999, *National Business Review*, 16 July, p.11.

'Black'. 2000, *YouTube*, viewed 24 August 2020, www.youtube.com/watch?v=aQ0_1wiSQv0

'Black collar "return to heritage": new look jersey explained'. 1999, *Otago Daily Times*, 12 July, p.17.

'Captains'. 1999, *YouTube*, viewed 20 August 2020, www.youtube.com/watch?v=5gAiOkMGx4g&t=2s

'Diversity is Strength'. 2018, *YouTube*, viewed 1 September 2020, www.youtube.com/watch?v=JI4_6-J8HXU

'Extra Time: why does New Zealand Rugby keep getting it wrong?' 2020, *Radio New Zealand*, October 9, viewed 13 November 2020, https://www.rnz.co.nz/news/sport/427968/extra-time-why-does-new-zealand-rugby-keep-getting-it-wrong

FitzSimons, P. 1996, *The rugby war*, HarperCollins, Sydney.

Gee, S. & Jackson, S. J. 2017, *Sport, promotional culture and the crisis of masculinity*, Palgrave Macmillan, London.

Goldman, R. & Papson, S. 1996, *Sign wars: The cluttered landscape of advertising*, Guilford Press, New York.

Hinton, M. 2020, *New Zealand Rugby reeling from $45m revenue hit: 'We have to seize chance for a reset'*. Stuff, viewed 13 November 2020, https://www.stuff.co.nz/sport/rugby/super-rugby/300150908/new-zealand-rugby-reeling-from-45m-revenue-hit-we-have-to-seize-chance-for-a-reset

Jackson, S. J. 2004, 'Reading New Zealand within the new global order: sport and the visualisation of national identity', *International Sport Studies,* Vol. 26, no. 1, pp. 13–29.

Jackson, S. J. 2013, 'Reflections on communication and sport: on advertising & promotional culture', *Communication and Sport*, Vol. 1, no. 1/2, pp. 100–112, https://doi.org/10.1177/2167479512472049

Jackson, S. J. 2019, 'Reflections on the 2019 Rugby World Cup: the state of the All Blacks and global rugby in the age of globalization', *Japanese Journal of Sport Sociology,* Vol. 27, no. 1, pp. 3–18.

Jackson, S. J., Batty, R. & Scherer, J. 2001, 'Transnational sport marketing at the global/local nexus: the Adidasification of the New Zealand All Blacks', *International Journal of Sports Marketing and Sponsorship*, Vol. 3, no.2, pp. 185–201, https://doi.org/10.1108/IJSMS-03-02-2001-B006

Jackson, S. J. & Hokowhitu, B. 2002, 'Sport, tribes and technology: the New Zealand All Blacks *Haka* and the politics of identity, *Journal of Sport and Social Issues*, Vol. 26, no. 1, pp. 125–139, https://doi.org/10.1177/0193723502262002

Jackson, S. J. & Scherer, J. 2013, 'Rugby World Cup 2011: sport mega-events and the contested terrain of space, bodies and commodities', *Sport in Society*, Vol. 16, no. 7, pp. 883–898, https://doi.org/10.1080/17430437.2013.791156

Kermeen, C. 2020, *NZ Rugby rejects South Africa's blame game over Super Rugby exit but won't buy into war of words*. Stuff, Viewed 13 November 2020, https://www.stuff.co.nz/sport/rugby/all-blacks/300120434/nz-rugby-rejects-south-africas-blame-game-over-super-rugby-exit-but-wont-buy-into-war-of-words?rm=a

Knowler, C. 2020, *The sorry tale of NZ Rugby and Rugby Australia's crumbling relationship*. Stuff, viewed 11 November 2020, https://www.stuff.co.nz/sport/rugby/all-blacks/122954493/the-sorry-tale-of-nz-rugby-and-rugby-australias-crumbling-relationship?rm=a

Laidlaw, C. 1999, *Rights of passage: Beyond the New Zealand identity crisis*. Hodder Moa Beckett, Auckland.

Lilley, R. 1999, 'Adidas thinks big over All Blacks', *National Business Review,* 16 July, p. 11.

Phillips, J. 1987, *A man's country: The image of the Pakeha male, a history,* Penguin, Auckland.

'Primal team'. 1999, *Admedia,* Vol. 14, no. 9, pp. 22–23.

'Pull up to the jumper'. 1999, *Admedia,* Vol. 14, no. 9, p. 30.

Reid, N. 2000, '$1.5m for haka', *Sunday News,* 11 June, p. 1.

Revington, M. 1997, 'Haka hooligans', *New Zealand Listener,* 6 December, p. 22.

Sam, M. & Jackson, S. J. 2015, 'Sport and small states: the myths, limits and contradictions of the legend of David and Goliath', *International Journal of Sport Policy and Politics,* Vol. 7, no. 3/4, pp. 319–327, https://doi.org/10.1080/19406940.2015.1031814

Scherer, J. & Jackson, S. J. 2007, 'Sports advertising, cultural production and corporate nationalism at the global-local nexus: branding the New Zealand All Blacks', *Sport in Society,* Vol. 10, no. 2, pp. 268–284. https://doi.org/10.1080/17430437.2013.791156

Scherer, J. & Jackson, S. J. 2008, 'Cultural studies and the circuit of culture: advertising, promotional culture and the New Zealand All Blacks', *Cultural Studies/Critical Methodologies,* Vol. 8, no. 4, pp. 507–526, https://doi.org/10.1177/1532708608321577

Scherer, J. & Jackson, S. J. 2010, *Sport, globalisation and corporate nationalism: The new cultural economy of the New Zealand All Blacks,* Peter Lang, Oxford.

Scherer, J. & Jackson, S. J. 2013, *The contested terrain of the New Zealand All Blacks: Rugby, commerce, and cultural politics in the age of globalisation,* Peter Lang, Oxford.

Silk, M., Andrews, D. & Cole, C. (eds.). 2005, *Sport and corporate nationalisms,* Berg, Oxford.

4
BRITISH TRADITIONS AND NEW FRONTIERS FOR NEW ZEALAND CRICKET

Greg Ryan

Introduction

On 6 January 2020, the record for most runs by a New Zealand male Test cricketer was exceeded by Ross Taylor, a player of Samoan heritage. Taylor's achievement in a sport that has been dominated by the Pākehā (European) middle class in Aotearoa New Zealand prompts questions about both the past and the future of cricket. Why, in view of a significant contribution to many sports and dominance of some, have Māori and Pasifika players had only a sporadic impact on cricket? Given recent and projected changes to New Zealand's population profile, what are the prospects for New Zealand Cricket (NZC) to achieve ethnic and gender diversity in its player base against a long-term trend of declining participation in the major team sports? Answers to these questions require examination of a range of demographic, geographic, socio-economic and cultural barriers to Māori and Pasifika engagement. They also involve an evaluation of recent strategies by NZC and its provincial affiliates to mitigate such barriers in the context of a dramatic transformation in the finances and global profile of cricket following the emergence of the twenty20 format from 2003.

While there have been some accounts of those sports, and especially the rugby codes, in which Māori and Pasifika dominate and excel (e.g., Grainger 2009), there has been little systematic explanation of their relative absence from others. At the height of a 2003 debate about Māori involvement in New Zealand cricket, following from a claim by former international captain Martin Crowe that they lacked the temperament, patience and concentration required for the game (Hoby 2003), journalist Richard Boock wrote: "Apathetic and sometimes-bigoted local associations, costs, the strangeness of the game and an understandable dislike of English colonialism had combined to repel almost anyone with brown skin" (Boock 2003, para. 3). But this explanation is equally

DOI: 10.4324/9781003034445-4

32 Greg Ryan

problematic in that it ignores colonial settings, especially in South Asia and the Caribbean, where cricket came to exert a powerful influence beyond its European introduction (e.g., Guha 2002, Beckles & Stoddart 1995). It also ignores the fact that the earliest reports of cricket in New Zealand during the 1830s involved Māori playing with missionaries at the Bay of Islands, that there were some exclusively Māori clubs by the 1880s and that several Māori players appeared in provincial representative teams before the end of the nineteenth century at a time when cricket, rather than rugby, was the "national game". There is no cultural reason why growth ought not to have continued given that Māori readily accepted other dominant nineteenth-century sports, for example, rugby and horse racing, and that sport emerged as one of the few ways for Māori, and later Pasifika, to interact with and gain acceptance from the dominant Pākehā population (Ryan 2004; Ryan & Watson 2018). Rather, it seems that the neglect of Māori within cricket was passive rather than active. There were also geographic and socio-economic factors at play whereby the largely urban base of organised cricket placed it out of reach of a mainly rural and economically vulnerable Māori population. Without the need for manicured grounds and expensive equipment, rugby was an easier and cheaper game to develop in a rural setting. It is no coincidence that the few Māori players who were visible in representative cricket before the late twentieth century were all atypical products of the elite and urban Pākehā education system (Ryan 2004; Potiki 1954). It is also evident that the communal emphasis of Māori society led to a preference for true team games rather than a game such as cricket with its emphasis on the performance of the individual within the team. Indeed, this is still the case as surveys of Māori sport and leisure involvement indicate a greater preference than Pākehā for group or team rather than individual activities, and especially those such as waka ama that also provide a context for the collective expression of resurgent Māori identity and culture (e.g., Sport New Zealand 2015; Wikaire & Newman 2014). Hokowhitu (2003) also argues that the physicality of rugby came to reinforce broader stereotypes of Māori. It was widely perceived that their sporting prowess was genetic, derived not from application and mental resolve but from a natural athleticism not far removed from the supposedly primitive, animalistic world of the pre-European period. Such arguments endure in claims that Māori and Pasifika prefer "high velocity" and "high impact" contact sports. But such assertions are countered by the fact that a dominant summer preference is softball, which is not a contact sport, while the success of all leading athletes requires a great deal of application rather than simply intrinsic "flair" (Ryan & Watson 2018). A 2005 analysis of "carded athletes", those formally aligned to the New Zealand Academy of Sport, revealed that cricketers were 85% Pākehā, 8% Māori, 3% Pasifika and 3% "other", with the surprisingly high figure for Māori suggesting a pattern whereby some players who claimed Māori identity were not publicly recognised as such by administrators and supporters of the game. In a revealing contrast, 43% of rugby union players identified as Māori and 18% as Pasifika, while the figures for rugby league were 28% and 58%, with 21% and

New Zealand cricket **33**

19% for netball (Palmer 2006). In sum, cricket was a game without traditions and role models to inspire Māori participation.

Rapid Māori urbanisation and relative economic improvement from the 1950s, followed by significant immigration by Pasifika peoples to New Zealand from the 1960s, did not translate to noticeable participation in cricket. For Pasifika, the explanation is less straightforward in that Kirikiti, an indigenous variant of cricket, was Samoa's national sport and also played in other parts of the Pacific from the late nineteenth century. Therefore, Samoan immigrants in particular were familiar with cricket (Sacks 2019). But for both Māori and Pasifika the barrier to cricket was and is socio-economic. The "Rogernomics" reforms of the 1980s liberalised trading hours and created new leisure opportunities for many, but they also produced wage stagnation, casualisation of the labour market, high unemployment by the early 1990s and significant wealth disparity (Roper 2005). In this setting, many had to weigh their income needs and employment patterns, not least being weekend work, variable hours and split shifts, against their desire to play sport. Notwithstanding that young Māori in particular have a higher rate of sporting involvement than other ethnicities in New Zealand (Sport New Zealand 2019a), the preference has been for activities that are cheaper, shorter or more flexible in their timing. By 2017 the average hourly wage for Māori employees was 82% of that for Pākehā while that for Pasifika was 77% of the Pākehā average (Treasury 2018). A 2018 survey revealed that 19% of Pasifika cited cost as a barrier to sporting participation against a national average of 12%. Other barriers above the national average were difficulties in getting into training or games and not having the necessary equipment or places nearby to participate (Sport New Zealand 2019a). For Pasifika, greater obligations to church and family have also been cited as a barrier to sporting participation (Gordon et al. 2013). Under these circumstances, a relatively expensive and time-consuming sport such as cricket was unlikely to attract new players.

From the 1980s onwards a handful of Māori and Pasifika players progressed to men's and women's provincial representative cricket. Beyond mention during the 1990s that two men's international players, Adam Parore and Heath Davis, had Māori ancestry, as did Maia Lewis who eventually captained the women's team, there was no analysis as to why this was a rarity. Nor was there meaningful discussion of Murphy Su'a as the first Samoan to play for New Zealand during the early 1990s (Ryan 2007). During 2000–2001 NZC lent its support to various initiatives for Māori and Pasifika cricket and Kirikiti tournaments, including the Pacific Cup, a tournament featuring other Pacific nations and won by the Māori team. But these produced no momentum as they were not accompanied by longer term player development strategies (Payne & Smith 2001).

It was not just that the rugby codes in particular satisfied Māori and Pasifika sporting preferences at a community level, but they also offered lucrative opportunities and enticements at an elite level where cricket did not. Within a decade of rugby union's move to open professionalism in 1995, Māori and Pasifika each constituted around a third of New Zealand Super Rugby players.

34 Greg Ryan

The establishment of the Māori- and Pasifika-dominated Auckland Warriors in 1995 reinforced similar pathways in rugby league. Other players found opportunities overseas in both rugby codes (Field 2013; Paul 2007; Te Puni Kōki 2006). As Samoan academic Damon Salesa observed, "If you have the potential to be a rugby or league player, male or female, they will find you. The pathways into the rugby system don't rest on self-navigation" (Chapman 2018, para. 8). By contrast, the pathways into cricket for anyone, let alone Māori and Pasifika, were haphazard. The game was slow to adopt professional structures and coherent development programmes to sustain periodic player growth (Astle 2014). The national men's team generally struggled throughout the 1990s and early 2000s and spectator interest dwindled. The nadir was undoubtedly the professional players strike during 2002 when what were essentially justified demands for improvements to pay and conditions entirely failed to generate public sympathy (Ryan 2002). Significantly, improved international results, such as appearances in successive men's World Cup finals in 2015 and 2019, certainly revived public support, but there is a lingering sense that such results are more the exception than the rule. Indeed, a survey of professional and semi-professional players in 2012 revealed that 64% were "not aware of, and do not understand, how the NZC high-performance programme works" (Alderson et al. 2012a, para. 10).

From the mid–2000s, an increasing number of elite players, both men and women, secured lucrative contracts in new international twenty20 leagues. But in other respects, the rise of twenty20 as a vehicle to attract new players may not have been a blessing for New Zealand cricket. As a consequence of the small domestic market and hence the limited broadcast and sponsorship resources available to attract talented overseas players, NZC's twenty20 competitions have become secondary to the Australian Big Bash League (BBL), and latterly the Women's Big Bash League (WBBL) played at the same time. While these and other international leagues in India, Britain and the Caribbean have received substantial live coverage in New Zealand, along with a plethora of international cricket from all parts of the world, only the final of the New Zealand men's domestic 50 over competition has ever been televised and until the 2019–2020 season coverage of the men's domestic twenty20 competition extended no further than one of the three fixtures in each round, with very little equivalent coverage of the women's competition before the 2018–2019 season. Nor does it help that cricket coverage has been confined to pay television since the late 1990s, thus limiting the audience to those who are willing and able to pay. An impressionable generation of potential players are therefore less likely than those in other countries to find their inspiration and role models from local competitions. In sum, it is unsurprising that 2018 Sport New Zealand (SNZ) survey results for those "interested in trying or doing more of an activity" reveal that while potential interest in basketball, netball, rugby and touch ranged between 5% and 9% for Māori and Pasifika, interest in cricket was less than 1% for both (Sport New Zealand 2019a).

Specific initiatives to promote adult Māori cricket began during the 2010–2011 season with the formation of the Northern Districts Māori Cricket team for a series of regional and later inter-provincial fixtures. The team was described as "dedicated to providing a pathway to encourage talented young Māori sportspeople to pursue achievement through cricket" (Northern Districts Cricket 2014). Its manager, Graeme Stewart, stated that there were more Māori playing cricket than was generally realised, but there was a need to increase their exposure in order to create role models and mentors. "At the moment, kids go to a test match and see a player like Black Cap Trent Boult and have no idea that he is Māori, and his whakapapa is from Wellington" (Mackenzie 2013, para. 11). Stewart's vision, as yet unfulfilled, is for Māori sides within New Zealand's six major associations and a national team on the model used by rugby to provide additional high-performance pathways for Māori players (Stutchbury 2014). Initially, the emphasis was on twenty20 as a format more easily accommodated amid other commitments. In 2015, NZC, in conjunction with the Māori Sports Awards, launched an annual Māori Cricket Scholarship to support the most promising young male player (Mackenzie 2013; Taipari 2015).

Meanwhile, the factors that had always militated most against cricket for Māori and Pasifika could be seen in declining support for the game more generally. Analysis by SNZ in 2019 indicated that participation in sport among 18–24-year-olds had declined by 13.9% during the previous 16 years. Although cricket remains the dominant summer sport in terms of both participation and coverage, and junior numbers had increased markedly in the wake of New Zealand's co-hosting of the 2015 World Cup, the number of secondary school players, mostly boys, dropped from nearly 18,000 in 2000 to under 9,000 by 2019. NZC attributed the decline to a growing perception among young people that cricket took too long to play, was expensive, was only played on a Saturday and contained long periods of inactivity for individual players (Hepburn 2019; Revealed 2018). Certainly, this decline was not unique to New Zealand, with similar trends evident in Britain and Australia especially (Hosken 2020), but as the smallest of the major cricket countries by population, New Zealand will likely experience a more pronounced impact on its future elite player pool.

The key response to these trends is the "One Cricket" project overseen by former international player and NZC Chief Executive Martin Snedden to broaden participation in the game at all levels and especially to retain and grow youth participation. Drawing from similar schemes in Australia, the aim was to develop abbreviated and hybrid forms of cricket and "age plus stage" rules to make junior cricket a more inclusive experience. The approach includes shorter pitches to reduce the bowling of wides and therefore keep the ball in play for longer, a reduction in team sizes and a requirement for all players to bat and bowl. Dual pitch formats were also promoted where teams of eight played two games at the same time – six players fielding on one pitch while the other two batted on the other as the opposing team did the same. At secondary school level and beyond, a number of regions have also developed mid-week and twilight competitions to shift the emphasis from the weekend (Harvey 2015; Hepburn 2019). More

36 Greg Ryan

controversial is the debate about removing all representative cricket below the under-15 age group and shifting the emphasis from talent identification to a broader programme of participation and skill development in line with Sport New Zealand's desire to discourage early specialisation. It is argued that talent identification at junior level is unreliable and exclusion of some players based on perception of a lack of talent at that age is detrimental to cricket as a whole (Cleaver 2019, Sport New Zealand 2019b).

While "One Cricket" does not explicitly target Māori or Pasifika, there is an implicit emphasis on diversity and inclusivity and a recognition that different groups require different approaches. As the NZC Strategic Plan stated in 2017: "Cricket will be a game for all New Zealanders; a game without barriers – a game that can be played anywhere, by anyone" (New Zealand Cricket 2017). The rapid growth in South Asian, especially Indian, migration since the early 2000s is certainly diversifying the game at all levels. But this is a matter of transplanting from very strong cricket cultures. The greater challenge for NZC is to attract those largely unfamiliar with the game (Spoonley and Taiapa 2009). With input from the New Zealand Cricket Players Association (CPA) and School Sport NZ, a tangible initiative came in early 2019 with the selection of the first New Zealand Māori secondary school boys' team for a fixture against a Governor General's XI at which the team were capped by Trent Boult. The New Zealand under-19 men's team selected later in 2019 also contained four Māori players and another of Cook Islands heritage (Geenty 2019a). But as with virtually all Māori players who have appeared in men's representative cricket since the late nineteenth century, all of the 2019 cohort were drawn from high decile, long-established and traditional cricket-playing boys' schools. The barometer of success for NZC, aside from ensuring this team endures, will be whether a wider cross section of schools eventually contribute to it.

Attracting Pasifika players is no less challenging. Certainly, in Ross Taylor New Zealand cricket possesses an exemplar for aspiring players (Hurihanganui 2018). But the barriers are less easily surmounted. From around 2010 former international bowler Kerry Walmsley worked in conjunction with the CPA to run the Hooked on Cricket programme to take the game into lower decile Auckland schools with a high proportion of Pasifika children. As he explained the strategy,

> The most important thing in the Polynesian community is convincing parents it's worthwhile. The kids are often big and strong; they have great eyes to smash the ball and natural, uncoached bowling actions. However, we believed it was vital to sit down to explain the bigger picture and the pathways cricket offers because it is not a sport they're accustomed to and can be quite expensive. It's always a battle in low decile areas because $10 buys you a rugby ball which can entertain 30 kids, just like that.
>
> *(Alderson et al. 2012b paras 15–16)*

By 2012 Auckland Cricket had appointed a Pasifika development officer and was using Kirikiti to assist in the transition to twenty20 cricket. Country of

Origin cricket tournaments were also staged with sides including Cook Islands, Niue, Samoa and Tonga along with others from South Asia (Moore 2012). In the context of the ICC's expanding international structure, it was also emphasised that there are teams other than New Zealand for players to aspire to. Fiji, Samoa and Cook Islands are affiliate members of the ICC East Asia-Pacific region, and cricket is active in Tonga although its national body was suspended from the ICC in 2013 for membership breaches (Northern Districts Cricket 2014). But, these are teams in the very lowest divisions of the ICC rankings and do not offer realistic career paths for aspiring players.

Encouraging Māori and Pasifika girls and women to choose cricket confronts added layers of complexity, not least in terms of a lack of supporting structures for female players and administrators at all levels. Despite a sharp increase in participation by girls at junior level since 2011–2012, 90.5% of clubs did not have girls-only teams and 57.6% did not offer any cricket for girls. In 2016, only 4% of all female players were adults compared to 23% of males (Beaman 2016). There had also been a marked decline in the presence of women in NZC's coaching and governance structure. An original reason for forming separate sporting organisations earlier in the twentieth century was that women were concerned they would lose control over their sport if they affiliated with men. The argument in favour of amalgamating the men's and women's cricket administration in 1992 was that it confirmed earlier amalgamations at club and provincial level and would ensure that funds from the wealthier men's game would help to promote women's cricket (Simpson 1998). While some objectives were met, an independent report commissioned by NZC in 2016 referred to female cricketers as "a species on the verge of extinction" and noted that fewer than 10% of coaches were female and the proportion of women involved in the governance structure had fallen from 38% in 1993–1994 to 6.4% in 2016. Those interviewed for the report also believed that NZC regarded women's cricket as an obligation and a cost centre with no apparent return on investment. In an accompanying press statement NZC conceded: "We have allowed women's cricket to be run by men for women; we have neglected the women's game on the basis of cost, and a perceived lack of interest. We have sidelined women's cricket both structurally and philosophically. We were wrong, and we now need to address the areas we've allowed to slip" (Beaman 2016, 12, 14). A global view also suggests that whereas New Zealand was long regarded as being third behind Australia and England in the development of the women's game and the performance of the national team, the rapid transformation of the 2010s, if judged by international results alone, has seen it slip behind India and South Africa and arguably the West Indies.

Efforts to close this gap, including the election of former international star Debbie Hockley as NZC's first female president in November 2016, were given further momentum in 2019 when SNZ and High Performance Sport New Zealand announced that as a formal condition for ongoing investment, all partner sports receiving funding of over $50,000 a year would need to achieve a minimum of 40% of women on their board by December 2021 (Froggatt 2019).

Having secured hosting rights for the Women's World Cup in 2021, NZC has a further incentive to increase the number of females playing the game (McFadden 2017). Hence it has also made significant progress in the provision of professional contracts for elite female players, although the number and value of these still lags well behind those for men (Geenty 2019b). Moreover, NZC argues that female provincial players are classed as "amateur" rather than professional, with their participation in cricket considered secondary to other employment. It is therefore cautious to expand the volume of women's cricket too quickly as it believes that players will be caught between the demands of cricket and other commitments and then leave the game (George 2020). A timeframe to achieve contractual parity with the men has not been set.

In early 2020, an inaugural Māori schoolgirls' team was assembled with Maia Lewis as coach. While largely drawn from high decile girls' schools, it contained some signs of a broader base. Lewis believes that the new professional opportunities within women's cricket and the considerable success of Māori players such as recent New Zealand captain Suzie Bates and leading bowler Lea Tahuhu obviously signal a career pathway for aspiring players. As with other advocates of Māori cricket, she hopes that the shorter formats will attract more players. "They like to hit the ball and to be aggressive … it's a natural part of our culture and instinct. The twenty20 format is really conducive to that, it sort of suits the temperament" (Tunnicliffe 2020). Of course, the risk with such assessments is to ensure that they do not become all pervasive to the point of pigeonholing Māori and Pasifika players into the shortest format of the game and not others. Another challenge is that Māori girls are prone to be whakamā (shy/embarrassed) to put themselves forward for unfamiliar sports. It is therefore important to attract them to cricket with whānau or friends (Tunnicliffe 2020). In a related context, the acknowledged barriers for many Pasifika females engaging in sport include perceptions and restrictions imposed by families and the community because of gender (Gordon et al. 2013).

Predictions for the ethnic composition of the New Zealand population to 2038 indicate that "European and Other" will be the only sector of the population to decrease its proportion with significant growth continuing for Māori, Pasifika and Asian broadly defined, but especially rapid growth in people of Chinese and Indian origin. It is estimated that Māori will comprise one third of all children and youth. Auckland, as New Zealand's largest city and the largest Pasifika city in the world, is likely to see its European population fall from around 75% in 1996 to less than 50% by 2038, while its Asian population will increase from 10% to 30% over the same period (Statistics New Zealand 2017). These trends, combined with the diversification and fragmentation of sport and leisure commitment, especially among the wealthier Pākehā population, provide a strong incentive for cricket to develop an ethnically diverse player base. Yet the challenge is not merely to provide cricket but to actively overcome the barriers to it. While twenty20 is an answer to the time constraint and certainly offers lucrative financial rewards for elite players, and NZC can now draw on a

New Zealand cricket **39**

number of talented Māori players as role models, it has less scope on its own to resolve entrenched socio-economic disparities confronting the wider Māori and Pasifika player base.

References

Alderson, A., Cleaver, D. & Leggat, D. 2012a, *The shame game: Plenty of opportunities at game's grassroots level*, New Zealand Herald, viewed 2 February 2020, https://www.nzherald.co.nz/sport/news/article.cfm?c_id=4&objectid=10851953.

Alderson, A., Cleaver, D. & Leggat, D. 2012b, *The shame game: Talented Polynesian players left behind*. New Zealand Herald, viewed 2 February 2020, https://www.nzherald.co.nz/special-report-the-shame-game/news/article.cfm?c_id=1503307&objectid=10851959.

Astle, A. 2014, 'Sport development – plan, programme and practice: A case study of the planned intervention by New Zealand Cricket into cricket in New Zealand', PhD Thesis, Massey University, Palmerston North, New Zealand.

Beaman, S. 2016, *Women and cricket, cricket and women*. New Zealand Cricket, Christchurch, viewed 27 January 2020, https://www.nzc.nz/media/7756/nzcr_j000080_women-and-cricket-document_digital_d1.pdf

Beckles, H. & Stoddart, B. (eds.). 1995, *Liberation cricket: West Indies cricket culture*, Manchester University Press, Manchester.

Boock, R. 2003, *Off the ball: Crowe's view on Maori unacceptable*. New Zealand Herald, viewed 6 April 2020 https://www.nzherald.co.nz/sport/news/article.cfm?c_id=4&objectid=3051941.

Chapman, M. 2018, *Where are all our Pacific cricket players?* The Spinoff, viewed 7 February 2020, https://www.barkersonline.co.nz/blog/pacific_cricket_players/.

Cleaver, D. 2019, *New Zealand cricket on junior rep teams: 'We don't believe it's the right thing to do'*. New Zealand Herald, viewed 26 January 2020, https://www.nzherald.co.nz/sport/news/article.cfm?c_id=4&objectid=12208166.

Field, M. 2013, *Polynesian men a global sports commodity*. Stuff, viewed 6 April 2020, http://www.stuff.co.nz/sport/8718872/Polynesian-men-a-global-sports-commodity.

Froggatt, R. 2019, *The strategic case for gender equity on sports boards*. Stuff, viewed 6 December 2019, https://www.stuff.co.nz/sport/other-sports/113595942/the-strategic-case-for-gender-equity-on-sports-boards.

Geenty, M. 2019a, *New caps and a Trent Boult Hongi greet first Māori schools cricket team*. Stuff, viewed 26 January 2020, https://www.stuff.co.nz/sport/cricket/111074653/new-caps-and-a-trent-boult-hongi-greet-first-mori-schools-cricket-team.

Geenty, M. 2019b, *New master agreement ushers in big changes for women's cricket in New Zealand*. Stuff, viewed 7 February 2020, https://www.stuff.co.nz/sport/cricket/114962558/new-master-agreement-ushers-in-big-changes-for-womens-cricket-in-new-zealand.

George, Z. 2020, *Cricket's gender gap: Female players miss out compared to their male counterparts*. Stuff, viewed 11 February 2020, https://www.stuff.co.nz/sport/cricket/118848914/crickets-gender-gap-female-players-miss-out-compared-to-their-male-counterparts.

Gordon, B., Sauni, P. & Tuagalu, C. 2013, 'Sport means 'family and church': sport in New Zealand Pasifika communities', *Asia-Pacific Journal of Health, Sport and Physical Education*, Vol. 4, no. 1, pp. 49–63.

Grainger, A. 2009, 'Rugby, Pacific peoples, and the cultural politics of national identity in New Zealand', *International Journal of the History of Sport*, Vol. 26, no. 16, pp. 2335–2357.

Guha, R. 2002, *A corner of a foreign field: The Indian history of a British sport*, Picador, London.

Harvey, S. 2015, *Decline in NZ school kids playing cricket calls for different approach*. Sunday News, viewed 2 February 2020, https://www.stuff.co.nz/sport/cricket/67468457/decline-in-nz-school-kids-playing-cricket-calls-for-different-approach.

Hepburn, S. 2019, *Cricket must adapt to the times*. Otago Daily Times, viewed 7 February 2020, https://www.odt.co.nz/sport/cricket/cricket-must-adapt-times.

Hoby, K. 2003, *Crowe: Cricket not the game for Maori*. New Zealand Herald, viewed 5 April 2020, https://www.nzherald.co.nz/nz/news/article.cfm?c_id=1&objectid=3052026.

Hokowhitu, B. 2003, '"Physical beings": stereotypes, sport and the "physical education" of New Zealand Maori', *Culture, Sport, Society*, Vol. 6, no. 2–3, pp. 192–218.

Hosken, J. 2020, *The disconnect tugging at Sydney cricket's grassroots*. The Roar, viewed 21 April 2020, https://www.theroar.com.au/cricket/longform/the-disconnect-tugging-at-sydney-crickets-grassroots-1070675/.

Hurihanganui, T. 2018, *Taylor going into bat for Pacific cricket*. Radio New Zealand, viewed 5 February 2020, https://www.rnz.co.nz/news/national/351607/taylor-going-into-bat-for-pacific-cricket.

Mackenzie, S. 2013, *Stewart wants to boost Maori cricket profile*. Stuff, viewed 5 April 2020, http://www.stuff.co.nz/sport/cricket/8666728/Stewart-wants-to-boost-Maori-cricket-profile.

McFadden, S. 2017. *Women in cricket: Back from the brink*. LockerRoom, viewed 7 February 2020, https://www.newsroom.co.nz/lockerroom/2017/11/21/61953/women-in-cricket-back-from-the-brink.

Moore, H. 2012. *Rise of pacific island cricket Heralds big future impact*. Pacific.Scoop, viewed 11 March 2020, http://pacific.scoop.co.nz/2012/03/rise-of-pacific-island-cricket-heralds-big-future-impact/.

New Zealand Cricket. 2017, *NZC strategic plan*, New Zealand Cricket, Auckland, New Zealand.

Northern Districts Cricket. 2014, *Northern Maori*, viewed 11 December 2020, https://northernmaoricricket.weekly.com.

Palmer, F. 2006, 'State of Māori Sport', in M. Mulholland (ed.), *State of the Māori nation*, Reed, Auckland, pp. 261–275.

Paul, G. 2007, *Rugby: Pasifika players dominating ranks*. New Zealand Herald, viewed 14 April 2020, https://www.nzherald.co.nz/sport/news/article.cfm?c_id=4&objectid=10426898.

Payne, F. & Smith, I. 2001, *2001 New Zealand cricket Almanack*, Hodder Moa Beckett, Auckland.

Potiki, P. 1954, 'Maoris and Sport', *Te Ao Hou*, Vol. 7, pp. 50–52.

'Revealed: The sports on the rise in New Zealand'. 2018. New Zealand Herald, viewed 2 December 2020, https://www.nzherald.co.nz/sport/news/article. cfm?c_id=4&objectid=11974676.

Roper, B. 2005, *Prosperity for all? Economic, social and political change in New Zealand since 1935*, Thomson, Southbank, Victoria, Australia.

Ryan, G. 2002, 'Amateurs in a professional game: player payments in New Zealand cricket c1977–2002', *Sport in History*, Vol. 25, no.1, pp. 114–135.

Ryan, G. 2004, *The making of New Zealand cricket 1832–1914*, Frank Cass, London.

Ryan, G. 2007, 'Few and far between: Māori and Pacific contributions to New Zealand Cricket', *Sport in Society*, Vol. 10, no. 1, pp. 84–100.

Ryan, G. & Watson, G. 2018, *Sport and the New Zealanders: A history*, Auckland University Press, Auckland.

Sacks, B. 2019, *Cricket, Kirikiti and Imperialism in Samoa, 1879–1939*, Palgrave Macmillan, London.

Simpson, A. 1998, 'New Zealand's Wicket Women', in B. Patterson (ed.), *Sport, society and culture in New Zealand*, Stout Research Centre, Wellington, 61–72.

Spoonley, P. & Taiapa, C. 2009, *Sport and cultural diversity: Responding to the sports and leisure needs of immigrants and ethnic minorities in Auckland*, Massey University & Auckland Regional Physical Activity & Sport Strategy, Auckland.

Sport New Zealand. 2015, *Sport and active recreation in the lives of New Zealand adults. 2013/14 active New Zealand survey results*, Sport New Zealand, Wellington.

Sport New Zealand. 2019a, *Active NZ 2018 participation report*, Sport New Zealand, Wellington.

Sport New Zealand. 2019b, *Why we need to tackle early specialisation*, viewed 21 April 2020. Available from: https://sportnz.org.nz/news-and-events/media-releases-and-updates/articles/why-we-need-to-tackle-early-specialisation-2.

Statistics New Zealand. 2017, *Subnational ethnic population projections: 2013(base)–2038 update*, viewed 13 April 2020, http://archive.stats.govt.nz/browse_for_stats/population/estimates_and_projections/SubnationalEthnicPopulationProjections_MR-13base-2038update.aspx.

Stutchbury, G. 2014, *First Maori matches considered catalyst for New Zealand game*. Reuters, viewed 13 April 2020, https://uk.reuters.com/article/uk-cricket-zealand-maori/first-maori-matches-considered-catalyst-for-new-zealand-game-idUKBREA-2J0EM20140320.

Taipari, G. 2015, *New cricket scholarship for Māori*. Sunlive, viewed 13 April 2020 https://sunlive.co.nz/news/114223-new-cricket-scholarship-maori.html.

Te Puni Kōkiri. 2006, *Te Māori i Te Whutupōro: Māori in Rugby*, viewed 13 April 2020, https://www.tpk.govt.nz/documents/download/195/tpk-maoriinrugby-2006-en.pdf.

Treasury. 2018, *Statistical analysis of ethnic wage gaps in New Zealand*, viewed 14 September 2020, https://www.treasury.govt.nz/sites/default/files/2018-08/ap18-03.pdf.

Tunnicliffe, B. 2020, *More Māori women can excel at cricket says former NZ captain*. Radio New Zealand, viewed 13 April 2020, https://www.rnz.co.nz/news/sport/408875/more-maori-women-can-excel-at-cricket-says-former-nz-captain.

Wikaire, R. & Newman, J. 2014, 'Neoliberalism as Neocolonialism? Considerations on the marketisation of Waka Ama in Aotearoa/New Zealand', in C. Hallinan and B. Judd (eds.), *Native games: Indigenous peoples and sports in the post-colonial world*, Emerald Group Publishing, Bingley, pp. 59–83.

5

NETBALL AND THE (RE)PRODUCTION OF A DOMINANT FEMININITY

The good game for kiwi girls

Amy Marfell

Introduction

Netball[1] is a team sport that was created *by* women *for* women and it is one of the few sports worldwide whose participants are, almost exclusively, female (Andrew 1997). Netball is currently the fourth most participated in sport in the country behind golf, football and tennis (Sport New Zealand 2018), with participation rates surpassing rugby union – traditionally lauded as New Zealand's national game (Pringle & Markula 2005). Netball is played in more than 80 countries across the globe, and in Aotearoa New Zealand in particular, it is, and has long been, the "major female sporting code" (Teevale 2008, p. 167; see also Sport New Zealand 2018) meaning, that unlike in other sports, female participation in netball has never really struggled for acceptance or legitimacy. Highlighting the dominance of netball in Aotearoa New Zealand and its links to sociocultural norms of gender, Hawes and Barker (1999) have pointedly suggested that netball is the national sport for New Zealand women.

The significance of netball as the ultimate women's game and "unambiguously" for women has gained attention and interest among a number of sport scholars (e.g., Andrew 1997; Nauright 1996, 1999; Nauright & Broomhall 1994; Taylor 2001; Treagus 2005). Many of these researchers have examined the history of netball and its alignment with traditional gender roles and relations. While unpacking the social acceptance of the game, the discussions have largely centered on netball's ability to provide what Andrew (1997, p. 3) terms "an island of female-centred sporting culture in the sea of masculinity that characterise[s] New Zealand sports".

In this chapter, I deepen and develop these discussions about netball and women's participation via a socio-spatial analysis that explores the ongoing and complex connections between netball, female participation and femininities in

DOI: 10.4324/9781003034445-5

Aotearoa New Zealand. That is, I move past dominant narratives of netball's significance as "female-centred" by unpacking the role of netball as an institutional force in the (re)production of a dominant and culturally valued conception of feminine identity. To help contextualise my argument, I first provide a brief overview of the development of a dominant femininity in Aotearoa New Zealand. I then briefly detail the methodological and theoretical underpinnings of this research, before presenting key findings.

A historical overview of femininity in Aotearoa New Zealand

The type of femininity celebrated in Aotearoa New Zealand is historically, geographically and culturally specific, and thus, has links to the country's colonial and rural roots (MacDonald 1999). Late-nineteenth-century European (or Pākehā) women lived in a patriarchal social structure, such that they were expected to marry and submit to their husbands. Importantly, however, the frontier nature of colonial New Zealand life also necessitated women work hard and engage in often remarkably physical forms of activity. As such, colonial New Zealand females did not, and could not, conform to Victorian expectations that suggested women "ought not be expected to lift anything heavier than pins and needles, and never more than a cotton reel" (Christian Observer 1870 as cited in Lineham 2011, p. 82). Raw, frontier New Zealand had little use for the "ornamental females" (Brooking 2004, p. 87) of Victorian middle-class society and instead required women be fit, strong, courageous, determined and unencumbered (Thompson 2003) such that those women "who acted as *a combination of* labourer, domestic servant, and child-producing machine" (Brooking 2004, p. 87, emphasis added) were widely valued and praised.

The need for females to work hard to contribute to the development of New Zealand society, therefore, functioned to privilege a particular type of femininity – one that celebrates characteristics of heteronormativity as well as physical fitness, determination, cooperation, stamina and strength. Of course, the colonisation of Aotearoa New Zealand by British settlers, was both a spatial and social process. In other words, not only did the British appropriate and gain control of land, but in so doing, they also imposed particular practices, values and social norms on the indigenous people of the country (Māori), including the reorganisation of gender roles and the formation of normative (white) discourses of femininity. For Māori women, identification with private spaces such as the home was a foreign concept, whereby sleeping was communal and food preparation was "the work of low-born women or slaves" and the structure of Māori dwellings "reflected hierarchies within and across genders" (Brookes 2016, p. 31). It was initially possible for Māori women to be selective about which aspects of the new European culture they adopted, "including the pressure to conform to a domestic ideal that centred on the home life of the nuclear family" (Brookes 2016, p. 40). However, colonisation, and subsequently, the prevalence of the Christian faith, eventually assisted in instilling "European

44 Amy Marfell

notions of domestic order" (Brookes 2016, p. 40) that prioritised the role of the female as keeper of the home and family alongside expectations to engage in hard physical labour.

Indeed, femininity in Aotearoa New Zealand has and continues to be "epitomised by 'usefulness'" (Hunter & Riney-Kehrberg 2002, p. 136), that is, the belief that women should embody heterosexuality, femininity and domesticity whilst *also* being ready, willing and able (fit) to perform demanding and physical chores and often in rural and rugged environments. Aotearoa New Zealand's colonial past has, therefore, worked to construct and privilege a particular and dominant type of feminine "ideal" that continues to be premised on European values that celebrate the performance of traditionally feminine traits (heterosexuality and domesticity) and a certain level of physical prowess. Therefore, it is important to note that when I refer to a "dominant femininity in Aotearoa/New Zealand", I am not only referring to gender, but also to race, and importantly, to the intersectionality (or overlapping nature) of these constructs. Although it is, unfortunately, beyond the scope of this chapter to delve more deeply into the relations between race and netball in New Zealand, it is important to note that sociocultural relations of whiteness do indeed inform the already complex relationship between netball and femininity in the country.

Brief notes on method and theory

Methodologically, this chapter draws upon my insider participant knowledge of netball, two years of ethnographic research (completed in 2013 and 2014) – including numerous observations and interviews with 16 female competitive and social recreational netballers – as well as extensive and ongoing analyses of media and secondary historical sources. The discussion, therefore, incorporates "insider" voices, as well as evidence gleaned from televised netball games, televised, online and print sports news coverage, magazines, webpages, netball-related advertising, and social media posts. All help to shed light on the intimate and complex socio-spatial relationship between netball and femininity. Further supporting this analysis is Lefebvre's (1991) theory of the production of space, which provides a useful framework for exploring the intersections between bodies, space and relations of power in this sport.

Lefebvre (1991) suggests that relations of power and human experience do not occur aspatially, that is, they do not exist independent of space, but rather are essentially formed, shaped, negotiated and contested *in and through* space. Specifically, Lefebvre (1991) positions space as comprised of the physical (spatial practices: boundaries, structures, interactions and movements), the mental (representations of space: ideas about space, thoughts, memories, rules, scientific theories and normative discourses on space) and the social (lived space: the space of the body, sensory phenomena and embodied experience – the space in which people simultaneously negotiate the material reality of perceived space and the social expectations of conceived space). In so doing, Lefebvre provides a systematic analytical framework that not only acknowledges, but also, importantly, helps to unravel the *mutually constitutive* and ongoing relationships between the moving body, space and social relations. Within netball in Aotearoa New Zealand there are a number of spatial practices and representations of space that produce the sport, not only as a social space that presents women and girls with a range of lived experiences and possibilities, but also as significant in the continued social construction of a particular feminine identity. Drawing inspiration from Lefebvre's spatial framework, and particularly his concepts of spatial practice and representations of space, I discuss how the physical spaces (that which can be perceived or seen such as the court, uniform, and the movements of women in this context) and mental spaces of netball (that which can be conceived or engaged with via thought such as the rules of the game and media representations of this sport and its players) facilitate the ongoing (re)production of particular and important relations of power that work to construct women's identities in line with dominant and culturally valued feminine ideals.

(Re)producing femininities: A socio-spatial analysis of netball

From the outset of netball's emergence in Aotearoa New Zealand over 100 years ago, the game was celebrated as not only acceptable, but also important for girls and women. Originating in the United States in 1891, before being adopted by England and then Aotearoa New Zealand in the late 1890s, netball quickly gained popularity as the "ideal" game for girls and young women (Ryan & Watson 2018). Indeed, as early as 1897, *The Otago Witness* wrote of the beauty of the sport and its fame in the United States where it was "completely eclipsing lawn tennis, and effectually nipping in the bud the threatened revival of croquet" (as cited in McFadden 2015, p. 2). Positive public perceptions of netball were also reflected in 1926 in an article in the *Christchurch Sun* where netball was praised for providing "splendid exercise for those engaged in it" whilst having "the added charm of not being too rough…which makes it so good a game for girls" as well as by the *Otago Daily Times* as "a game eminently suitable for every girl" (as cited in Nauright & Broomhall 1994, p. 394). As the dominant narrative suggests, netball prospered during this time, largely because of the restrictions placed on women's moving bodies: the game offered women an important opportunity to participate in team sports without engaging in typically "masculine" behaviour (Burroughs & Nauright 2000; Nauright 1996). Indeed, the rules of netball in its infancy ensured that women's movements were very small – the division of the court into thirds and the confinement of each of the nine players on each team to only one of these thirds, and the extreme restrictions on contact between players worked to ensure the alignment of women's participation in this sport with feminine ideals of decorum and delicacy. Interestingly, however, women's participation in netball during this time, also aligned with expectations on females to build and maintain levels of physical fitness in ways that ensured the production of "healthy" female bodies. That is, netball helped to produce bodies capable

46 Amy Marfell

of engaging in physical domestic labour alongside the carrying of children, and thus, the embodiment of useful femininity.

In addition to restricting women's movements, netball also ensured players were "nothing if not sticklers to the strictest sense of modesty" (Grundy 2001 as cited in Grundy and Shackelford 2005, p. 29) in dress. Wearing either "bloomers", an early version of women's gym clothes, or long skirts and shirts, netball ensured only slightly modified versions of conventional feminine dress and therefore, did not require women to step very far outside the bounds of the accepted feminine fashion standards of the time. As Thompson (2003) points out, the game of netball neither competed with men for space nor challenged dominant ideals of masculinity or femininity, and as such, women were not only let to simply "get on" with their participation in this sport, but they were encouraged towards it (see also Burroughs & Nauright 2000). Martin et al. (2020, p. 179) declare that netball was seen, by and large, as a viable "solution to the problem of providing exercise for the growing number of young urban women" and thus, it promptly became celebrated as the game for *good* Kiwi girls during a time where women's participation in a number of other sports remained contested. As such, netball not only grew in popularity during this time, but it quickly became an important vehicle for (re)producing the type of female body and feminine identity (modest and restrained, but physically capable) valued in Aotearoa New Zealand society.

Despite significant advancements in the game of netball, in the contemporary moment it very much remains a game of restraint that confines women's movements and defines their behaviours in ways that align with an idealised conception of traditional femininity. For example, the spatial boundaries of netball, and more particularly, the division of the court into thirds and the restrictions of players to particular areas (according to their designated position), remains a fundamental component of the game. Equally, the rules of the sport, which have remained relatively unchanged, ensure there continues to exist a collective understanding about what seems like "normal" behaviour in the space and what is tolerated/accepted (van Ingen 2002). Despite becoming faster and more skillful, netball is still considered a women's game in Aotearoa New Zealand. This is also notwithstanding some participation in the game among males, which has been largely contested because of, among other things, the feminine undertones of the sport (see Tagg 2016). Indeed, although some physical contact (deemed "fair contesting"[2]) is now permitted between players in netball, by and large, the game is still premised on many of the values of appropriate femininity that informed its creation. As Gordon (2008) points out, the restrictions on the movement of players, high levels of intervention from the umpires who consistently penalise transgressions (e.g., contact, stepping with or "replaying" the ball, going "offside" and defending too closely), and the stand-down rule following player contact continue to align women's behaviours in this sport with dominant beliefs about the performance of gender and more particularly, the types of movements and interactions deemed culturally acceptable for a woman (Marfell 2019; Nauright 1996; Nauright & Broomhall 1994; Treagus 2005).

Interestingly, while most other team sports encourage women to behave in traditionally masculine ways (e.g., to tackle one another, inflict and accept pain, and/or kick, hit and throw great distances), netball actually discourages (and punishes) these behaviours, and in so doing, the game helps to (re)produce female players in accordance with accepted and dominant standards of traditional femininity. In her comparison between rugby and netball players, Sarah, a recreational, competitive netballer, highlights this point suggesting that in netball "you play hard and compete without purposely causing contact or hurting anyone" which means that "there is definitely a stereotype with women rugby players that isn't there when you think about netballers". Certainly, contemporary netball is a far cry from the relatively static game introduced during the early twentieth century, requiring players be fit, strong and athletic. However, via the rules of the sport, netball continues to encourage women to perform their bodies in accordance with a dominant femininity. As Jess, a competitive recreational netballer, notes:

> I think if you look at netball in comparison to other sports like rugby it's a lot more graceful. The movements you make are a bit more graceful, not in terms of dance but, you know, going up for those intercepts. It's quite a nice, lovely sport to watch whereas rugby is more like "bang", "hit" and you don't usually see women in those aggressive contact type situations. I'm not saying netball isn't aggressive, because it is extremely aggressive, but in a different way. I guess it is quite a pretty sport (laughs), as bad as that sounds. I think there is a sense of elegance with some of the stuff you do, the ability to jump and pluck those balls out of the air and stretch and all that kind of stuff.

What Sarah and Jess' comments emphasise are the connections between the mental and physical spaces of netball in the (re)production of femininities. More particularly, what you see in netball, and of course what you don't, are not only defined by the rules of the sport but they also work to shape the ways players are read in relation to norms of gender and (hetero)sexuality. In this sense, the rules of netball continue to act as techniques of control – they influence how women perform their bodies in and through netball, while at the same time producing females who embody characteristics of a dominant and celebrated femininity, such as grace, agility and finesse, but also control, cooperation, restraint, and remorse for stepping too far outside the bounds of a normative gender performance. While these characteristics are also hallmarks of other feminine sports, such as gymnastics, figure skating and synchronised swimming (e.g., see Kerr 2008; Kestnbaum 2003), netball remains the only non-aesthetic sport in which notions of femininity are, quite literally, written into the rules of the game.

As the game of netball and its players have become more physical, and alongside broadening conventions of appropriate femininity that have made acceptable less restrictive forms of dress, the netball uniform has also changed in ways that

48 Amy Marfell

ensure it continues to (re)produce women's bodies as materially feminine. When discussing the netball uniform with the women I interviewed, all recognised the part played by these garments in (re)producing their sporting bodies in accordance with a dominant femininity. Natasha, a former regional representative netballer put it bluntly: "[netballers are considered] feminine because of how players present themselves in dresses". Indeed, the uniform plays an important part in establishing and reinforcing netballers' feminine identities despite increasing displays of typically masculine characteristics such as (controlled) aggression, strength and speed. For example, Jess suggests that the ways in which her netball uniform emphasises her womanly "curves" (e.g., her breasts, buttocks and thighs) and reveals her flesh work to accentuate and reinforce her femininity and heterosexuality despite her athletic prowess. She explains:

> Today [netball uniforms] are becoming quite fitting and the design gives you that silhouette look, you know, it really emphasizes your curves, and it's kind of showing off a lot more skin than you used to. No one would question your femininity or your sexuality wearing something like that! We wear dresses, we look pretty (laughs). Definitely the more competitive you get, like the uniform gets shorter, tighter and sexier … in more competitive netball, the shorter the dress the better and the tighter the dress the better.

Jess' comments point to the importance of the netball uniform for feminising and heterosexualising women's bodies in contemporary netball. More particularly, she speaks to how the design of the modern netball uniform, instead of covering women's bodies as it did in the past, works to reveal the female body in such a way that it embellishes and accentuates women's feminine physical features, thus reinforcing normative discourses of femininity.

Interestingly, the (re)production of a dominant femininity in and through women's netball performances is also supported by a national conversation that positions netballers as capable and credible athletes who *simultaneously* embody heteronormative feminine traits. Just as the New Zealand media played an important role in the acceptance of netball in the country during its infancy, it continues to play a significant part in (re)producing female players in accordance with a culturally valued femininity. Indeed, netball receives plentiful media coverage in Aotearoa New Zealand such that depictions of netballers "in action" feature regularly in the sports media. At face value, the media is responsible for ensuring that New Zealand's elite netball players (the Silver Ferns) are household names and known to most, young and old alike. Close and critical attention to coverage of netball, however, reveals the role of the media in (re)producing netballers, through images, text and representations, as adhering to heteronormative and appropriately feminine practices and protocols, despite their athletic status and prowess.

Indeed, televised representations of netballers working up a sweat and pushing their bodies to their physical limits in regional franchise games and international test matches are regularly positioned alongside mentions of their male partners supporting from the stands or images of the players holding their children at the end of the game. In a recent example, Sky Sport New Zealand spoke with one of New Zealand netball's most capped and regarded players, Casey Kopua, about her impending retirement from domestic netball (Sky Sport NZ 2019). The piece covers her rise to stardom in the sport and the triumphs and tribulations of her almost 20-year career. While there is plenty of footage of the goal defense plying her trade on the court, her interview and commentary of her time in the game also features her sitting on a bench outside her home stadium, daughter Maia bouncing in her lap. Similarly, following the Silver Ferns' dramatic World Cup victory in 2019, Kopua again faced the camera post-match with her daughter, who was beamed around the globe cheekily licking the sweat from her athlete mother's chest (Sky Sport NZ 2019). Importantly, these types of depictions not only humanise these female athletes, but they also work to shape dominant discourses that position these women as appropriately and normatively feminine.

Mainstream media (e.g., women's magazines, online news sites) also regularly celebrate New Zealand netballers, but often while emphasising their bodies and attractiveness, personal lives, relationships and families (including children). Indeed, numerous Silver Ferns have filled the pages of women's magazines such as *New Zealand Woman's Weekly*, whereby the perspiration and gritty determination these female athletes pride themselves on regularly takes a back seat to pretty (and sometimes revealing) clothes, lashings of makeup and expertly styled hair. For example, an article featuring player Casey Kopua and ex-player turned coach Amigene Metcalfe in celebration of the 20-year history of the Waikato/Bay of Plenty Magic netball franchise, largely omits imagery of the two women "in action" (there is one image of Metcalfe with ball in hand during her playing days, but on her own and looking relatively passive in the shot). The omissions are in favour of a series of glamourised shots highlighting the pair's feminine beauty, slim figures and "girl next door" appeal (Bertrand 2019).

While the article labels the pair "the belles of netball" (Bertrand 2019) and focuses significantly on their friendship and family lives (both are mothers), it also makes an interesting juxtaposition between netball and the performance of the type of "useful" and rural femininity celebrated in Aotearoa New Zealand. As Kopua explains, she believes the secret to her and her fellow players' success has been "the farm life" whereby "just like on the farm, we have an attitude that we just have to do what needs to be done, with no excuses" (Bertrand 2019, para. 4–5). This coverage works to temper the representation of the powerful, strong and physically capable netballer, with that of a conception of appropriate, desirable and heteronormative femininity.

Other prominent examples of the (re)production of a dominant femininity in netball include corporate sponsorship and associated messaging, which has consistently married ideas about domesticity with the famous faces of the Silver Ferns in targeted advertising campaigns. As far back as the late 1990s, the New Zealand national netball team have been linked to whiteware brand Fisher and Paykel, where they were regularly depicted using an array of domestic "tools" such as washing

50 Amy Marfell

machines, driers and dishwashers in a series of satirical, tongue and cheek advertising campaigns. More recent advertising has seen netball and its elite players linked to grocery giant New World, McCains Frozen Foods and LG Appliances – the latter featuring a depiction of a front loader washing machine merged with a netball goal and the caption: "Dedicated supports of the LG Mystics on court…and off" (ANZ Championship Souvenir Guide 2012, pp. 3–4). In leveraging netball's brand to reach an audience of women in Aotearoa New Zealand, the media has played an important role in the continued (re)production of the rhetoric of netballers as normatively feminine domestic labourers.

Netball and femininity in Aotearoa New Zealand: A summary

There is little doubt that the social acceptance of netball in Aotearoa New Zealand is intimately linked to the game's close alignment with feminine ideals. Despite the game being recognised by some as "a symbol of female emancipation" (McLachlan & Boucher 2016, p. 22) for women and girls during a time when their sport participation was rare, it is also interesting to consider how this sport has quite literally kept New Zealand females "in their place" with respect to the performance of a culturally valued and dominant femininity. As one participant put forth, "[playing] netball is the equivalent of being married with kids" (Natasha) in that participation in netball aligns with what is considered a typical gender performance helping to reinforce the behaviours and traits considered appropriate for a New Zealand woman.

Indeed, the very construction of netball (both physically and culturally) has worked to keep the feminine identities of its players intact by ensuring the embodiment of particular and culturally accepted gender ideals. Whilst the male-dominated sport of rugby is largely considered the "glue of masculine culture in New Zealand" (Booth 2000, p. 54) because of the demands it places on players to demonstrate their "manliness" by putting their bodies on the line to tackle their opponents in violent confrontations, netball can be considered an important institutional force in the (re)production of what some may term a type of "hegemonic femininity" in Aotearoa New Zealand. Indeed, this sport, by way of its spatial practices and representations of space, regulates, controls and defines women's moving bodies in accordance with the (re)production of feminine and heterosexual subjectivities, whilst at the same enabling them to perform a type of "useful" femininity underscored by physical fitness and athleticism. That is, netball helps to (re)produce and maintain the physically capable but simultaneously restrained femininity prioritised and celebrated in Aotearoa New Zealand society.

Notes

1 The term "netball" typically refers to a non-contact (or semi-contact in the contemporary moment) ball sport that is played either inside or outdoors by two opposing teams consisting of seven on-court players. In recent years, however, a number of hybrid forms of netball (e.g., Indoor Netball, Fast5) have developed that look very

different from the traditional game. It is important to note, therefore, that whilst I acknowledge that "netball" no longer describes a singular game, I use the term in this chapter to define the traditional seven-a-side version of this sport.

2 The International Netball Federation (2018) suggests that when attacking, defending or playing the ball, opposing players *can* come into physical contact with one another provided that the players do not interfere with each other's play or use their bodies to gain an unfair advantage over their opponent – this is deemed as a "contest" or "fair contesting". Conversely, "contact" (which is punishable within the rules of the game) occurs when a player's actions either accidentally or deliberately interfere with an opponent's play.

References

Andrew, G. 1997, '"*A girls' game-and a good one too*": *A critical analysis of New Zealand netball*', PhD thesis, University of Canterbury, Christchurch, New Zealand, viewed 26 June 2020, https://ir.canterbury.ac.nz/handle/10092/5701

ANZ Championship Souvenir Guide. 2012, viewed 26 June 2020, http://rugbynewsnz.realviewdigital.com

Bertrand, K. 2019, 'Casey Kopua and Amigene Metcalfe celebrate Magic's 20th anniversary', *The New Zealand Women's Weekly,* viewed 26 June 2020, https://www.nowtolove.co.nz/health/fitness/casey-kopua-amigene-metcalfe-waikato-magics-20th-anniversary-40892

Booth, D. 2000, 'Modern sport: emergence and experiences', in C. Collins (ed.), *Sport in New Zealand Society*, Dunmore Press, Palmerston North, New Zealand, pp. 45–63.

Brookes, B. 2016, *A history of New Zealand women*, Bridget Williams Books, Wellington.

Brooking, T. 2004, *The history of New Zealand*, Greenwood Publishing Group, Westbort, CT.

Burroughs, A. & Nauright, J. 2000, 'Women's sports and embodiment in Australia and New Zealand', *The International Journal of the History of Sport*, Vol. 17, no. 2–3, pp. 188–205, https://doi.org/10.1080/09523360008714133

Gordon, B. 2008, 'The feminine mistake?' *New Zealand Listener*, viewed 26 June 2020, https://www.noted.co.nz/archive/archive-listener-nz-2008/the-feminine-mistake

Grundy, P. & Shackelford, S. 2005, *Shattering the glass: The remarkable history of women's basketball*, The New Press, New York.

Hawes, P. & Barker, L. 1999, *Court in the spotlight: History of New Zealand netball*, A&H Book Packaging, Christchurch, New Zealand.

Hunter, K. & Riney-Kehrberg, P. 2002, 'Rural daughters in Australia, New Zealand and the United States: an historical perspective', *Journal of Rural Studies*, Vol. 18, no. 2, pp.135–143.

International Netball Federation. 2018. *Rules of Netball,* viewed 26 June 2020, https://www.sporty.co.nz/asset/downloadasset?id=16828cd8-9b55-4638-a6e6-42aa8740195f

Kerr, R. 2008, 'Doing gender right but doing sport wrong: rhythmic gymnasts' experiences of playing a "feminine" sport', in C. Obel, T. Bruce & S. Thompson (eds.), *Outstanding: Research about women and sport in New Zealand*, Wilf Malcolm Institute of Education Research, Hamilton, New Zealand, pp. 95–112.

Kestnbaum, E. 2003, *Culture on ice: Figure skating and cultural meaning*, Wesleyan University Press, Middletown, CT.

Lefebvre, H. 1991, *The production of space*, Blackwell, Oxford.

Lineham, P. J. 2011, 'The gender issue in New Zealand Evangelical history', in M. Habets & B. Wood (eds.), *Reconsidering gender: Evangelical perspectives*, Pickwick Publications, Eugene, OR, pp. 75–103.

Macdonald, C. 1999, 'Too many men and too few women: gender's "fatal impact" in nineteenth-century colonies', in C. Daley & D. Montgomerie (eds.), *The gendered kiwi*, Auckland University Press, Auckland, New Zealand, pp. 17–35.

Marfell, A. 2019, '"We wear dresses, we look pretty": the feminisation and heterosexualisation of netball spaces and bodies', *International Review for the Sociology of Sport*, Vol. 54, no. 5, pp. 577–602, https://doi.org/10.1177/1012690217726539

Martin, A., McCarthy, L. & Watson, G. 2020, *Will to win: New Zealand netball greats on team culture and leadership*, Massey University Press, Palmerston North.

McFadden, S. 2015, *Story: Netball*, viewed 26 June 2020, https://www.teara.govt.nz/en/netball/page-2

McLachlan, F. & Boucher, L. 2016, 'Is netball a feminist triumph? Let's discuss', *The Conversation*, viewed 26 June 2020, https://theconversation.com/is-netball-a-feminist-triumph-lets-discuss-62889

Nauright, J. 1996, 'Netball and the creation of a female sporting culture in New Zealand', *Journal of Physical Education New Zealand*, Vol. 29, no. 2, pp. 13–17.

Nauright, J. 1999, 'Netball, media representation of women and crises of male hegemony in New Zealand', in J. Nauright (ed.), *Sport, power and society in New Zealand: Historical and contemporary perspectives*, The Australian Society for Sports History, Queensland, pp. 47–65.

Nauright, J. & Broomhall, J. 1994, 'A woman's game: The development of netball and a female sporting culture in New Zealand, 1906–70', *The International Journal of the History of Sport*, Vol. 1, no. 3, pp. 387–407, https://doi.org/10.1080/09523369408713870

Pringle, R. & Markula, P. 2005, 'No pain is sane after all: a Foucauldian analysis of masculinities and men's experiences in rugby', *Sociology of Sport Journal*, Vol. 22, no. 4, 472–497, https://doi.org/10.1123/ssj.22.4.472

Ryan, G. & Watson, G. 2018, *Sport and the New Zealanders: A history*. Auckland University Press, Auckland.

Sky Sport NZ. 2019, *A kind of magic: Casey Kopua*, viewed 26 June 2020, https://www.facebook.com/watch/?v=415555029281056

Sport New Zealand. 2018, *Active NZ survey*, viewed 26 June 2020, https://sportnz.org.nz/managing-sport/research-and-insights/active-nz/active-nz-survey-2018/

Tagg, B. 2016, 'Macho men in a girls' game: masculinities and the Otago men's netball team', *Sport in Society*, Vol. 19, no. 7, pp. 906–922, https://doi.org/10.1080/17430437.2015.1067782

Taylor, T. 2001, 'Gendering sport: the development of netball in Australia', *Sporting Traditions*, Vol. 18, no. 1, pp. 57–74.

Teevale, T. 2008, 'Pacific women's netball: a question of style', in C. Obel, T. Bruce & S. Thompson (eds.), *Outstanding: Research about women and sport in New Zealand*, Wilf Malcolm Institute of Education Research, Hamilton, New Zealand, pp. 167–191.

Thompson, S. M. 2003, 'Women and sport in New Zealand', in I. Hartmann-Tews & G. Pfister (eds.), *Sport and women: Social issues in international perspective*, Routledge, London, pp. 252–265.

Treagus, M. 2005, 'Playing like ladies: Basketball, netball and feminine restraint', *The International Journal of the History of Sport*, Vol. 22, no. 1, pp. 88–105, https://doi.org/10.1080/0952336052000314593

van Ingen, C. 2002, *Unmapping social space: The Toronto front runners, Lefebvre and geographies of resistance,* PhD thesis, The University of Alberta, Alberta, Canada.

6

MĀORI (INDIGENOUS) KNOWLEDGE IN SPORT AND WELLBEING CONTEXTS

"Tūturu whakamaua kia tina!"

Farah Palmer, Bevan Erueti, Angelique Reweti, Chrissy Severinsen and Jeremy Hapeta

Introduction

The examination of Māori wellbeing in relation to Māori participation in sport and active recreation as players and leaders in Aotearoa New Zealand[1] has been researched from a Māori perspective by several scholars and practitioners (e.g., Erueti 2015; Hapeta 2019; Hippolite & Bruce 2010; Hokowhitu 2009; Palmer & Masters 2010; Te Rito 2006; Wikaire & Newman 2014). Some scholars have been critical of how sport is used as a tool for colonisation (see Hokowhitu 2009), while others have focused on how sport may benefit indigenous empowerment and wellbeing (e.g., Hapeta 2019).

Sport and its impact on Māori wellbeing have also gained attention from government agencies such as *Te Puni Kōkiri* (Ministry of Māori Development) and Sport New Zealand (SNZ)/Ihi Aotearoa[2] (Te Puni Kōkiri 2005, 2006; SNZ 2017). For instance, in June 2020 (see Sport New Zealand Annual Report 2020) SNZ stated its aim was to contribute to the wellbeing of everybody, including Māori in Aotearoa New Zealand and that

> the Māori-Crown relationship underpins our work with Māori. We work to promote play, active recreation and sport in a way that is appropriate for Māori. Sport N[ew] Z[ealand] is committed to upholding the mana of Te Tiriti o Waitangi [Te Tiriti] and the principles of partnership, protection and participation.
>
> *(p. 35)*

While there are distinct differences between the Māori (Te Tiriti o Waitangi) and English versions (The Treaty of Waitangi), both sustain that a strong bicultural foundation is critical to Aotearoa New Zealand's national identity

DOI: 10.4324/9781003034445-6

and wellbeing.[3] The SNZ annual report provides examples of SNZ's commitment to Te Tiriti principles (expressed as partnership, protection, participation) by making specific reference to key priorities and activities that promote the development and implementation of active recreation and sport in a way that is culturally responsive for Māori (see Sport New Zealand 2020, p. 35). These key priorities and activities include a *te reo me ōnā tikanga* (Māori language and cultural traditions) strategy; the launch and roll out of a *marae*[4]-based physical activity prospectus called *MaraeFit Aotearoa*; and the *He Oranga Poutama* (Stairway to Wellbeing) programme (see McKegg et al. 2013 for an evaluation of this programme) that is strongly centred on Māori cultural distinctiveness and supports community leadership and participation in play, active recreation and sport as Māori. These initiatives identify that SNZ has devised an investment approach to enact its Te Tiriti outcomes, however, with limited resources, capacity and capability it is unclear whether SNZ by themselves can adequately address the variety of priorities and aspirations Māori have across the expansive approaches of sport and active recreation. This chapter illustrates three examples of how sport and active recreation entities beyond the scope of SNZ's priority initiatives may assist Māori aspirations for wellbeing to be realised by Māori for Māori.

Case study one showcases *Waka Ama* (canoe vessel activity) and explores the experiences of a group of participants from the *Heretaunga Ararau o Ngāti Kahungunu Waka Ama Roopu*[5] based in the region of Hawke's Bay.[6] The participant narratives supplied by paddlers, *whānau* (family) and the wider community identify that the affective and holistic health benefits traverse beyond "the physical" to include spiritual and environmental *hauora* (wellbeing), and illustrate how *te ao Māori* (the Māori world) can be integrated into sport management and experiences at the club level to enhance the wellbeing of participants. Case study two explores the experiences and narratives of *rangatahi* (youth), *rangātira* (leaders) and *pūkenga* (elite athletes) participating in rugby programmes and teams targeting Māori within New Zealand Rugby (NZR), the national sport organisation (NSO) for rugby. Their narratives support the notion that Māori-centred rugby programmes and teams within an NSO structure can be a site to affect cultural (re)engagement and wellbeing when Māori worldviews and practices are holistically integrated. The third and final case study is focused at the level of global multi-sport events and discusses the perspectives of Māori athletes who have competed at the Olympic and Commonwealth games identifying the reciprocal (and at times detrimental) interactions between Māori athletes and high-performance staff (who are often non-Māori). The significance of cultural safety in establishing effective Māori athlete-coach relationships and thus wellbeing is also examined.

To assist in determining whether these distinct sporting and active recreational contexts enhance Māori wellbeing from a Māori perspective, we integrate a framework of wellbeing developed by the Ministry of Health referred to as the *Whakamaua: Māori Health Action Plan 2020–2025* (Ministry of Health 2020). This Whakamaua[7] framework was initially constructed for the general health

Māori knowledge in sport **55**

and disability sectors, and sets out a suite of outcomes, objectives and priority areas for action that contribute to the achievement of healthy futures for Māori. Notable within the Whakamaua framework is the term *mana,* a concept that is well-known in Aotearoa New Zealand vernacular and is generally translated as "prestige, authority, control, power, influence, status, spiritual power, charisma" and is further defined as "a supernatural force in a person, place or object" (maoridictionary.co.nz). The Whakamaua framework provides a more nuanced illustration of Te Tiriti principles (i.e., partnership, protection and participation) in mana terms and how these could be applied to sport and active recreation initiatives by Māori for Māori to enhance Māori wellbeing. The mana concepts as applied to sport and active recreation are:

- **Mana whakahāere (stewardship):** The effective and appropriate *kaitiakitanga* (stewardship) and exercise of control in sport and active recreation, beyond the management of assets or resources in accordance with *tikanga* (traditional protocols and cultural practices), *kaupapa* (Māori interests) and *kawa* (rites and rituals). Succinctly, Mana whakahāere gives Māori control and independence over the sport and active recreation system.
- **Mana motuhake (self-determination):** Expresses the right for Māori to self-determine and exercise their authority in sport and recreation, and to participate in sport and active recreation on Māori terms and according to Māori philosophies, beliefs, values and practices.
- **Mana tangata (equity):** Describes achieving equity in sport and active recreation outcomes for Māori, across their life course and contributing to the overall health and wellbeing of Māori, which may involve distributing resources based on needs of Māori in sport and active recreation
- **Mana Māori (customary rituals):** Sport and active recreation contexts are framed by *te ao Māori* (the Māori world), enacted through *tikanga Māori* (Māori philosophy and customary practices) and encapsulated within *mātauranga Māori* (Māori knowledge).

These four expressions of mana are applied to the three case studies in this chapter to aid in understanding the tangible and intangible ways sport and active recreation may enhance Māori wellbeing at the club, NSO and sport event level.

Case study one: Waka Ama

You get to know the different states of the water, you know when it's wrong, and to me that's a real Māori thing, you know everything is connected to the land, connected to the water. [Participant]

It is appropriate we start with Waka ama because *waka* (canoe vessels) hold historic, symbolic and spiritual meanings for Māori as they represent tribal identity, mana and territory (Walker 2004). Furthermore, many Māori can trace their *whakapapa* (genealogy) back to specific named waka attributed to the migration

56 Farah Palmer et al.

across the Pacific to Aotearoa New Zealand with the first accounts dating back to 1100–1300 AD (Taonui 2005). The (re)introduction of Waka ama as a recreational activity in Aotearoa New Zealand in the early 1980s was a demonstration of Mana motuhake, as Māori embraced the cultural significance of this sport and played a key role in establishing Waka ama as one of the fastest growing sports in Aotearoa New Zealand with over 85 clubs spread across the country, and with a high percentage of Māori participants getting the opportunity to connect with their culture through their involvement and connection with the sport (Waka Ama NZ 2018).

Ngā Kaihoe o Aotearoa (Waka Ama New Zealand) is unique as an NSO in Aotearoa New Zealand in that it is founded on principles of te ao Māori and fully embraces the concept of Mana Māori reflected in the four key values underpinning Ngā Kaihoe o Aotearoa; *manaakitanga* (reciprocity and inclusivity), *hauora* (wellbeing), *whanaungatanga* (belonging, identity, and collective strength), and *tū tangata* (accountability, respect, integrity and passion) (Waka Ama NZ 2018).

This case study highlights how involvement in Waka ama has created a pathway to learn and engage in te ao Māori and enhance the wellbeing of participants from Heretaunga Ararau o Ngāti Kahungunu Waka Ama Roopu, a "club" established in 2001 on the Clive River in Hawke's Bay. Their mission statement reads:

> To provide Community-based Waka Ama programs that encourage both whānau and individual participation, competition and healthy lifestyle, promoted within a safe, nurturing and fun environment.

As the mission statement states, involvement in Waka ama brings whānau members from different generations together in the spirit of *whanaungatanga* (inclusiveness). It is not unusual to see parents, grandparents children and *mokopuna* (grandchildren) all paddling at the same event (Waka Ama NZ 2018). This intergenerational participation aligns with the concept of Mana tangata, thus enabling equity, wellbeing and achievement across the life course of participants, as the following quotes from participants illustrate:

> Ko tōna painga, he hākinakina mō te whānau kātoa. It's a sport that the whole whānau can enjoy.
>
> Going to the waka ama nationals at Lake Karapiro is one of the most positive large events that I've ever been to. It's just like such a cool event and such a positive experience. It was really amazing.

Participants referred to whanaungatanga and *manaakitanga* (reciprocity and inclusivity) as aspects of Waka ama that made the experience enjoyable and positive. Manaakitanga involves caring for a person's mana through an expression of *aroha* (love and compassion), generosity and mutual respect. Much like all team sports and recreational activities, Waka ama requires that each individual has a role and responsibility, while contributing harmoniously to a common collective agenda that is vital to progress. As a result, members become strengthened in their bonds

Māori knowledge in sport **57**

of friendship and kinship "both on and off the water" and support for one another often extends "outside the waka" into the different circumstances that life brings. This reinforces that manaakitanga, whanaungatanga and aroha creates social cohesion within their community and provides participants with a sense of wellbeing and connectedness as noted by these statements:

> So you go there with a mindset of sharing, supporting each other, working together, working hard.
>
> It's actually a lifestyle for me … it's not only the sport, that keeps you healthy, but this other side of it, the camaraderie, all this is really good for the soul and the spirit.
>
> I just think that waka is a community-building activity. It just forces you to be in community. You can't paddle on your own. You can't win the race on your own. You have to work with other people…and I think, yeah… there's a lot that we gain from that.

The Heretaunga Ararau o Ngāti Kahungunu Waka Ama Roopu also demonstrate Mana motuhake or authority over the way in which they manage their club by incorporating Māori philosophies, beliefs, values and practices at the centre of club activity. For example, the club incorporates *tikanga* such as *karakia* [prayer] before engaging with activities on the water and *waiata* [songs] within the club environment to demonstrate Mana motuhake. It is also evident that relationships and a sense of connectedness is not only about people but also refers to the connection experienced between an individual and the geographical location, place and local environment (Barlow 1991; Metge 1990). For instance, the club's name refers to Heretaunga Ararau which is the Māori ancestral name of the region now known as Hastings, and Ngāti Kahungunu is the local iwi of the region. Participants expressed how their connection to the environment impacts positively on their wellbeing:

> You're outside. You're connecting with the awa [river] and the moana [ocean]. And just connecting with nature, so that has a really positive effect on your mental health.
>
> I can't sing the praises enough for the health benefits, and they're health benefits that you probably didn't know were going to be a benefit when you started.

This philosophy of wellbeing embraces *hauora* (a holistic view of health) that not only embodies the positive association with mental health and wellbeing, but also influenced their growing awareness of environmental issues. One participant noted that

> …a lot of people that are into waka ama are also very much into protecting these waterways or fixing them or getting change to happen, because they're in direct contact with them … and so that part I really value as well.

58 Farah Palmer et al.

These narratives highlight the concept of Mana whakahāere that goes beyond the mere stewardship over decisions and authority of the activity itself, but extends to this group's status as *mana whenua* (sovereign hosts of the region) and collective members of *Ngāti Hori ki Kohupatiki*[8] *hapū* (sub-tribe)[9] to act as active protectors and "stewards" of the waterways. By caring for their local waterscapes, its integrity as a natural resource is maintained and therefore remains safe to be used by this group guaranteeing the continuation of Waka ama as a viable activity that ensures intergenerational prosperity at both (bio)physical and environmental sustainability levels.

Case study two: Māori Rugby

Māori rugby is unique, it is not primarily about creating a rugby pathway, but it is about a Māori pathway and access into te ao Māori [the Māori world]. [Rangitira]

Rugby was introduced to Aotearoa New Zealand in 1870 and has become engrained within New Zealand's national as well Māori identity, whether we like it or not. More recently this connection between rugby, Māori identity and pride has been explored from a Kaupapa Māori perspective by both functional and critical scholars (e.g., Hapeta 2018; Hapeta & Palmer 2014; Hirini & Flett 1999; Hokowhitu 2005, 2009; Hokowhitu & Scherer 2008; Mulholland 2009; Palmer 2017). Although Māori empowerment through rugby is challenged and critiqued by both Māori and non-Māori scholars (e.g., Falcous 2007; Hokowhitu 2009; Hokowhitu & Scherer 2008) rugby continues to be an alluring pathway for Māori due to historical narratives (Hokowhitu 2005; Ryan 1993), the mana or elevated status that comes with success in rugby (Mulholland 2009), and the lure of professionalism providing upward social mobility (Scherer & Jackson 2013).

These elements have influenced the high participation rates of Māori in rugby which suggest rugby helps to achieve Mana tangata or equity in rugby. Although the overall Māori population was ≤15% in 2019, >43,000 (27%) of registered players identified as Māori (NZMRB 2019), Māori participation at the elite level in NZR was estimated at 27% in 2017 (NZMRB 2017), and despite the onset of a global pandemic, Māori player numbers decreased to just under 25% in 2020 (NZMRB 2020). On the surface it appears rugby enhances Māori wellbeing, but with regards to Mana whakahāere and Mana motuhake, anecdotal evidence suggests Māori participation at the decision-making level in rugby is well below the player participation percentages. Furthermore, a review of rugby culture that took place in 2017 (Cockburn & Atkinson 2017) highlighted the need for NZR to construct a strategic document that safeguards Māori so that "[Māori] do not have to 'switch modes' to a mono-cultural environment or suppress the very things [Māori] value most" (Cockburn & Atkinson 2017, p. 41). And despite adopting a charter in 2018 that became known as *"Te Ara Ranga Tira*[10] *- The Rugby Way"* (NZR 2021), which aimed to make rugby a more inclusive environment for people from diverse ethnicities, genders, sexualities, religions

Māori knowledge in sport   **59**

and abilities, there are still ongoing concerns about racism and cultural misappropriation in NZR (Blair 2020; Kahi 2017; Taonui 2019). Nonetheless, within NZR there are Māori rugby initiatives which may enhance Māori wellbeing that include some of the mana elements from the Whakamaua model. The narratives provided in this case study illustrate the ways in which a sample of Māori male *rangatahi* (youth), *rangatira* (leaders) and *pūkenga* (elite Māori players) felt rugby experiences that embraced Mana Māori contributed to their wellbeing, particular with regards to embracing their Māori identity.

One rangatahi athlete articulated how Mana Motuhake was integrated into a Māori rugby camp that helped them to perceive their Māori identity as a source of strength:

> We had a kōrero-a-roopu [team meeting] and established our team value… one I have implemented into my everyday life, was "Mana motuhake". For me this re-affirmed my cultural identity. I feel it guided me towards a deeper connection to my roots. In a rugby sense this experience is one of the standouts, because compared to the other mainstream [NZR] camps… this related to me and my cultural background. At the other camps we discussed values, however none accommodated for tikanga [cultural protocols] that we hold as Māori people. Mana motuhake was the value that helped to bring us together and for me is a taonga [treasure] I still carry with me today.

Two other *rangatahi* involved in Māori rugby camps also shared how the inclusion of *te reo*, *tikanga* and *mātauranga Māori* in rugby (both on and off the field) enhanced Mana Māori:

> …There was a pōwhiri [traditional welcome] held for us. I'm no stranger to pōwhiri, but to engage in this ritual at a high-performance rugby camp is something I had never experienced before …after our pōwhiri there was a hākari [feast] for us and we had the opportunity for kōrero [discussion] and whakawhanaungatanga [making connections]. The rest of the day was taken up by waiata [singing] and haka [dance] practices… …Overall, it was a very unique and inspiring week for me, further sparking my passion for not only rugby but Te Ao Māori [Māori world] and its place in modern day rugby.
>
> [The referee] informed us that the game would be refereed entirely in te reo which was a big surprise to me and was an awesome experience and a great way to incorporate te ao Māori [the Maori world] into the game.
>
> The difference that I felt at this [Maori] camp, compared to the others, was that although we may come from different backgrounds, we still share that connection that only Māori have with each other through whakapapa [genealogy] and culture.

60 Farah Palmer et al.

This appreciation of Mana Māori in rugby contexts was also appreciated by a *pūkenga* involved with the Māori All Blacks (MABs) team:

> Everything was amazing. Our kaumatua [respected elder] was awesome at bringing out the Māori side of the players. I really learnt a lot from him about my people which I never knew but loved it. The Māori side bound us together.

The integration of the Māori world with the rugby world appears to have created a sense of pride in Māori identity that then influenced effort, and a sense of unity which also enhanced team performance. This was expressed by a *pūkenga* who played in the MABs when they claimed playing for a Māori team made them *"grow another arm and leg, another heart and lung".*

A *rangatira* involved with the Māori All Blacks also explained how they got a sense of wellbeing from helping *pūkenga* on their cultural journey which was often not revealed until after a tour:

> … selfies … I receive from the [MABs] players, who have returned home to their marae [meeting house] saying – "look at me and my whānau [family] – we have come back home to our maunga [mountain], awa [river] and tūrangawaewae [place of belonging]" – this is a highlight for me.

These anecdotes from *rangatahi, rangatira* and *pūkenga* suggest that Mana Māori integrated into Māori rugby teams, programmes and initiatives enhances the experience of Māori in rugby. This also highlights that high participation rates among Māori in rugby may indicate equity of opportunities (Mana tangata); however, providing opportunities to engage in rugby that are centred on *mātauranga Māori, tikanga Māori* and *Te Ao Māori* will enhance the overall wellbeing of Māori wanting to bring their "whole" selves to the rugby experience (Mana motuhake).

Ultimately, ensuring that Māori wellbeing in rugby is a priority requires Mana whakahāere or stewardship. This is demonstrated through having Māori in decision-making roles at the management and governance level. For more than a decade there has been a Māori Rugby development manager in the NZR, and in 2019, a kaihautū Māori (Māori cultural advisor) was appointed. Despite the many job losses that occurred in 2020 (25%), the only two Māori-specific roles in NZR were maintained through the assistance of funding from *Te Puni Kōkiri* (Ministry of Māori Development) and the Accident Compensation Corporation (ACC) for programmes that targeted *rangatahi* resilience and mental wellbeing. At the governance level, there is currently a Māori Representative on the NZ Rugby Board, who then becomes the Chair of the New Zealand Māori Rugby Board (NZMRB). As an Incorporated Society, the NZMRB works in partnership with the NZRU and Affiliated Unions to promote and develop rugby pathways amongst Māori whether playing, coaching, refereeing, administration or governance and advocating on behalf of Māori Rugby to the NZRU and other appropriate bodies regarding strategic issues relating to Māori rugby. This Mana whakahāere, however, is not necessarily reflective of complete autonomy for Māori in rugby and Māori rugby at this point in time, and the introduction of a potential private equity investor buying 12.5% in NZR's commercial interests, does put Mana whakahāere at risk (Knowler 2021). The achievement of Mana whakahāere relies heavily on Māori stakeholders in the game continually insisting on a seat at the decision-making table/s in rugby. As this case study has demonstrated, the wellbeing of *rangatahi, rangatira* and *pūkenga* relies on the consideration of all the *mana* elements of the Whakamaua model for the future of Māori wellbeing in and through rugby.

Case study three: Olympic and commonwealth games

> The Olympic experiences were quite special. When I think about it now the emotions that flood back, and there are certain emotions that come to mind, it gives me shivers just thinking about it – a tingling sensation it just felt absolutely awesome. It touches you in a special way but for the first time I felt that my culture was being respected and that it had some value because it was being connected to my sport and to me as an elite athlete. [Participant]

Māori have had a distinctive presence in mainstream sport in Aotearoa New Zealand, and more recently at the elite level of the Olympic (and Commonwealth) Games (Erueti & Palmer 2013; Erueti 2014). New Zealand first attended the 1908 Summer Olympic Games in London as part of an "Australasian" team, with the first Māori (Indigenous) athletes, John Hoani MacDonald and Lawrence "Jumbo" Jackson competing in the rowing eights at the Los Angeles Summer Olympic Games in 1932. In the 64-year period between 1932 and 1996 (Atlanta), only 10 Māori athletes competed at the Summer/Winter Olympic and Paralympic Games. However, in a 16-year period for those same events between 2000 (Sydney) and 2016 (Rio) 109 Māori athletes have competed alongside an additional eight Māori participants who attended as officials, referees and coaches.

At the 2016 Olympic Games in Rio, 43 athletes from Aotearoa NZ identified as Māori in the Summer Olympics, as well as seven officials and four Paralympians. In total, Māori participation at the 2016 Rio Olympics and Paralympics numbered 58 due to some participants from Australia also identifying as Māori. The ≥21% of athletes competing at Rio who identified as Māori is slightly above the Māori population of ≤15% of New Zealand's total population (Statistics NZ 2017), an indicator that is generally used to assess Māori societal advancement and prosperity. This supports the Mana tangata principle of equity. In total, Māori athletes have contributed towards the winning of 13 gold medals, four silver medals and four bronze medals.

62 Farah Palmer et al.

Prior to the positive progress of Māori participation at the Olympic Games since Sydney 2000, tensions and misunderstandings between Māori athletes and managers and administration staff at the Olympic Games was more pronounced during the 1980s and 1990s (Erueti 2015). One athlete commented:

> Outwardly we would be able to show other countries our culture mainly through haka. But otherwise, you were not allowed to show anything Māori. Absolutely not!

Another athlete expressed:

> There wasn't much integration of Māori concepts...let alone a whānau feeling. That stuff was non-existent! It was very difficult for an individual athlete to connect with anyone...it was quite tough.

From these examples it is evident that the pre-dominantly non-Māori managers, administrators and coaches at that time did not give full consideration to "cultural needs" of Māori athletes who interpreted their experiences as "lonely", "isolated" and made to feel "pretty much on [their] own". The New Zealand Olympic team management tended to appropriate decontextualised elements of Māori culture such as Haka to mark a specific narrative about New Zealand's national identity, rather than genuinely and holistically embrace Māori identity in the Olympic context. This tokenism was demonstrated by selecting certain aspects of tikanga Māori that preserved the interest of the dominant culture rather than the interests of the indigenous culture. As a result, Māori participants expressed feelings of being marginalised. Such examples contradict the notion of Mana motuhake, the right for Māori to participate in sport on Māori terms and according to Māori philosophies, beliefs, values and practices.

A Māori athlete who joined the Athletes Commission in 1995 started the conversation about bringing in some tikanga Māori principles into the New Zealand Olympic environment (Erueti 2014). As a result of this Mana whakahāere demonstrated by this Māori athlete's persistence, in preparation for the Sydney Olympic Games in 2000, the Chef de Mission and the New Zealand Olympic Committee (NZOC) took on some of these ideas and embarked on an approach to integrate Māori cultural practices and concepts as a vehicle to create a sense of intra-personal connection and to develop an understanding of what it means to represent Aotearoa New Zealand at the Olympic Games (Erueti 2014). To ensure the safe application and integration of these Māori cultural practices, two Māori cultural advisors were appointed (to ensure Mana whakahāere) and travelled with the New Zealand team to Sydney. The advisors identified the Māori concepts of *whānau* (familial ties), *whanaungatanga* (developing connections) and *kōtahitanga* (community or unified vision) as essential elements to their approach. The shift to develop this approach certainly aligns with the principle of Mana

Māori (customary practices). This included practices such as *haka* (ritualistic dance) and *waiata* (song or chant) used during the process of *pōwhiri* (welcoming ritual) and performed to celebrate the success of NZ athletes. Additionally, there were a number of carefully selected symbols such as *korowai* (ceremonial cloak made of feathers) worn by the flag-bearer and *pounamu* (jade or greenstone) jewellery gifted to each athlete.

The result was the establishment of a single team entity of identity, meaning, belonging and cohesion (Hodge & Hermansson 2007). Since its inception in Sydney 2000, the integration of Māori cultural practices has become a fundamental component for all subsequent able-bodied New Zealand Summer and Winter Olympic and Commonwealth Games teams competing at these mega-events.

A surprising and unexpected outcome has been the profound impact the integration of Māori cultural practices has had upon Māori athletes (Erueti 2015). They testify that

> it is hard to put into words what it actually felt like because I believe that you needed to have been a part of it all and be there to experience the feeling…but it was certainly very special and something I will never ever forget… it was pretty powerful. It also gave you a sense of home and being very Kiwi.
>
> To have those who are non-Māori perceive what we were doing as being special made it even more special for me because they were recognizing a part of who I am and to the best of their ability trying to connect with that part of what makes New Zealand unique. On a deeper level the obvious and main effect that was happening was the construction and building of a team foundation and bringing us closer together. It just makes you so proud to be a New Zealander.

The integration of some aspects of tikanga Māori within the NZ team at the Olympic games has various impacts on those involved. First, for non-Māori involved with the NZ Olympic (and Commonwealth) Games team, it demonstrates how Māori cultural practices in elite sporting environs can "bring people together" with the potential for all involved to increase their awareness of Aotearoa New Zealand's bicultural heritage. Additionally, when attempts are made by non-Māori coaches, administration and management staff to understand cultural differences, close long-term relationships followed (Erueti 2014). Second, and more importantly from a Māori wellbeing perspective, when Māori athletes experience their culture being reflected in their sporting environment, a reaffirmation of the value of Māori culture and personal identity occurs. Succinctly, the narrative evidence overwhelmingly encourages the notions expressed by the principle Mana Māori (customary practices) and the positive impact this can have on Mana motuhake.

In 2018 the NZOC Māori Advisory Committee was established, to provide advice on "tikanga – general behaviour guidelines for daily life and interaction

64 Farah Palmer et al.

in Māori culture and ensuring its 'seamless' inclusion across the organisation and its activities" (Etchells 2019, para. 29). Although the acceptance of a bicultural approach was non-existent in Aotearoa New Zealand's first century of participation at the Olympic Games, the last two decades indicate that the extent to which the NZOC continues to support Māori athlete participation, and embrace Māori political resurgence and bicultural advancement within policy and strategy, seems outwardly at least, to be very progressive and embracing of Mana whakahāere (stewardship) and Mana tangata (equity).

Conclusion

The title of this chapter "Whakamaua[11] kia tina!" is taken from a well-known *whakataukī* (proverb):

> Ko te pae tawhiti, whāia kia tata. Ko te pae tata, whakamaua kia tīna!
> Seek out the distant horizons, while cherishing our achievements at hand!

Hence, the *Whakamaua* model and the *whakataukī* it is inspired by, conveys a sense of acting to take hold of those goals within our reach, as well as working to secure outcomes, objectives and priority areas for action that will contribute to the achievement of healthy futures for Māori. It is with this proverb in mind in which we hope that this chapter has expressed the ways in which sport and active recreation can be a site of resistance and revitalisation for Māori. The focus of this chapter was on how sport and active recreation could enhance Māori wellbeing. There were however, elements of the three case studies that did demonstrate aspects of resistance through the Māori narratives shared.

Resistance in waka ama occurred through the formation of an NSO in the 1980s that had at its centre, a Māori worldview that embraced te reo Māori and tikanga Māori, something that would have been quite unique at the time, when most NSOs were well-established in NZ from a colonial perspective in the late 1800s and early 1900s (Watson et al. 2017). Within rugby, resistance occurred through Māori rugby stakeholders, and other high-profile Māori figures challenging the NZR to better serve Māori in rugby through reviews, commissioned reports, and representation at the governance and management levels within the organisation. In the NZ Olympic (and Commonwealth) Games teams, Māori athletes (past and present) challenged the NZOC to move beyond tokenistic inclusion of *tikanga* Māori and *taonga* (treasures) and to understand that the inclusion of *tikanga* and *taonga* not only benefitted national identity and wellbeing but Māori identity and wellbeing as well.

Through the application of the Whakamaua model and the mana concepts of *Mana whakahāere* (stewardship); *Mana motuhake* (self-determination); *Mana tangata* (equity); and *Mana Māori* (customary rituals) illustrated how sport and active recreation revitalises Māori wellbeing through the perspective of Māori participants in waka ama (at the club level), rugby (at the NSO level), and as part of the NZ Olympic (and Commonwealth) Games team (at the global event level).

Mana whakahāere (stewardship) and Mana motuhake (self-determination) often went hand-in-hand in all case studies. Māori play a key role in Mana whakahāere in waka ama, and Mana motuhake is thus demonstrated as a result. It could be argued that waka ama at the national and club level is an act of Mana motuhake for Māori that not only benefits Māori but non-Māori as well who value the *whanaungatanga* (connection) and *kaitaikitanga* (guardianship) of the environment that are integral to waka ama practices and philosophies. Mana whakahāere in rugby is demonstrated through the NZ Māori Rugby Board and the two roles within NZR with a specific Māori *kaupapa* (purpose). Unlike waka ama, this stewardship is more precarious and often depends on a spirit of partnership between the NZR and NZMRB, as well as Mana whakahāere coming from Māori stakeholders outside the organisation who keep those within NZR aware of their role as stewards. Within the NZ Olympic and Commonwealth environments, Māori have some opportunities to demonstrate Mana whakahāere as cultural advisors and Committee members, and Māori athletes have appreciated their efforts as stewards in a way that enhances their Mana motuhake. There is room for improvement in terms of Mana whakahāere and Mana motuhake in both rugby and the Olympic movement, in order for these efforts to be sustained into the future.

Mana Māori was evident in all three case studies. It was integral and central to the waka ama case study, included wholeheartedly in Māori rugby initiatives within NZR, and embraced more recently by the NZOC in a way that benefitted national as well as Māori identity and pride. The inclusion of Mana Māori also impacts directly on Mana motuhake of Māori participants who appreciate the bringing together of the sport world with their Māori world.

Mana tangata was evident in waka ama with a high percentage of Māori engagement at all levels – from kaihoe (paddler) to kaihautū (leader). On the surface, Mana tangata appeared to occur in rugby at the player level in both the community and professional game but reports and anecdotal evidence suggest equity at the leadership level, and in terms of resource allocation and club culture is still out of reach. Mana tangata at the Olympics and Commonwealth Games for Māori has improved more recently, especially with the inclusion of sports such as basketball, rugby and netball where Māori participation is strong. In terms of Mana tangata at the decision-making level of NZR and NZOC specifically, equity is still on the distant horizon, but recent diversity and inclusion strategies embraced by SportNZ (see https://sportnz.org.nz/diversity-and-inclusion/) may bring that horizon closer.

In summary, the application of the Whakamaua model and mana principles appears to be a useful tool for sport and active recreation systems and structures who genuinely want to explore how Māori wellbeing could be enhanced now and in the future. The three case studies provide a snapshot of how, when sport and active recreation contexts are framed by *te ao Māori* (the Māori world) perspective, enacted through *tikanga Māori* (Māori philosophy and customary

66 Farah Palmer et al.

practices) and encapsulated within *mātauranga Māori* (Māori knowledge) Māori wellbeing can be enhanced.

Notes

1 The Māori name for New Zealand, translated as "Land of the Long White Cloud". For this chapter the unified term of Aotearoa New Zealand is used.
2 Ihi Aotearoa is the te reo Māori (Māori language) designation for Sport New Zealand.
3 In 1840 representatives of the British crown and some (but not all) Māori chiefs signed a treaty of cession called Te Tiriti o Waitangi (Māori version) or the Treaty of Waitangi (English version). There are four articles of the Māori version that are respectively manifested by the terms kāwanatanga (governorship), tino rangatiratanga (chieftain-ship), ōritetanga (equity and equality) and ritenga/wairuatanga (spirituality).
4 Geographical locations of significance based on whānau (familial) and hapū (sub-tribal) connections.
5 The name (designation) is in reference to their history and ancestral connections to the area in which the club is located. *Heretaunga Ararau* refers to the Māori Ancestral name of the Hastings District region. *Ngāti Kahungunu*, is the name of the local *iwi* (tribe) of the region of Hawkes Bay (see below).
6 A region of Aotearoa New Zealand located on the east coast of the North Island. The region's name derives from Hawke Bay, which was named by Captain James Cook in honour of Admiral Edward Hawke. The Māori designation of Hawke's Bay is *Te Matau-a- Māui*/the Fishhook of Māui which is in reference to the *pūrākau* (Māori historical narrative) of the demigod Māui and his discovery of Aotearoa.
7 *Whakamaua* means "to secure, to grasp, to take hold of, to wear". It is also widely associated with the whakataukī "Ko te pae tawhiti, whāia kia tata. Kote pae tata, whakamaua kia tīna" – "Seek out the distant horizons, while cherishing those achievements at hand".
8 Ngāti Hori ki Kohupatiki is a *hapū* of Ngāti Kahungunu ki Heretaunga, the larger governing iwi. Ngāti Hori ki Kohupatiki are kaitiaki of the lower Karamu Stream and have a close historic and traditional relationship with the Karamu stream and the former course of the Ngaruroro River.
9 The basic foundation of Māori life was based on the familial societal structure of the *whānau* nuclei, with many whānau contributing amongst one another to form *hapū* (sub-tribes). The process of reciprocity between communal *hapū* formed *iwi* (tribes) that became particularly functional especially during periods of warfare or expansion (see Erueti 2015).
10 More accurately translated as "the way that unites people" (see NZR 2021).
11 The word *whakamaua* contains the root word *mau* that has several descriptions. As a verb it denotes to "lay hold of, grasp, wield, to put on" and as a stative it describes to be "held, established, taken, comprehended, understood" (see māoridictionary. co.nz). Adding the prefix "*whaka*" enhances the word *mau* as a concept that advocates it to be "caused to happen" while the suffix "*a*" is merely a particle used in passive endings (mainly with verbs).

References

Barlow, C. 1991, *Tikanga whakaaro: Key concepts in Māori culture*, Oxford University Press, Auckland.
Blair, N. 2020, *Super Aotearoa: New Zealand Rugby miss a trick as Māori players suffer.* Stuff, viewed 20 January 2021, https://www.stuff.co.nz/sport/rugby/opinion/300173111/ super-aotearoa-new-zealand-rugby-miss-a-trick-as-mori-players-suffer

Cockburn, R. & Atkinson, L. 2017, *Respect and responsibility review. A commissioned report for New Zealand Rugby*, NZ Rugby, Auckland, viewed 30 January 2021 https://www.nzrugby.co.nz/assets/NZR-RRR-Final-Review-Report.pdf

Erueti, B. 2014, 'Mātauranga Māori at the Olympic and Commonwealth Games', *MAI Journal*, Vol. 3, no. 1, pp. 60–73.

Erueti B. 2015, *'Ngā kaipara Māori: Ngā pūmahara o te tuakiri Māori me te ao hākinakina Māori athletes: Perceptions of Māori identity and elite sport participation'*, PhD thesis, Massey University, Palmerston North, New Zealand.

Erueti, B. & Palmer, F. R. 2013, 'Te whāriki tuakiri (the identity mat): Māori elite athletes and the expression of ethno-cultural identity in global sport', *Sport in Society*, Vol. 17, no. 8, pp. 1061–1075.

Etchells, D. 2019, *New Zealand Olympic Committee President acknowledges successful year as 2018 annual report presented*, viewed 7 June 2020, https://www.insidethegames.biz/articles/1078995/new-zealand-olympic-committee-president-acknowledges-successful-year-as-2018-annual-report-presented.

Falcous, M. 2007, 'The decolonizing national imaginary: Promotional media constructions during the 2005 Lions tour of Aotearoa New Zealand', *Journal of Sport and Social Issues*, Vol. 31, pp. 374–393.

Hapeta, J. 2019, *'An examination of cultural inclusion and Māori culture in New Zealand rugby: The impact on well-being'*, PhD thesis, Massey University, Palmerston North, New Zealand.

Hapeta, J. & Palmer, F.R. 2014, 'Māori culture counts: a case study of the Waikato Chiefs', in T. Black (ed.), *Enhancing mātauranga Māori and global Indigenous knowledge*, New Zealand Qualifications Authority, Wellington, pp. 101–116.

Hippolite, R. H. & Bruce, T. 2010, 'Speaking the unspoken: racism, sport and Māori', *Cosmopolitan Civil Societies Journal*, Vol. 2, no. 2, pp. 23–45.

Hirini, P. & Flett, R. A. 1999, 'Aspects of the Māori All Black experience: the value of cultural capital in the new professional era', *He Pukenga Korero: A Journal of Māori Studies*, Vol. 5, no. 1, pp. 18–24.

Hodge, K. & Hermansson, G. 2007, 'Psychological preparation of athletes for the Olympic context: the New Zealand Summer and Winter Olympic Teams', *The Online Journal of Sport Psychology*, Vol. 9, no. 4, pp. 1–4.

Hokowhitu, B. 2005, 'Rugby and tino rangātiratanga: early Maori rugby and the formation of traditional Maori masculinity', *Sporting Traditions*, Vol. 21, no. 2, pp. 75–95.

Hokowhitu, B. 2009, 'Māori rugby and subversion: creativity, domestication, oppression and decolonization', *International Journal of the History of Sport*, Vol. 26, no. 16, pp. 2314–2334.

Hokowhitu, B. & Scherer, J. 2008, 'The Māori All Blacks and the decentering of the white subject: hyperrace, sport, and the cultural logic of late capitalism', *Sociology of Sport Journal,* Vol. 25, no. 2, pp. 243–262.

Kahi, H. 2017, *Heart of Dark(y)ness: Negotiating race and racism in New Zealand rugby: Club rugby players talk rugby*, Masters thesis, University of Canterbury, Christchurch, New Zealand.

Knowler, M. 2021, *Rugby: NZ Māori Rugby Board boss won't allow Silverlake to hijack haka*. Stuff, viewed 1 April 2021, https://www.stuff.co.nz/sport/rugby/all-blacks/300265878/rugby-nz-mori-rugby-board-boss-wont-allow-silver-lake-to-hijack-haka

McKegg, K., Wehipeihana, N., Pipi, K. & Thompson, V. 2013, *He Oranga Poutama: What have we learned. A report on the developmental evaluation of He Oranga Poutama*, Sport NZ, Kennect Group (46pp).

Metge, J. 1990, 'Te rito o te harakeke: Conceptions of the whānau', *Journal of the Polynesian Society*, Vol. 99, no. 1, pp. 55–92.

Ministry of Health. 2020, *Whakamaua: The Māori Health Action Plan 2020–2025*, Ministry of Health, Wellington.

Mulholland, M. 2009, *Beneath the Māori moon: An illustrated history of Māori Rugby*, Huia Publishers, Wellington.

New Zealand Māori Rugby Board. 2017, *Annual report*, New Zealand Rugby, Wellington.

New Zealand Māori Rugby Board. 2019, *Annual report*, New Zealand Rugby, Wellington.

New Zealand Māori Rugby Board. 2020, *Annual report*, New Zealand Rugby, Wellington.

New Zealand Rugby. 2021, *Rugby toolbox: The rugby way*, viewed 22 February 2021, https://www.rugbytoolbox.co.nz/the-game/the-rugby-way

Palmer, F.R. 2017, 'The Māori All Blacks and ethnicity in Aotearoa New Zealand in the professional era', in J. Nauright & T. Collins (eds.), *The Rugby World in the professional era*, Routledge, New York, pp. 62–77.

Palmer, F. R., & Masters, T. M. 2010, 'Māori feminism and sport leadership: Exploring Māori women's experiences', *Sport Management Review*, Vol. 13, no. 4, pp. 331–344.

Ryan, G. 1993, *Forerunners of the All Blacks: The 1888–89 New Zealand Native football team in Britain, Australia and New Zealand*, Canterbury University Press, Christchurch, New Zealand.

Scherer, J. & Jackson, S. J. 2013, *The contested terrain of the New Zealand All Blacks: Rugby, commerce, and cultural politics in the age of globalisation*, Peter Lang, Oxford.

Sport New Zealand. 2017, *Māori participation in community sport review*, KTV Consulting (38 pp). https://sportnz.org.nz/resources/maori-participation-in-community-sport-report/

Sport New Zealand. 2020, *Annual report*, viewed 1 February 2021, https://sportnz.org.nz/media/3577/201920-sport-nz-annual-report-12_22-web.pdf

Sport New Zealand. n.d., Growth of Waka Ama case study, viewed 2 February 2021, https://sportnz.org.nz/resources/growth-of-waka-ama/

Statistics New Zealand. 2017, *New Zealand population summary figures 1991–2017*, Statistics New Zealand, Wellington.

Taonui, R. 2005, *Tribal organisation*, viewed 30 January 2021, https://teara.govt.nz/en/tribal-organisation/print.

Taonui, R. 2019, *Rugby, racism and xenophobia*, viewed 30 January 2021, https://www.waateanews.com/waateanews/x_news/MjMzODI/Opinion/Rugby,Racism-and-Xenophobia.

Te Puni Kōkiri. 2005, *Te Māori i te whutupōro: Māori in rugby* (Fact Sheet 23), Te Puni Kōkiri, Wellington.

Te Puni Kōkiri, 2006, *Ngā Māori in ngā mahi Tākaro. Māori in sport and active leisure* (Fact Sheet 25), Te Puni Kōkiri, Wellington.

Te Rito, P. 2006, 'Leadership in Māori, European cultures and in the world of sport', *MAI Review*, Vol. 1 (Intern Research Report 8), pp. 1–19, retrieved from http://www.review.mai.ac.nz/index.php/MR/article/view/17/17.

Waka Ama NZ. 2018, *Waka ama New Zealand*, viewed 30 September 2020, https://www.wakaama.co.nz/stories.

Walker, R. 2004, *Ka whawhai tonu mātou: Struggle without end*, Penguin, Auckland.

Watson, G.D., Palmer, F.R. & Ryan, G.J. 2017, 'Aotearoa/New Zealand', in J. Nauright & D. Wiggins (eds.), *Routledge handbook of sport, race and ethnicity*, Routledge, Oxon, pp. 131–145.

Wikaire, R. & Newman, J. 2014, 'Neoliberalism as neocolonialism? Considerations on the marketisation of Waka Ama in Aotearoa/New Zealand', in C. Hallinan & B. Judd, B. (eds.), *Native games: Indigenous peoples and sports in the post-colonial world*, Vol. 7, Emerald Group Publishing, pp. 59–83.

7

POLICY, MODERNISATION AND THE POLITICS OF SPORT INTEGRITY

Michael P. Sam and Timothy M. Dawbin

Introduction

As with all public sector programmes aimed at achieving some form of development/growth, sport is a "tricky" endeavour. For many states, achieving the dual aims of "getting more people to play more" and "getting more people to play better" is difficult not least because these aims rely on a complex set of interdependent organisations (cf. Sam 2016; Sam & Ronglan 2018). To the degree that organisations in the sports sector are autonomous and span public, private and non-profit sectors at national/regional/local levels, it is not surprising to see persistent efforts towards coordinating and steering their activities. From a central government agency's perspective, this sectoral coordination is impor-tant to reduce duplication, distribute resources efficiently and generally foster a competent system.

The devil is in the detail as they say, and it is widely understood that any at-tempt to lead, control or coordinate a system will generate side effects (Hood & Peters 2004; Margetts et al. 2012). For instance, it appears fairly evident that centralised, politically controlled and hierarchical systems of elite sport develop-ment are susceptible to doping, just as commercial, free-market-oriented systems have a tendency to treat sport as an entertainment commodity (with its attendant inequities). For a country like New Zealand, the way in which sport has been governed lies somewhere in between these extremes, yet this is not to say that deliberate interventions aimed at steering the sector have been without effects.

The New Zealand media deemed 2018 "the year of sports reviews" (Cleaver 2018; Johannsen 2018). Five national sport organisations (Netball, Cycling, Hockey, Football and Rowing) announced they had undergone or would be commissioning, independent reviews to assess aspects of their respective pro-grammes, cultures and strategies (Alderson 2018; Anderson 2018; Gourdie 2018;

DOI: 10.4324/9781003034445-7

70 Michael P. Sam and Timothy M. Dawbin

Johannsen 2018; Napier 2018; Prendiville 2018). The reviews of cycling, hockey and football were particularly high profile since they shared a critical view of organisational cultures said to tacitly accept bullying, harassment and athlete maltreatment. In the same year, the government's crown agency Sport New Zealand (SNZ), commissioned a scoping investigation on the subject of "integrity" in the sector (Sport New Zealand 2018), resulting in a discussion paper, a survey and a separate report on elite athletes' rights and welfare (Cottrell 2018). A year later, SNZ issued a joint statement with the country's five largest NSOs suggesting that "it's time to change our approach to youth sport". Among its stated commitments, the group advanced changes in competitions structures and promoted a *developmental* (rather than a professional) approach to youth sport.

Given New Zealand's small size, its social "two degrees of separation" and sport's interdependency (Sam 2015b), it would be hard to claim these reviews, discussions, deliberations and joint commitments are not in some way connected. The subject of integrity has emerged rather suddenly in the New Zealand sport landscape. While the concept has its roots in "good governance", and the corruption in international sport governing bodies such as the International Olympic Committee and FIFA (Chappelet 2018), integrity has become a catch-all for a range of issues including athlete welfare, child protection, sexual harassment/violence, illegal betting, doping and fan hooliganism (Gardiner et al. 2017).

Against this background, this chapter aims to trace the policy reforms that have led to the emergence of integrity as a contemporary governance issue in New Zealand sport. This analysis spans the last two decades of sport policy in New Zealand and focuses particularly on the state's relationship vis-à-vis its partner national governing bodies. It is argued that while the recent concern for integrity in sport may be recognised as part of a larger (and global) social movement, it can nevertheless also be viewed as the outcome of successive attempts to direct the affairs of NSOs in line with outputs, targets and audits.

The following analysis is informed principally by political variants of institutional theory (see Peters 2012). From this perspective, institutions are understood to comprise the policies, rules, regulations, procedures and patterns of interaction that shape the behaviours of organisations and individuals. Institutions enable/constrain these behaviours not only by signalling what *should* be done but by also limiting what one can *imagine* doing (Hall & Taylor 1996; March & Olsen 1989). For example, sport organisations are likely to operate far differently if they are guided by a *market* (an institution characterised by a logic of competition) versus a *network* (characterised by a logic of cooperation) versus a *federation* (characterised by a logic of democratic representation). Importantly then, institutions have inertia and are resistant to change, owing to their reproduction and incremental development over time. However, institutions also contain the seeds of their own reconstruction due to their inherent imperfections (and tradeoffs), as well as their susceptibility to "critical junctures" and societal changes (Baumgartner & Jones 1993; Lowndes & Roberts 2013). With these basic principles in mind, it is suggested here that the institutions surrounding elite sport (e.g., contracts, target setting and monitoring) have induced a "tipping point" at which the actions and practices of NSOs now face scrutiny around integrity.

This chapter proceeds as follows. The first section highlights the link between sport and the new public management (NPM), where NPM refers to the global movement in which governments have been recast to adopt private sector principles and practices. This section further highlights the two main institutions that together have served to modernise sport over the last two decades: (1) the system of contracts, performance measurement and targeted funding, and (2) the deployment of training, consultancy services and reviews. Focusing on high-performance sport, the next section corroborates extant research on New Zealand sport policy with evidence drawn from the Cottrell report to suggest that the funding regime elicits a number of side-effects related to integrity. Finally, this chapter concludes by suggesting that given the focus on compliance both historically and through institutions modernising NSOs, we can expect the emerging national policy frameworks to include further performance-based remedies.

Sport, NPM and modernisation

Emanating from the mid-1980s, NPM was a set of doctrines within the public sector that effectively sought to make government "more business-like". The use of NPM (as distinct from the term "neoliberal" per other sections of this volume) is useful because it encapsulates a number of specific structural reforms that are particular to governments and their operations (Pollitt & Bouckaert 2004). A dominant element in NPM reforms is that creating markets (and competition) can induce efficiencies and reduce costs. Hence from 1984 onwards, successive New Zealand governments oversaw the creation of markets for electricity (by unbundling line ownership from line charges), markets for tertiary education (via the proliferation of private training establishments) and other markets from the sale of state assets (like railroads, telecommunication and airlines). The underpinning logic in these markets is that citizens are best served by their rational decision-making as consumers. By extension, the government itself can cut costs and increase its efficiency if it also becomes a consumer and "shops around" to get the best buy. The government should thus purchase or more particularly "contract out" its goals to a range of private and non-profit organisations (Boston et al. 1996).

Reflecting this new doctrine, sport moved from within a government ministry into a Crown agency at arms-length, resulting in the Hillary Commission (HC) in 1987. By the early 1990s, the HC began contracting national sport organisations (NSOs) and newly established regional sports trusts (RSTs) to deliver central programmes. The entrenchment of this contracting continued with the establishment of Sport and Recreation New Zealand (SPARC), a new Crown agency formed from the amalgamation of the New Zealand Sport Foundation, the Office of Tourism and Sport and the Hillary Commission.

The importance of this background lies in understanding the tightening accountability around partner organisations and the increasing use of contracts, audits and other tools of "inspection" to discipline them (Houlihan & Chapman 2015; Sam 2009). Internationally, New Zealand governments throughout the 1980s and 1990s were amongst the most enthusiastic adopters of performance measurement, a ubiquitous feature of NPM that has been widely applied in sport (Fahlén 2017; Sam 2012). Generally, these regimes involve the use of targets/benchmarks to "sweat assets" into performing better. In the sport sector, these schemes work alongside the creation of "quasi-markets" that pit providers (NSOs) against one another for contestable funding. Thus, shortly after its establishment in 2002, SPARC initiated a range of reforms, chief among them that the distribution of funds to sport organisations be more tightly controlled and targeted to those that could deliver on key outcomes. This new investment regime meant that the central agency increasingly relied on targets and output measures as conditions for effective contracts. While output measures were applied to RSTs in relation to participation growth, the new performance regime was most stringently applied in relation to high-performance sport.

Indeed by 2009, SPARC noted that it had to "be uncompromising in applying criteria based on past performance and the likelihood of future success" (Worthington 2009, para. 5). The result was an increasingly selective funding model aiming to "place money, investment and support where you think you will get outcomes" (Cleaver 2009, para. 13). Performance-based allocations remain a key principle of High Performance Sport New Zealand (HPSNZ) where investment is: "Targeted and top-down [and] prioritises resources to NSOs and campaigns with the greatest probability of success" (High Performance Sport New Zealand 2017, p. 7). Importantly, this regime emanated directly from SPARC/SNZ's own targets and the need to show value for money to its principals – the government and its institutions (e.g., Parliament and Treasury).

Given SPARC/SNZ's reliance on RSTs and NSOs, the agency has long aimed to modernise them, under the logic that well-functioning, professional organisations are likely to produce greater outputs (Sam et al. 2018). SPARC/SNZ has sought to improve the governance capabilities of partner organisations, through its publications (e.g., *Nine Steps to Effective Governance*) and programmes (e.g., SportsMark, Organisational Development Tool, Sport Compass, Governance Quality Mark). While these programmes change periodically, they share common elements such as the achievement/maintenance of a "quality standard", via regular external evaluations by accredited assessors (see for example, Sport New Zealand, 2016). Governing boards are the typical target for these training and consultancy services (Hill et al. 2016). Delivered via SNZ's "business capability team", services like these bring NPM back to the fore, inasmuch as they aim to make public sport organisations more efficient and business-like (Hill et al. 2021; Sam et al. 2018; Sam & Schoenberg 2020). For NSOs more particularly, these "nudges" are backed to some degree by their contract agreements with SNZ (Dawbin et al. 2021). Indeed, SNZ stipulates that as part of the agreement, it can

> request in writing that a review be undertaken of [an NSO's] governance, management and/or financial administration by Sport New Zealand or, at Sport New Zealand's election, by an independent person.
>
> *(Sport New Zealand 2013, p. 9)*

The agreement also stipulates that the NSOs must "co-operate fully in the completion of any Audit or Review"; refusing to do so or "fail[ing] to implement any recommendations" may result in Sport New Zealand "suspend[ing] any investment or provision of other support" (Sport New Zealand 2013, p. 9). These reviews thus advance NPM ideas by heightening accountability, transparency, and reporting practices, as well as emphasising performance-based results (Dawbin et al. 2021).

SNZ thus tries to coordinate sector activities through both its formal contracting and various benchmarking exercises/tools for organisational "self-assessment". These tools indirectly set the shared understandings and expectations of the sector. These expectations are manifest in SNZ's focus and support of "capable organisations", targeting those that "can effectively and efficiently deliver" and those best able to demonstrate outputs (Sport New Zealand 2012, 2013, p. 15). While output measures and the push towards making sport more "modern" appear across the sector, these two elements are most explicitly applied with respect to elite sport.

Targets and modernisation: sowing the seeds of the integrity movement?

Globally from the late 1990s it became increasingly evident that NPM in general and the systems of performance measurement, audit and inspection more particularly, could elicit distortions and unintended consequences. In the UK health sector, for instance, decreased emergency room wait times (the target) became emblematic of the "gaming" behaviours these targets could induce (e.g., making patients wait in ambulances or corridors to meet the target) (Bevan and Hood 2006). In this vein, the following section suggests how the modernisation project has precipitated the contemporary demands for athlete welfare and integrity.

It has long been understood that performance regimes can have effects other than the efficiency gains they are designed for (Van Dooren et al. 2010). While early reviews, strategies and programmes emphasised high-performance results, in alignment with the broader dominant paradigm, they paid little (if any) attention to athlete welfare or broader sports integrity issues. The effects of New Zealand sport's performance-based funding model feature both in scholarly research and in SNZ's more recent reviews.

As part of its Sport Integrity Review, SNZ commissioned a separate report to focus on high-performance sport and athlete welfare. The report's investigator (Steve Cottrell, a solicitor and former athlete) drew from interviews and submissions from 107 athletes, coaches, administrators, campaign personnel and the Athletes' Commission. The Cottrell (2018) report entitled *"Elite Athletes' Rights and Welfare"* yielded many insights and observations, many of which suggest a link between integrity issues and the system of targets and performance-based funding.

One observation has been that since HPSNZ/SNZ fund NSOs on the "probability of success", this can favour the purchase of an existing environment rather than the development of a less efficient and effective one (Sam, 2012). The concern, as Cottrell (2018) observes is that, *"with the current funding model…it drives Sporting Organisations to focus on short term results at the expense of developing players or creating a sustainable high performance system within each sport"* (p. 115). Indeed this precarious sustainability can be traced back to over a decade ago when HPSNZ decreased the number of sports and carded athletes it supported from 24 sports and 950 athletes in 2006 down to 14 sports and 440 athletes in 2013 (Sam 2015a). Thus, under this funding model, Sam and Macris (2014) have noted that the central agencies tend to operate as would a corporate sponsor, cherry-picking the NSOs and high-performance campaigns they think will reap medal outputs. Reflecting this point, a para elite athlete speaking to Cottrell (2018) suggested there were "[para] sports which are funded because it is perceived to be easier to win a medal in that sport's classification" (p. 115).

Picking the "low hanging fruit" is a practice that has subsequently been adopted by the NSOs themselves – Sam and Macris (2014) reported evidence of an NSO abandoning a women's programme because administrators did not feel they could "get a return out of that" (p. 523). From this, it follows that cherry-picking may also become evident within the HP "entourages", where support personnel (e.g., mental skills, strength & conditioning, etc.) start to focus their attention on athletes most likely to yield a return (Sam 2015a). As it relates to integrity, one of Cottrell's (2018) interviewees suggested that for support personnel, the risk is that performance might be prioritised over health. Cottrell (2018) wrote, *"I was told that there is a potential for increased risk-taking behaviour, related to a performance outcome perspective, the more closely aligned practitioners are with sport outcomes and the further they are from their professional colleagues"* (p. 116).

There is also the propensity for performance-based funding to result in athletes taking risks so as not to lose their grant support. More particularly, and with respect to the propensity for such systems to foster integrity problems, Cottrell (2018) observes that the threat of "being cut by the system" increased the pressure to compete:

> One interviewee spoke of the need to retain her PEGs [performance enhancement grants] as being one of the considerations behind her decision to race while carrying an injury (she ended up making the injury worse and having to have surgery.
>
> (p. 117)

Research has noted in this context that "rewarding the winners and punishing the losers" has had very real effects on NSOs and their operations. Perhaps best encapsulating the connection between the performance funding regime and its effects, Cottrell (2018) recounts:

> An example given to me was where HPSNZ wants medal outcomes from an NSO. The NSO says it needs more resources and expertise to achieve those outcomes. HPSNZ's response is that its [the NSO's] performance does not warrant more resources but it needs to improve to get funding. The coach is then under pressure to improve performance so his or her only option is to train the athletes harder. This in turn leads to athlete welfare issues. When they arise, HPSNZ stands back and says, "Sport owns sport" and the NSO says, "We are just doing what it takes to achieve the performance outcomes set by HPSNZ". No one takes responsibility for the consequences.
>
> *(p.115)*

On the other side of the risk equation, the system makes NSOs risk-averse (Sam 2012). One of Cottrell's (2018) respondents for example pointed out that the risk for "when things go wrong" lies with the athlete, coach and NSO, leading to "a blame culture" (p. 117). This culture in turn can have perverse effects, chief among them the propensity for NSOs to protect the brand. Indeed Cottrell noted that NSOs are "incentivised to make the future look bright", quoting one interviewee who said, "*the current HPSNZ funding model encourages sports to paint a positive picture in an attempt to secure more or retain funding*" (p. 115). As an example of this kind of "brand protection", Swimming New Zealand once claimed success for an altitude training camp with "no major illness", but at which the sport's top medal hopeful being hospitalised from exhaustion and dehydration (Sam 2015a, p. 24). To an extent, such behaviours are an expected outcome of a system in which mistakes can affect a sport's reputation, funding and support. Beyond this, immersing the sports sector in blame cultures potentially leads to NSOs embedding accountability in formal structures and policies. However, this arguably reinforces a cycle of risk-aversion, organisational opaqueness and ineffectual learning, characterised by Swimming New Zealand's frequent reviews in the last decade (cf. Dawbin et al. 2021; Sam 2012). Despite being reviewed in 2005, 2008, 2011 and, with "damning" recommendations in 2012 (advising for the resignation of the board and chief executive), Swimming NZ was once again reviewed in 2017.

According to Cottrell (2018), four independent reviews had been underway during the time of his investigation: cycling, hockey, football and triathlon. He observed that all of the reviews appeared "to have been driven at least in part, by concerns raised by Elite Athletes about how they have been treated by their NSO and/or coach" (p. 14). Importantly, where problems have been brought to the fore publicly (e.g., most recently in hockey, canoe racing), the narrative appears increasingly to suggest both a dysfunctional NSO, as well as a dysfunctional system. Cycling's review (Heron 2018) for example, released within a month of Cottrell's report, levelled criticism at the wider system for that sport's inability to address its integrity problems. The investigator stated:

> Underlying this situation is a high performance system which requires further reflection as to whether it adequately protects the welfare of athletes and others involved. There is an absence of a functioning and confidential method of escalating and dealing with situations such as these. That absence appears in other areas of high performance sport in New Zealand. The system needs review in that respect.
>
> *(Heron 2018, p. 6)*

The cycling review furthermore connected athlete welfare with modernisation reforms and high-performance funding arrangements:

> After the performances at [the] Rio [Olympics], the base funding was reduced to $4.2m by HPSNZ. Because of this investment model, it was expressed to me that there is pressure, be it conscious or unconscious, to act in a way that gives the organisation the best chance at producing medals (so that funding can be maximised). This could lead to an environment where negative behaviour is tolerated and overlooked in the short term.
>
> *(Heron 2018, p. 45)*

In New Zealand Football's (2018) review, the investigator also acknowledged the current challenges for sport regarding athlete/ player welfare and engagement, noting "a number of other reviews of NZ national sports organisations have recently taken place, or are underway (indicating that the issues facing NZF are not isolated)" (Muir 2018, p. 6). According to this same report, Peter Miskimmin (CEO of SNZ) said that:

> …national sports organisations are having to grapple with redefining what success looks like for their organisation in 2018 and beyond. It can no longer be just about winning. It needs to be a much more balanced view, which includes the wellbeing of athletes.
>
> *(p. 6)*

Though other reports are not publicly available, it stands to reason that they would report similar systemic issues, given the probable overlapping of submitters and witnesses across the various reviews. Taken together, SNZ's reports and discussion papers, along with the recent reviews of particular sports, appear to signal a changing view of NSOs – from one initially concerned with outputs and performance to a view perhaps acknowledging the latter's distorting effect on culture and integrity (Dawbin et al. 2021).

Sport integrity **77**

The future: integrity governance

In recognising integrity issues as systemic, it follows that the central agencies are likely to develop and advance a system-wide response. Indeed, SNZ's (2018) Sport Integrity Review sought submissions/views regarding the effectiveness of institutional instruments such as an ombudsman, whistleblowing mechanisms and other protection protocols/measures. To an extent, these discussions bring the issue of integrity back towards NPM and its predilection for measurement, audits and secure contracting.

In the United Kingdom, for example, the remedies for ensuring athlete welfare and integrity are firmly situated within an additional layer of managerial control and auditing. NSOs are to "benchmark" their practices against a checklist, develop actions plans and, where needed, capitulate to an independent panel with powers to monitor their activities for a period of three days (Cottrell 2018). These are thus early signals that New Zealand NSOs may face new compliance costs, potentially demanding additional human and capital resources. Indeed, new education and training workshops for coaches and volunteers are likely to be matched with other measures including codes of conduct, complaints registries and integrity officers. Perhaps in anticipation of this, Cottrell (2018) warned against imposing new key performance indicators (KPIs) as a means of introducing reforms. He also cautioned that "it is important not to homogenise what are very different environments when considering the rights and welfare of their elite athletes" (p. 27).

Drawing from institutional theory, however, the inertia of the existing modernisation project likely holds too much momentum to discount. Given the historical focus on compliance and the existing funding model for NSOs, we can expect the emerging national policy frameworks to include further performance-based remedies. Interestingly, these coordinated mechanisms would mirror the existing structural arrangements for disciplining partner NSOs, in that they would rely on the contractual resolution to a systemic problem.

Conclusion

Over the last two decades, New Zealand has overhauled its sport policy structures, enabling government to adopt a broader leadership role in the sector. Persistent efforts in that time have gone towards modernising partner organisations (such as National Sport Organisations) ultimately in the hope of generating continuous improvement and performance.

The growth of NPM and its attendant demands for outputs have been enthusiastically adopted in the sport sector with the introduction of quasi-markets, contestable funding and targets. This performance measurement system has coincided with the deployment of training, consultancy services and reviews aimed at making organisations more "business-like". Cumulatively, these institutions

78 Michael P. Sam and Timothy M. Dawbin

appear to have impacted NSOs and their delivery of high-performance sport, raising the prospect of distortions such as cherry-picking and risk aversion.

We suggest that the contemporary sport sector likely generates the conditions precipitating "integrity" breaches (particularly linked to athlete welfare) with recent evidence from NSO reviews and SNZ. The New Zealand case is significant as it has historically been an eager adopter of NPM reforms, embraced simultaneously by other Western states including Australia, Canada and the UK. Likewise, in terms of sport, the systems in these countries are undergoing similar reviews of their structures and concerns around integrity and athlete welfare.

As systemic issues of athlete welfare and sports integrity breaches grow and gain recognition, so does the likelihood that central agencies will pursue system-wide responses. It is likely that emerging national policy frameworks will include further performance-based remedies such as "ethical governance audits" (McNamee & Fleming 2007) and benchmarking exercises, given the historical focus on compliance within the sector. However, since the policies around integrity mark a further effort to modernise sport, it is unknown how they will develop or disrupt the systems they are intended to reform over the coming 20 years.

References

Alderson, A. 2018, *Cycling: High performance sport New Zealand review release delayed.* New Zealand Herald, viewed 10 August 2020, https://www.nzherald.co.nz/sport/news/article.cfm?c_id=4&objectid=12116445

Anderson, I. 2018, *Rowing New Zealand high performance boss Alan Cotter resigns.* Stuff, viewed 20 August 2020, https://www.stuff.co.nz/sport/other-sports/106177715/rowing-new-zealand-high-performance-boss-alan-cotter-resigns

Baumgartner, F. R. & Jones, B. D. 1993, *Agendas and instability in American politics,* University of Chicago Press, Chicago, IL.

Bevan, G., & Hood, C. 2006, 'What's measured is what matters: targets and gaming in the English public health care system'. *Public administration, Vol. 84, no.3, pp.* 517-538.

Boston, J., Martin, J., Pallot, J. & Walsh, P. 1996, *Public management: The New Zealand model,* Oxford University Press, Auckland.

Chappelet, J. L. 2018, 'Beyond governance: the need to improve the regulation of international sport', *Sport in Society,* Vol. 21, no. 5, pp. 724–734, https://doi.org/10.1080/17430437.2018.1401355

Cleaver, D. 2009, *Kiwi funding strikes right chord.* New Zealand Herald, viewed 20 August 2020, http://www.nzherald.co.nz/dylan-cleaver/news/article.cfm?a_id=193&objectid=10610654

Cleaver, D. 2018, *Big read: The year of the review – New Zealand's broken system and broken athletes.* New Zealand Herald, viewed 10 August 2020, https://www.nzherald.co.nz/sport/big-read-the-year-of-the-review-new-zealands-broken-system-and-broken-athletes/773ZRE6PGSV545GOV2W7MGXMHQ/

Cottrell, S. 2018, *Elite athlete's rights and welfare,* viewed 5 August 2020, https://sportnz.org.nz/media/3193/elite-athlete-right-and-welfare.pdf

Dawbin, T. M., Sam, M. P., & Stenling, C. (2021). 'National sport organisation responses to independent reviews', *International Journal of Sport Policy and Politics, Vol. 9, no. 1,* pp. 29-43. https://doi.org/10.1080/19406940.2021.1877168

Fahlén, J. 2017, 'The trust–mistrust dynamic in the public governance of sport: exploring the legitimacy of performance measurement systems through end-users' perceptions', *International Journal of Sport Policy and Politics*, Vol. 9, no. 4, pp. 707–722, https://doi.or g/10.1080/19406940.2017.1348965

Gardiner, S., Parry, J. & Robinson, S. 2017,' Integrity and the corruption debate in sport: where is the integrity?' *European Sport Management Quarterly*, Vol. 17, no. 1, pp. 6–23, https://doi.org/10.1080/16184742.2016.1259246

Gourdie, A. 2018, *Hockey NZ plan independent review into women's Black sticks culture.* Newshub, viewed 10 August 2020, https://www.newshub.co.nz/home/sport/2018/08/hockey-hockey-new-zealand-to-conduct-independent-review.html

Hall, P. A., & Taylor, R. C. R. 1996, 'Political science and the three new institutionalisms', *Political Studies*, Vol. 44, pp. 936–957.

Heron, M. 2018, *Independent review of cycling New Zealand high performance programme*, viewed 20 August 2020, http://mhqc.co.nz/wp-content/uploads/2018/10/CNZ-Review-Final.pdf

High Performance Sport New Zealand. 2017, *Strategic plan 2017–2020*, viewed 10 August 2020, https://hpsnz.org.nz/content/uploads/2018/03/HPSNZ-Strategic-Plan-2017-2020.pdf

Hill, S., Kerr, R. & Kobayashi, K. 2016, 'Questioning the application of policy governance for small-scale sports clubs in New Zealand', *Managing Sport and Leisure*, Vol. 21, no. 4, pp. 203–217, https://doi.org/10.1080/23750472.2016.1252686

Hill, S., Kerr, R. & Kobayashi, K. 2021, 'Around the kitchen-table with Bourdieu: understanding the lack of formalization or professionalization of community sports clubs in New Zealand', *Sport in Society*, Vol. 24, no. 2, pp. 115–130, https://doi.org/10.108 0/17430437.2019.1615893

Hood, C. & Peters, B. G. 2004, 'The middle aging of new public management: into the age of paradox?' *Journal of Public Administration Research and Theory*, Vol. 14, no. 3, pp. 267–282, https://doi.org/10.1093/jopart/muh019

Houlihan, B. & Chapman, P. 2015, 'Modernisation and elite sport development in England and the United Kingdom', in S. S. Anderson, B. Houlihan & L. T. Ronglan (eds.), *Managing elite sport systems: Research and practice*, Abingdon, Routledge, pp. 31–48.

Johannsen, D. 2018, *All you need to know about all of New Zealand's sport reviews.* Stuff, viewed 5 August 2020, https://www.stuff.co.nz/sport/other-sports/104983154/all-you-need-to-know-about-all-of-new-zealands-sport-reviews

Lowndes, V. & Roberts, M. 2013, *Why institutions matter: The new institutionalism in political science*, Palgrave, Basingstoke.

March, J. G. & Olsen, J. P. 1989, *Rediscovering institutions: The organizational basis of politics*, Free Press, New York.

Margetts, H., Perri 6 & Hood, C. (eds.). 2012, *Paradoxes of modernization: Unintended consequences of public policy reform*, Oxford University Press, Oxford.

McNamee, M. J. & Fleming, S. 2007, 'Ethics audits and corporate governance: the case of public sector sports organizations', *Journal of Business Ethics*, Vol. 73, no. 4, pp. 425–437, https://doi.org/10.1007/s10551-006-9216-0

Muir, P. 2018, *Independent review into NZ football*, viewed 5 August 2020, https://www.sporty.co.nz/asset/downloadasset?id=3c273e4a-ccfe-4648-8cb1-f65440730857

Napier, L. 2018, *Netball NZ reveal panel to review Silver Ferns.* New Zealand Herald, viewed 5 August 2020, https://www.nzherald.co.nz/sport/netball-nz-reveal-panel-to-review-silver-ferns/BUUTTLEOH7POWSYTL5AE33UAOE/

Peters, B. G. 2012, *Institutional theory in political science: The new institutionalism*, Continuum, New York.

Pollitt, C. & Bouckaert, G. 2004, *Public management reform: A comparative analysis*, 2nd edn., Oxford University Press, Oxford.

Prendiville, M. 2018, *'We want clear governance' – Football NZ not off the hook despite Heraf's exit*. One News, viewed 5 August 2020, https://www.tvnz.co.nz/one-news/sport/football/we-want-clear-governance-football-nz-not-off-hook-despite-heraf-s-exit

Sam, M. P. 2009, 'The public management of sport: wicked problems, challenges and dilemmas', *Public Management Review*, Vol. 11, pp. 499–514, https://doi.org/10.1080/14719030902989565

Sam, M. P. 2012, 'Targeted investments in elite sport funding: wiser, more innovative and strategic?' *Managing Leisure*, Vol. 17, pp. 206–219, https://doi.org/10.1080/13606719.2012.674395

Sam, M. P. 2015a, 'Big brother and caring sister: performance management and the athlete's entourage', in S. S. Andersen, B. Houlihan & L. T. Ronglan (eds.), *Managing elite sport systems: Reseach and practice*, Routledge, London, pp. 16–30.

Sam, M. P. 2015b, 'Sport policy and transformation in small states: New Zealand's struggle between vulnerability and resilience', *International Journal of Sport Policy and Politics*, Vol. 7, no. 3, pp. 407–420, https://doi.org/10.1080/19406940.2015.1060715

Sam, M. P. 2016, 'Sport development', in R. Hoye & M. M. Parent (eds.), *Sage Handbook of Sport Management*, Sage, London, pp. 227–240.

Sam, M. P., Andrew, J. & Gee, S. 2018, 'The modernisation of umpire development: Netball New Zealand's reforms and impacts', *European Sport Management Quarterly*, Vol.18, no. 3, pp. 263–286, https://doi.org/10.1080/16184742.2017.1377272

Sam, M. P. & Macris, L. I. 2014, 'Performance regimes in sport policy: exploring consequences, vulnerabilities and politics', *International Journal of Sport Policy and Politics*, Vol. 6, no. 3, pp. 513–532, https://doi.org/10.1080/19406940.2013.851103

Sam, M. P. & Ronglan, L. T. 2018, 'Building sport policy's legitimacy in Norway and New Zealand', *International Review for the Sociology of Sport*, Vol. 53, no. 5, pp. 550–571., https://doi.org/10.1177%2F1012690216671515

Sam, M. P. & Schoenberg, G. 2020, 'Government policy and sport governance in Canada, New Zealand and Australia', in D. Shilbury & L. Ferkins (eds.), *Routledge handbook of sport governance*, Routledge, Abingdon, pp. 65–78.

Sport New Zealand. 2012, Strategic plan 2012-2015, Wellington.

Sport New Zealand. 2013, *Relationship agreement*, Sport New Zealand, Wellington.

Sport New Zealand. 2016, *Governance mark for sport and recreation launched*, viewed 5 August 2020, https://sportnz.org.nz/resources/governance-mark-for-sport-and-recreation-launched/

Sport New Zealand. 2018, *Sport integrity review discussion document*, Wellington, New Zealand.

Van Dooren, W., Bouckaert, G. & Halligan, J. 2010, *Performance management in the public sector*, Routledge, Abingdon.

Worthington, S. 2009, *Olympic-medal sports get funding boost*. The Dominion Post, viewed 23 August 2020, http://www.stuff.co.nz/sport/1755161/Olympic-medal-sports-get-funding-boost

8

SYMBOLIC EQUALITY IN AOTEAROA NEW ZEALAND SPORTS ORGANISATIONS

Alida Shanks, Sarah Leberman, Sally Shaw and Geoff Watson

Introduction

Gender equity in sports organisations remains elusive despite national and international moves to address this through legislation, reports and strategies (e.g., Shaw 2013). To date, such initiatives have delivered little more than superficial change and a fundamental shift is required to address persistent gender inequity. This chapter argues that sports organisations in Aotearoa New Zealand are failing to address gender equity because initiatives, to date, have not addressed the practices of gendered relations across all four aspects of production, power, symbolism and emotional relations. Although gender is the focus of this chapter, it is important to note that gender is non-binary and women have many aspects to their identity, including sexual orientation, ethnicity, age, ability, faith and social-economic background.

Symbolic equality

A critical reason for ongoing gender inequity in sports organisations is that although national sports organisations (NSOs) create policies that promise diversity, they do not address everyday practices that maintain the inequity (Edelman 2016). Over time, the organisational policies symbolise compliance with human rights laws, irrespective of their effectiveness. Diversity policies become symbols of equal opportunity, yet often hide ongoing discrimination and essentially help to perpetuate inequity (Edelman 2016). This phenomenon is called symbolic equality. It highlights how laws and policies may be introduced to address overtly discriminatory behaviour; however, discrimination and inequality persist because the actual practices are not addressed and therefore do not change.

DOI: 10.4324/9781003034445-8

82 Alida Shanks et al.

Connell's four-dimensional framework

Connell (2002) argues that interactions at a sectoral, organisational or personal level are made up of a set of gendered relationships. When these gender relations are not consciously addressed, then the way they are exercised, for example, allocation of roles or informal practices, are based on pre-existing perceptions or beliefs of "masculine" and "feminine" or (un)conscious bias. Connell (2002) proposed a four-dimensional theoretical framework that identifies a pattern of gender relations in an organisation established through social actions or practices of production, power, symbolism, and emotional relations. In order to develop transformational equality that is deeply embedded in an organisation and not simply symbolic equality, all four aspects of Connell's framework need to be addressed by sports organisations. The first social practice is production, or the gender division of labour, which covers the proportion of men and women involved in the organisation, the gendered distribution of roles within that organisation or sector, and how those roles are remunerated (Connell 2002). Connell (2002) argues that power relations, such as organisational hierarchy are the way authority is exercised. Power can be demonstrated through decision-making processes, particularly those based on preconceived ideas of gender, which might appear to be impersonal at a macro level, but can have a very personal impact. Symbolism highlights the ways gender identities are defined and represented publicly and includes the casual use of gender stereotypes. These preconceived beliefs can influence the roles that women hold (or are given) in sports organisations, usually by men, and these roles impact the type of work (or production) that women carry out (Connell 2002). Emotional relations examines the connection and interaction between men and women in an organisation, for example, how supportive they are of each other. This also includes identifying where certain emotional responses are expected based on gender, for example, sympathy from females and aggression from males (Connell 2002).

Connell's (2002) theoretical framework provides a mechanism to identify and understand how gender is manifested in organisational processes and examines how the processes and relations operate to determine the impact (or lack thereof) on gender equity. Connell (2002) suggests that gender relations are not always dichotomous or binary and maybe manifested directly or indirectly. Critically, the four factors of Connell's (2002) framework are dynamic, which means there is space for action and change. All four factors can also be present simultaneously in one situation. Connell (2002) notes the four dimensions are distinguished individually to explain the "complex reality" of gendered relations, but they do not operate independently and are interwoven and continually interact with each other (Adriaanse & Schofield 2013; Connell 2002, p. 68). For example, simply identifying the lack of gender equality on the board of a sports organisation is production. However, when gender quotas or targets are introduced to address the existing gender inequality, there is often no review or guidance to address aspects such as what roles were held by men and women on the board or in organisations (symbolism and production), the organisational hierarchy or decision-making process (power), or how women and men could or should be supported with the implementation of the quotas (emotional relations). Consequently, by not addressing all four aspects of Connell's (2002) framework, production, power, symbolism, and emotional relations, the result is little significant change.

International context

Since the 1970s, sports and non-government organisations, as well as central governments, have sought to address gender inequity in sport. For example, in 1972 the United States introduced the Title IX amendment which prohibited gender discrimination in all publicly funded educational organisations and had a significant impact in lifting funding for, and participation in, women's sport, but consequently resulted in fewer women in coaching and leadership positions (Boutilier & San Giovanni 1994). In 1994, the Brighton Declaration was signed by 82 countries to advocate for gender equity on and off the sports field, and the International Working Group (IWG) on Women and Sport was formed. Conferences have been held every four years since, with the next IWG conference to be hosted by Aotearoa New Zealand in 2022 (Women in Sport Aotearoa 2018).

In 1996, the International Olympic Committee (IOC) made a resolution that for all member sports, 10% of decision-making positions were to be held by women by 2000, increasing to 20% by 2005. In 2013, the New Zealand Olympic Committee (NZOC) and Sport New Zealand (SNZ), the Crown entity responsible for governing sport and recreation in Aotearoa New Zealand, further extended this to 33% by 2015 and 40% by 2020 (Ryan & Watson 2018). As at December 2020, the NZOC board is the exception to many of its international counterparts with 63% female representation. However, the president of the NZOC board remains a male and many of the NZOC's member sports have not met these targets. In 2007, the NZOC examined 47 NSOs and found only half had reached the 2005 target of 20% women on their boards (Cockburn et al. 2007). By 2018, a report examining 14 NSOs found only 8 organisations had more than 40% female board members (Archibald et al. 2018). While it is challenging to compare reports that use different methodologies and examine different NSOs, it is clear the targets imposed by the NZOC and SNZ have largely been symbolic, with women remaining under-represented in leadership roles.

Independent reviews of National Sports Organisations (NSOs)

The lack of attention to the gendered power relations, symbolism and emotional relations in initiatives like these policies has been exposed with recent events revealing concerning behaviour in some NSOs in Aotearoa New Zealand, particularly with respect to gender and culture. Between 2016 and 2019 significant reviews were conducted in ten NSOs. Gender inequity was highlighted in eight

84 Alida Shanks et al.

of the ten reviews either through explicit statements on the lack of gender diversity within organisations or analyses of the behaviour of male coaches towards female athletes. The eight sports were cricket (NZ Cricket 2016), rugby (Cockburn & Atkinson 2017), football (Muir 2018), cycling (Heron 2018), triathlon (Triathlon NZ), hockey (Hockey NZ 2019), plus rowing and swimming who did not release their reports. All ten NSOs discussed organisational cultural issues such as bullying and player welfare, those already listed plus netball (Netball NZ) and rugby league (Castle & Castle 2018). It is worth noting that although most NSOs, with the exception of rowing and swimming, released something akin to a report, there was significant variability in how extensive these reports were. NZ Rugby's (NZR) report was the most open and detailed (Cockburn & Atkinson 2017). All the other NSOs had two reports, a public summary and a more detailed private report, for example, NZ Cricket had an elaborate public report with quotes and key findings and also had a 428-page private report (NZ Cricket 2016). Triathlon NZ had a four-page summary that was undated with no letterhead or author (Triathlon NZ). While Hockey NZ's (2019) four-page summary was dated and on letterhead, it was essentially a highlights package with little detail.

Of the publicly available reviews, only cricket and rugby paid particular attention to gender inequity within their organisations. Few of the reports identified detailed measures to address gender diversity which would align with Connell's (2002) gendered relations of production, power, symbolism or emotional relations within their organisation, instead focusing on high-performance programmes and implementing basic human resource-type policies. The details of these policies are not specified in the reports or summaries, for example, a "dedicated HR Advisor [is appointed] to provide ongoing support for its policies and procedures" and "[Hockey NZ] to ensure training for staff and players on [anti-]discrimination, [anti-]harassment and [anti-]bullying" (Hockey NZ 2019, p. 3). This is not a surprise because even though independent reviews are purported as a tool by NSOs and SNZ for accountability, modernity, and change, historically many NSOs have made little to no change as a result of the reviews (Dawbin 2018). There is a lack of engagement or acknowledgement of the aspects articulated in Connell's (2002) framework, in particular the critical role of gender relations in discrimination, harassment and bullying. Consequently, the reviews are largely symbolic.

Notable exceptions that made more substantial changes include, NZR which made constitutional changes to increase the number of appointed board directors, NZ Cricket which increased the number of women on their board from 11% in 2016 to 37.5% in 2020 and appointed their first female president in 2016 (Sport NZ 2018), and NZ Football appointed their first female president in 2019 ("NZ Football appoints" 2019). However, these appointments are rare and represent the few changes that were a result of the reviews. While increasing the proportion of men and women involved (production), the reviews did not discuss and there were no known steps taken to address organisational hierarchy or decision-making processes, challenge existing beliefs about gender and how roles are allocated, or what support is available, particularly for an organisation which has a female president for the first time. Also, the longevity of these changes is uncertain owing to the financial pressure caused by the COVID-19 pandemic. In 2020 NZR announced an organisational restructure that impacted half of the 180 full-time roles, including absorbing dedicated women's development officers with community development (Johannsen 2020).

Merging of female and male NSOs

One of the reasons progress in diversity has been glacial is because the structure of many NSOs have remain unchanged since they were first formed. Formerly separate men's and women's national sports bodies merged between the 1980s and early 2000s (Macdonald 2018; Ryan & Watson 2018). Similar mergers also occurred in the United States, United Kingdom and Australia (Kihl et al. 2013). As with the mergers between gender affiliated sport organisations internationally, little is known about many of the mergers of Aotearoa New Zealand NSOs except they appear to have been motivated largely by desires to achieve administrative and financial efficiencies, or to encourage promotion of family sport (Kihl et al. 2013; Macdonald 2018; Ryan & Watson 2018).

The mergers were an opportunity for NSOs to address their structure and diversity; however, when the men's and women's hockey organisations merged in 1988, it was one of only three NSOs along with bowls and golf that acknowledged gender representation in their new, post-merger constitution. Hockey NZ's new constitution stipulated that of the eight board members, in addition to two appointed board members, there must be six members who are elected and the board must have a 50% gender split. In addition, the positions of president and vice president must be one female and one male, and they must alternate every three years (Hockey NZ 2016).

The men's and women's national bowls organisations merged in 1996 following extensive consultation (Sinclair 2018). Initially, all board members from the men's and women's organisation stayed, but that meant 52 councillors governing one sport, which was problematic. It took a further four years before a constitutional change was agreed on to reduce the number of councillors to 26 in total. In 2019, there were seven people on the board and the constitution stipulates that, like Hockey NZ, the positions of president and vice president must be one female and one male, and they must alternate (Bowls NZ 2019).

The men's and women's national golf organisations merged in 2005 after extensive negotiations, to be more efficient administratively and to address the decreasing membership numbers (Cox 2018). The new constitution noted that the appointments panel, who make recommendations on the election of the president, elected board members and selects the appointed board members of NZ Golf, must ensure that of the four appointed members, one needs to be of "each gender" (NZ Golf 2019, p. 28). There is also a clause stating a preference for board diversity in terms of gender, geography, age and ethnicity (NZ Golf 2019). Together with these measures, in 2018 NZ Golf adopted a two-page inclusion charter to address gender, ability, age, ethnicity and sexuality at a national, regional, industry, commercial and club level, as well as a one-page women and girls-specific charter (NZ Golf 2018).

In all three cases, while there was a gesture towards addressing the proportion of women and men involved on the board when the women's and men's organisations merged, there was no examination of the way authority was exercised, what roles women and men held, or how men and women from the previously separate organisations were now expected to work together. The measures introduced were largely symbolic, which was further revealed when, despite NZ Golf announcing the diversity charters, women's golf was undermined at national and local levels when the NZ Women's Golf Open was discontinued in 2017 and women continue to struggle to have equal playing rights to men at some golf clubs ("Misogyny gone mad" 2019).

The men's and women's cricket and football organisations merged in 1992 and 1999 respectively, with apparently little significant changes to the men's organisations. Both mergers were motivated at least in part by the desire to retain government funding. The Hillary Commission, the predecessor to SPARC and then SNZ, would only fund a new cricket academy in Christchurch if the organisations merged (Ryan & Watson 2018). Similarly, the Hillary Commission would only provide financial support to the beleaguered men's football organisation if they merged with the women's organisation (Gryphon Governance Consultants 2011). Other factors included a directive from Fédération Internationale de Football Association (FIFA) to all national bodies to take control of women's football (Cox 2010; Gryphon Governance Consultants 2011). Following the merger, the administration of women's football was transferred to an advisory committee. However, this proved to be a symbolic move, because within 18 months the seven members of the women's committee were told that the all-male NZ Soccer board and the seven federation male chairs had decided to disestablish the women's committee (Cox 2010). It was only re-established following mediation along with a sole female administrator in charge of women's football (Cox 2010).

Concerns that women would lose control of their sport if they affiliated with men's organisations soon proved prophetic (Ryan & Watson 2018). For example, with one exception, all the coaches of the Aotearoa New Zealand women's hockey team between 1935 and 1992 were female, but since 1992, four years after the merger, every head coach has been male (Ryan & Watson 2018). Similarly, in cricket, the number of women in governance roles decreased from 38% in 1993 to 6.4% in 2016, and only 10% of coaches were female (NZ Cricket 2016). Apart from some symbolic measures that were introduced to address the proportion of women and men involved, the mergers gave scant attention to any actions that related to gender relations within the organisations.

Government reports

In Aotearoa New Zealand, there have been at least three government reports that address gender equity in sports organisations. The Recreation and Government in New Zealand report (1985) that accompanied the *Sport on the Move* report, included one paragraph acknowledging barriers to women's involvement in sport. This report was influential in establishing the Hillary Commission in 1987, along with the first regional sports trusts (RSTs) to manage government funding for sport. Later, *Women's sport, fitness and leisure: The inside story* (Hillary Commission 1994) provided a snapshot of women involved as athletes, coaches, administrators, and women's sport in the media. Another 24 years later, in October 2018, the government announced the Women and Girls in Sport and Active Recreation strategy, the first ever strategy in Aotearoa New Zealand dedicated to women and girls and included funding of $10 million over three years to support its delivery (Sport New Zealand 2018). The strategy included nine measures under three pillars; participation, value and visibility, and leadership, and SNZ released a report to accompany the strategy with 24 commitments to meet those measures which captured the existing status of women and girls in sport (Sport New Zealand 2018). Using the three pillars from the 2018 strategy, we can compare the three reports to examine if there has been any change in women's involvement in sports organisations.

Table 8.1 looks at participation, focusing on time spent being active, the number of girls and women who are participating and how confident they feel while taking part. All three reports discuss these issues, with many similarities.

The second pillar is value and visibility, outlined in Table 8.2, examining commercial and media aspects, which are addressed by all three reports. The gender pay gap is a heading in the 2018 strategy but is not addressed in any of the reports.

It is worth noting that the figures cited for media coverage in both the 1994 and 2018 reports focused on the Olympics, which is a high point in coverage of women in sport. Generally, coverage of women's sport in mainstream media, both print and television, hovers around the 10% mark annually (Bruce 2008; Brunner et al. 2018; French 2013).

The third pillar is leadership, detailed in Table 8.3, which examines representation of women at a governance level, in senior management and coaching.

It is important to note that the 2018 figures of 39% of leadership and management roles and 76% of administration and support service roles cover organisations from across the whole sector including NSOs, regional sports organisations, RSTs, territorial authorities, national recreation organisations, government agencies and Crown entities, and only 24% (90) of those who responded were from NSOs (Sport New Zealand 2017). The leadership and administration figures in the *Women's sport, fitness and leisure* report (1994) examined 116 NSOs.

The measures under the three pillars of participation, value and visibility, and leadership in the 2018 strategy all focused on women and girls' involvement in

88 Alida Shanks et al.

TABLE 8.1 Participation of women and girls in sport and active recreation

Measure in the Women and Girls in Sport and Active Recreation strategy (Sport New Zealand 2018)	Recreation and government in New Zealand report (1985)	*Women's sport, fitness and leisure: The inside story* (Hillary Commission 1994)	Women and Girls in Sport and Active Recreation strategy (Sport New Zealand 2018)
Time spent by women and girls being physically active.	"Women are less active in physical activities". "Recreation facilities should … include such issues as childminding facilities".	On average, women are 15% less involved in formal or informal sport compared to men. 60% of women want to increase their participation.	On average, women spend 12% less time participating in a week, than men. 77% of women want to participate more.
Number of girls and women meeting physical activity guidelines (through play, active recreation and sport).	"More affirmative action is required to ensure women's groups, women not in groups and women's recreation in general receive more attention and gain their fair share of recreation resources".	38% of women belong to a sports club compared to 61% of men.	Women are more likely than men to be dissatisfied with their sports club experience.
Levels of confidence and competence women and girls feel about taking part in activities.	"A great deal of women's recreation …. activities are not recognised or valued".	"Women are more likely than men to be constrained from participating in sport and leisure due to a lack of confidence and a perception that they do not have the skills or abilities to participate well".	"Barriers to participation are significantly higher for women compared to men".

Symbolic equality in organisations **89**

TABLE 8.2 Value and visibility of women and girls in sport and active recreation

Measure in the Women and Girls in Sport and Active Recreation strategy (Sport New Zealand 2018)	Recreation and government in New Zealand report (1985)	*Women's sport, fitness and leisure: The inside story* (Hillary Commission 1994)	Women and Girls in Sport and Active Recreation strategy (Sport New Zealand 2018)
Percentage of media coverage (traditional and social media) dedicated to women and girls	*No information*	Media coverage of women's sport during the 1992 Olympics – newspaper coverage was 11.3% and television coverage was 20%.	Online coverage of the Rio Olympics from a major NZ media site dedicated 28.2% of its coverage to women.
Percentage of investment from funding agencies into women and girls in sport and active recreation	Men's and mixed organisations received twice as much mean per capita allocations as did women's organisations. "The process of attracting funds for women's organisations is a more difficult process…"	"Many women either have little discretionary income to spend on sport activities, or they … [spend it on] activities for their family. Women are more likely than men to be concerned about, and affected by, the cost of facilities, … transport, … and that few facilities or activities are available close to their homes".	
Pay gap between women and men	*No information*	*No information*	*No information*

sport and active recreation, that is, production. However, the strategy does not address power relations, symbolism, or emotional relations, and in fact, the strategy reinforced outdated beliefs about gender, using a binary definition of gender for the targets and throughout the document. Concerns were raised almost immediately by some NSO chief executives about meeting the governance gender

90 Alida Shanks et al.

TABLE 8.3 Leadership of women and girls in sport and active recreation

Measure in the Women and Girls in Sport and Active Recreation strategy (Sport New Zealand 2018)	Recreation and government in New Zealand report (1985)	*Women's sport, fitness and leisure: The inside story* (Hillary Commission 1994)	Women and Girls in Sport and Active Recreation strategy (Sport New Zealand 2018)
Number of Boards (national, regional and local) meeting gender diversity target – a minimum of 40% of each gender	"The 'system' is not sensitive to the circumstances and needs of women".	27% of NSO board roles are held by women.	27% of NSO board roles are held by women.
Number of organisations meeting gender diversity target for management teams – a minimum of 40% of each gender	"In women's organisations, there are fewer paid administrators". "There is a need for advocacy and advocates for women's aspirations and needs in recreation and sports at all levels".	37% of women were employed as Executive Directors, Marketing Directors and Senior Coaching roles in NSOs. 70% of women employed in NSOs were in administration, clerical and accounting positions.	39% of leadership and management roles are held by women [across the whole sector]. 76% of administration and support services roles are held by women [across the whole sector].
Women and girls coaching and volunteering at all levels	*No information*	20% of the coaches and administrators that attended the 1994 Commonwealth Games were women.	30% of High Performance coaches are women.

target of 40% (McFadden 2019). The strategy says SNZ-affiliated organisations must ensure their board meets the gender diversity target of a minimum of 40% of self-identified female and male. SNZ later confirmed that those organisations that receive more than $50,000 in funding from SNZ must reach this target by December 2021 ('Sport NZ to sports bodies' 2019). It is not clear why the criteria

Symbolic equality in organisations **91**

is $50,000, what that means for the gender diversity of those sports organisations who receive less than that, or what happens if that target is not met. In addition, while officially linking the target to funding is new, the target itself is not a new initiative for those NSOs of Olympic sports. Recent research with Spanish sports organisations shows that the threat of economic sanctions was effective in increasing the proportion of women on boards (production) and made gender inequality more visible, however there was no increase in the number of women chairs (symbolism) (Valiente 2020).

Although both the Recreation and Government in New Zealand report (1985) and the Hillary Commission report (1994) on women's sport had identified significant gender inequities in sport, the ministerial taskforce report on sport, fitness and leisure (2001) did not prioritise gender equality as an issue to be addressed. Indeed, it recommended devolving policy-making on women's sport to the Ministry of Women's Affairs, rather than making gender equity the responsibility of NSOs and SPARC. SPARC's ambivalence towards promoting women's sport contrasted with commitments Aotearoa New Zealand governments had made towards gender equity in sport, such as introducing the Winning Women programme to support women leaders in sports organisations. The programme was introduced in 1998 as part of the Hillary Commission's commitment to the Brighton Declaration (Leberman & Palmer 2009).

When the Hillary Commission transitioned to SPARC in 2002, the focus for NSOs moved to general participation at a community level and some funding became linked to winning medals for high performance. This has led to a high performance "winning at all costs" model that has historically justified overriding equity policies, such as dropping the Winning Women programme in 2002, and did not challenge existing organisational structures and gendered relations that ultimately led to the NSO reviews between 2016 and 2019 (Burton & Leberman 2017; Leberman & Palmer 2009; Shaw 2013). The 2018 Women and Girls strategy is the first time the government has focused on wellbeing and explicitly moved away from a community versus high-performance structure (Sport New Zealand 2018). It is also worth noting SNZ appointed Raelene Castle as their first female chief executive in 2020 ("Castle named first female chief executive" 2020).

Conclusion

While there are greater opportunities for women and girls to participate in sport, women remain under-represented in leadership roles at both a professional and amateur level. Like the reports from 1985 and 1994, neither the independent reviews of the NSOs or SNZ's Women and Girls strategy (2018) examine the existing organisational structures or processes of sports organisations. There is still an expectation to increase the number of women in sports organisations without addressing the structure or culture. This view ignores the gendered nature of sport and its organisations, where male leadership is considered normal and masculine behaviour and gender stereotypes are reinforced. Even with recent

92 Alida Shanks et al.

appointments of women to the roles of president in cricket and football and chief executive at SNZ, this is still considered atypical and newsworthy. There needs to be a fundamental shift in focus on the structure and actions of sports organisations by examining the gendered relations in production, power, symbolism, and emotional relations. If there is not, there is a risk of not only history repeating, but the 2018 strategy becoming yet another case of symbolic equality.

References

Adriaanse, J. & Schofield, T. 2013, 'Analysing gender dynamics in sport governance: a new regimes-based approach', *Sport Management Review*, Vol. 16, no. 4, pp. 498–513 https://doi.org/10.1016/j.smr.2013.01.006.

Archibald, K., Collins, S., Shanks, A. & Smith, B. 2018, *More great women in sport governance: Let's walk the talk*, New Zealand Women's Sport Leadership Academy, New Zealand.

Boutilier, M. & San Giovanni, L. 1994, 'Politics, public policy and Title IX: some limitations of liberal feminism' in S. Birrell & C. Cole (eds.), *Women, sport and culture*, Human Kinetics, Illinois, pp. 97–109.

Bowls New Zealand 2019, *Constitution of Bowls New Zealand Incorporated*, viewed 5 January 2020, https://bowlsnewzealand.co.nz/wp-content/uploads/2020/02/BC10064773005-1.pdf.

Bruce, T. 2008, 'Women, sport and the media: a complex terrain' in C. Obel, T. Bruce & S. Thompson (eds.), *Outstanding: Research about women and sport in New Zealand*, Wilf Malcolm Institute of Educational Research, School of Education, University of Waikato, New Zealand, pp. 51–71.

Brunner, C. Compain, M. Cowley Ross, S. Smith, J. & Wong, R. 2018, *Improving the media coverage of our sportswomen*, New Zealand Women's Sport Leadership Academy, New Zealand.

Burton, L. & Leberman. S (eds.) 2017, *Women in sport leadership: Research and practice for change*, Routledge, New York.

Castle, T. & Castle, R. 2018, Independent review of the Kiwis 2017 Rugby League World Cup campaign: A summary.

'Castle named first female chief executive of Sport New Zealand', 2020, *Stuff.co.nz*, viewed 4 November 2020, https://www.stuff.co.nz/sport/women-in-sport/300149575/castle-named-first-female-chief-executive-of-sport-new-zealand

Cockburn, R. & Atkinson, L. 2017, Respect and responsibility review: New Zealand Rugby.

Cockburn, R. Gray, K. & Thompson, R. 2007, *Gender balance in New Zealand Olympic sports*, New Zealand Olympic Committee, New Zealand.

Connell, R. 2002, *Gender,* Blackwell, Cambridge.

Cox, B. 2010, *Issues of power in a history of women's football in New Zealand: A Foucauldian genealogy,* PhD Thesis, University of Waikato, New Zealand.

Cox, E. 2018, *Women's Golf New Zealand, 1911–2005*, viewed 5 January 2020, https://nzhistory.govt.nz/women-together/womens-golf-new-zealand.

Dawbin, T. 2018, *National sport organisation responses to independent reviews*, Master's Thesis, University of Otago, New Zealand.

Edelman, L. 2016, *Working law: Courts, corporations, and symbolic civil rights*, University of Chicago Press, Chicago, IL.

Symbolic equality in organisations **93**

French, S. 2013, 'Still not there: the continued invisibility of female athletes and sports in the New Zealand print media', *Media International Australia*, Vol. 148, no. 1, pp. 39–50, https://doi.org/10.1177/1329878X1314800105.

Gryphon Governance Consultants. 2011, *Organisational change in seven selected sports: What can be learnt and applied?* Sport and Recreation New Zealand, Wellington.

Heron, M. 2018, Independent review of Cycling New Zealand High Performance programme.

Hillary Commission. 1994, *Women's sport, fitness and leisure: The inside story*, Wellington.

Hockey New Zealand. 2016, *Constitution of Hockey New Zealand Incorporated (updated 2016)*, viewed 5 January 2020, http://hockeynz.co.nz/wp-content/uploads/HNZ-Constitution.pdf.

Hockey New Zealand. 2019, Summary of review findings.

Johannsen, D. 2020, 'Coronavirus: fears NZ Rugby's bold plans for women's game in 2021 will be put on hold', *Stuff.co.nz*, viewed 18 May 2020, https://www.stuff.co.nz/sport/121534889/coronavirus-fears-nz-rugbys-bold-plans-for-womens-game-in-2021-will-be-put-on-hold.

Kihl, L. Shaw, S. & Schull, V. 2013, 'Fear, anxiety, and loss of control: analyzing an athletic department merger as a gendered political process', *Journal of Sport Management*, Vol. 27, no. 2, pp. 146–157, https://doi.org/10.1123/jsm.27.2.146.

Leberman, S. & Palmer, F. 2009, 'Motherhood, sport leadership, and domain theory: experiences from New Zealand', *Journal of Sport Management*, Vol. 23, no. 3, pp. 305–334, https://doi.org/10.1123/jsm.23.3.305.

Macdonald, C. 2018, *Organisations in sport, recreation and leisure,* viewed 9 September 2019, https://nzhistory.govt.nz/women-together/theme/sport-and-recreation.

McFadden, S. 2019, 'Sports struggling to appoint more female directors as diversity deadline looms', *Newsroom*, viewed 26 April 2019, https://www.newsroom.co.nz/@lockerroom/2019/04/26/553666/sports-call-for-help-to-get-more-women-on-boards.

Ministerial taskforce of sport, fitness and leisure. 2001, *Getting set for an active nation,* Wellington.

'"Misogyny gone mad": Women banned from Queenstown golf comp'. 2019, *NZ Herald*, viewed 15 February 2019, https://www.nzherald.co.nz/index.cfm?objectid=12204113.

Muir, P. 2018, Independent review into NZ Football: Public findings and recommendations.

Netball New Zealand. undated, Appendix B – Review announcement: 2018 Commonwealth Games campaign review.

New Zealand Cricket. 2016, *Women and Cricket. Cricket and Women,* NZ Cricket, Christchurch.

'NZ Football appoints first female president' 2019, *1 News*, viewed 2 April 2019, https://www.tvnz.co.nz/one-news/sport/football/nz-football-appoints-first-female-president-says-its-time-game-move-forward.

New Zealand Golf. 2018, *New Zealand Golf Inclusion charter,* viewed 7 February 2020, https://www.golf.co.nz/uploads/Inclusion%20Charter%20-%20June%202018.pdf.

New Zealand Golf. 2019, *New Zealand Golf Incorporated, Constitution,* viewed 5 January 2020, https://www.golf.co.nz/About/Constitution.aspx.

Recreation and government in New Zealand: Change in relationships. 1985, Ministry of Recreation and Sport, Wellington.

Ryan, G. & Watson, G. 2018, *Sport and the New Zealanders: A history,* Auckland University Press, Auckland.

Shaw, S. 2013, 'Managing gender equity in sport', in D Hassan & J Lusted (eds.), *Managing sport: Social and cultural perspectives*, Routledge, New York, pp. 186–200.

Sinclair, J. 2018, *New Zealand Women's Bowling Association*, viewed 9 September 2019, https://nzhistory.govt.nz/women-together/new-zealand-womens-bowling-association.

Sport New Zealand. 2017, *2017 Sport and recreation paid workforce survey*, Sport NZ, Wellington.

Sport New Zealand. 2018, *Women and girls in sport and active recreation: Government strategy*, Sport NZ, Wellington.

'Sport NZ to sports bodies – reach board gender equity or risk funding'. 2019, *Stuff.co.nz*, viewed 14 June 2019, https://www.stuff.co.nz/sport/other-sports/113420512/sport-nz-to-sports-bodies--reach-board-gender-equity-or-risk-funding.

Triathlon New Zealand. undated, Triathlon NZ's High Performance review: Board summary.

Valiente, C. 2020, 'The impact of gender quotas in sport management: the case of Spain', *Sport in Society*, pp. 1–18, https://doi.org/10.1080/17430437.2020.1819244.

Women in Sport Aotearoa 2018, *IWG 2018–2022*, viewed 5 January 2020, https://womeninsport.org.nz/iwg-2018-2022/

9

SPORTS COACHING, EDUCATION AND DEVELOPMENT

A continually contested terrain

Tania Cassidy

Introduction

Timing is everything. When I began writing this chapter it was, as Sergeant Pepper said, "twenty years ago today" (plus 10 days) that Trevor Mallard, the then New Zealand's Minister of Sport, Fitness and Leisure, announced the terms of reference for a Ministerial taskforce review of sport and recreation in New Zealand. As I complete this chapter COVID-19 has changed the landscape in ways that would have been unimaginable a few months earlier. In pre-COVID-19 times I concluded the proposed abstract of this chapter with Sport New Zealand's (SNZ) position that it would "not force changes on sports and it could take a generation for people to fully support changes occurring in junior sport....The leaders had to buy into the changes and then work it through the volunteers" (Hepburn 2019, para 2). What a difference a pandemic makes. Seven months ago the time line for change was discussed in terms of a generation. Now, all sectors of New Zealand are expected to be able to adapt to rapid change within hours. This was illustrated in March 2020 when the New Zealand population was given little over 48 hours to prepare for the COVID-19 inspired State of National Emergency.

Rapid change is often associated with a crisis, which can in turn provide opportunities for the status quo to be challenged. This was evident in the following statement from a member of SNZ's Diversity and Inclusion team.

> COVID-19 forced all sport to stop. If we use this pause in play to proactively reimagine our future, we can shed old priorities, choices, habits, and exclusionary behaviours, and clear the slate for new, better ones that benefit all New Zealanders.
>
> *(White 2020, para. 1)*

DOI: 10.4324/9781003034445-9

96 Tania Cassidy

While I applaud the desire to design practices for the betterment of all New Zealanders, the changes needed to do so will undoubtedly intensify the contested terrain around sports coaching in Aotearoa New Zealand. To highlight this the chapter is organised two-fold: the first section comprises two parts, which reflect the common adage that to understand/create the future it is necessary to know the past; the second section also comprises two parts and examines the potential impact the New Zealand government's Wellbeing Budgets, UNICEF reports and COVID-19 has, and will have, on the terrain in which sports coaching operates in Aotearoa New Zealand. The discussion throughout the chapter highlights the debates that have occurred, and continue to occur, around the philosophies, models and language used to inform the education and development of sports coaches.

Part 1: Setting the scene

While Sergeant Pepper may have "taught the band how to play" the Ministerial taskforce review of sport and recreation in New Zealand changed how sport and recreation were "played" in Aotearoa New Zealand.

> On 29 June 2000 the Minister of Sport, Fitness and Leisure, Trevor Mallard stated that the Government had set the taskforce a major challenge... [for a sector that] is in desperate need for leadership and a vision for the future... Our Government's overall objectives for the sporting sector [in the next 25 years] are to increase participation and support excellence.
> *(New Zealand Government 2000, paras. 4–6)*

In 2005 Trevor Mallard gave a presentation about the impact the Ministerial taskforce review of sport and recreation had on the sport and recreation sector in New Zealand (New Zealand Government 2005). To set the scene he described the situation in New Zealand prior to the taskforce thus; there were "three main organisations responsible for promoting and supporting sport and recreation (para. 3)...there was little coordination between organisations and the sector was fragmented and ineffective" (para. 7). He then described a key recommendation of the Ministerial taskforce, which was that these organisations (the Hillary Commission, the Office of Tourism and Sport and the New Zealand Sports Foundation) "be replaced by a single Crown entity, Sport and Recreation New Zealand (SPARC)" (para.16), which would have "three key areas of focus – participation, high performance and sports systems" (para. 17). Mallard went on to explain that the establishment of SPARC was not just a merger of the previous organisations, rather it "signalled a fresh start for government intervention in the sport and recreation sector...[and] it was a clean sheet of paper to rewrite the way sport and recreation were administered in New Zealand" (New Zealand Government 2005, para. 18). Another finding of the Ministerial taskforce (2001), not mentioned by Mallard but central to this chapter, was the attention given to the sports system; "Coaching is in urgent need of support and development" (p. 10).

Insight into why the Ministerial taskforce made this finding about the state of coaching can be gained by Kidman and Keelty's (n.d.) overview of coach education in Aotearoa New Zealand. In the two decades prior to the Ministerial taskforce, the organisation of coach education appeared to be in a constant state of flux. For example, in the late 1970s the New Zealand Association of National Sports Coaches was developed, but by the middle of the 1980s the Coaching Association of New Zealand (CANZ) was created and "identified as the key provider of coach education" (Kidman & Keelty n.d., p. 4). In 1985 the first national CANZ level I coaching programme was implemented. Six years later CANZ became Coaching New Zealand (CNZ), which was funded by the Hillary Commission to "develop a multi-level coach education standardised, accredited scheme" (p. 4). This continued until 1997 when CNZ was disestablished and the "Hillary Commission became the governing body for coach education" (p. 4).

With the disestablishment of the Hillary Commission SPARC had the mandate to provide "urgent" support for sports coaching in Aotearoa New Zealand. Despite the so-called urgency, it took four years before the *New Zealand Coaching Strategy* (SPARC 2004) was launched. The *New Zealand Coaching Strategy* identified 10 coaching areas needing attention, six of which specifically identified a need for "coach development" (SPARC 2004). Unsurprisingly two of the three objectives of the *Strategy* related to coach education. When describing how to implement the objectives the authors established five tactics for future action. Tactic three – "improve coach education requirements and qualifications" – was the driver for the establishment of a working party to design what was to become known as the *Coach Development Framework (CDF)* (Cassidy & Kidman 2010).

Part 2: Strategic documents

Having the mandate to review and upgrade sports coaching practice and resourcing, SPARC subsequently published two policy documents: *The New Zealand Coaching Strategy* (SPARC 2004) and the *CDF* (SPARC 2006). Upon examining these documents Cassidy and Kidman (2010) contended a paradigmatic shift had occurred

- *from* coach education *to* coach development;
- *from* generic courses for all coaches *to* recognising the nuances of coaching communities; and
- *from* formalised, accredited, certified and standardised programmes *to* an ongoing professional development process informed by an applied athlete-centred philosophy.

98 Tania Cassidy

When paradigmatic shifts occur, resources are redirected and terrain becomes contested.

This shifting and contested terrain was evident in the change of language being used, for example from coach *education* to coach *development*. This was apparent in the advancement of what eventually became known as the *CDF* (SPARC 2006). At the first meeting of the working party tasked with writing the *Framework* there was agreement "that previous orthodox coach *education* programmes in New Zealand had not worked" (Cassidy & Kidman 2010, p. 314, *emphasis in original*) and the working party should focus on coach *development* and not coach *education*. The working party also held the common view that the failures of the previous coach education programmes were due to them primarily being "formal, classroom and theory orientated practices that focused on the 'what' (knowledge) in coaching and not the 'how' (skills) and 'why' (understanding)" (p. 314). Additionally, there was a 'desire' to use language that emphasised coach *development* and provide opportunities for coaches to access "formal and informal coach *development* learning opportunities...that will support wider personal development and growth" (SPARC 2006, p.6, *emphasis added*). Finally, the working party was able to successfully argue for the *Framework* to be called the *CDF* because of its focus on athlete-centred coach development and its shift away from a multi-level coach education standardised, accredited scheme that had existed prior to the Ministerial taskforce (Cassidy & Kidman 2010). Consequently, coach development became the responsibility of each National Sporting Organisation, with opportunities to collaborate across sporting codes and draw on generic coaching content offered by SPARC.

Another area of contestation occurred around the interpretation and utilisation of the concept of "coaching communities". In the *CDF* the concept is expressed in an inconsistent and potentially confusing manner (Cassidy & Kidman 2010). For example, "coaching communities" initially appeared, at the request of SPARC, in *The New Zealand Coaching Strategy* (SPARC 2004) to describe the age of the groups of athletes, for example, late teenage (ages 17–19), early teenage (ages 13–16), and late childhood (ages 9–12). However, another associated working party, which SPARC had commissioned to write the *Talent Development Pathway (TDF)*, had conceptualised "communities" "around a broader understanding of development, one that focused on the needs of the athletes (i.e., stage and phase) rather than their age" (Cassidy & Kidman 2010, p.316). This differing interpretation required a compromise to be reached between the members of the *CDF* working party and SPARC, and saw the addition of a qualifier appearing in the *Framework* which stated: "[t]he coaching communities will be aligned to the stages of athlete development but 'descriptions are indicative only'" (SPARC 2004, p.9).

Part 3: Talent development

The *Talent Development Pathway (TDF)* was to be the catalyst for subsequent coaching strategies and initiatives to adopt an athlete-centred philosophy. Yet

Sports coaching, education and development **99**

this shift also became contested terrain. Due to personal and political agendas it took nearly a decade before a participant centred sports system was mandated, with the publication of SNZ's[1] Strategic Plan 2015–2020 (Sport New Zealand, n.d.a). In another re-branding exercise in 2011 SPARC became Sport New Zealand (SNZ). Arguably this re-branding was a contentious exercise because the day after SNZ began "trading" under its new name the Ministry of Culture and Heritage put out a statement stating "[t]here's no change to what we do"[2] (New Zealand Government 2012). But change they did. The authors of SNZ's Strategic Plan 2015–2020 argued that opportunities existed to change the way community sport was delivered and advocated for the adoption of a "participant centred, world-leading community sports system that enriches lives and ultimately increases sport participation amongst New Zealanders" (Sport New Zealand n.d. a).

A possible explanation for the extensive delay in the publication of the *TDF* is the contested terrain around what constitutes athlete development. In the mid-2000s, when the initial discussion began on the *TDF*, the work of Istvan Balyi and his Long Term Athlete Development (LTAD) model was getting considerable global attention from sport governing organisations. His model prescribed early and late specialisation pathways, with suggested windows of optimal trainability and accelerated adaptability that were based on age and biological maturation (Balyi & Hamilton 2004). It did not take long before such a view of LTAD was so ingrained in many sport governing organisations that it had become viewed by some as a "global law that must be adhered to for athletes to be internationally competitive" (Day 2011, p.181). Yet, increasingly Balyi's conceptualisation of LTAD was challenged. Initially the challenges came from the sport psychology community. For example, Côté and Hancock (2016) as well as Ford et al. (2011) critiqued the above view of LTAD because it primarily focused on physiological paradigms and was not based on supporting empirical evidence unlike other models of development (see Abbott & Collins 2004; Bailey & Morley 2006; Côté et al. 2012; Lloyd & Oliver 2012). Additionally, they claimed that Balyi's LTAD model created anxiety in parents, young athletes and coaches with its suggested windows of opportunity. Finally, they were critical of the attempts of Balyi and others to unashamedly commercialise an important life event. The International Society for Sport Psychology (ISSP) published a position paper in which they also challenged Balyi's LTAD model by critiquing its prescribed early specialisation pathways, which were based on age and biological maturation. One of the ISSP's recommendations was that people working with young people be aware that development occurs within a complex interplay between the environment, the task and the young person themselves (Côté et al. 2009).

Increasingly, as SNZ moved to draw on research and make evidence-based decisions the focus turned to descriptive, rather than prescriptive, models of development. In other words, they moved away from drawing on a Balyi inspired LTAD model and began gaining inspiration from models such as the Developmental Model of Sport Participation (DMSP; Côté et al. 2012; Côté &

100 Tania Cassidy

Vierimaa 2014), with its key concepts of deliberate practice and deliberate play and the importance it placed on the sampling phase during ages of 6–12 years. When developing the DMSP the authors drew on evidence of what elite athletes had done in their development phase. This is powerful data and a growing number of organisations working with elite athletes are acknowledging the value to youngsters of them adopting a sampling approach to sport participation in their early years of playing sport. For example, the Sevilla Football Club in Spain, one of the world premier football clubs, does not designate athletes to a particular position until the ages of 16 or 17 (Gilbert 2017) and the International Olympic Committee identified sport sampling as a key recommendation on its consensus statement on athlete development (Bergon et al. 2015).

Yet talent development is still a contested terrain in Aotearoa New Zealand. SNZ's Athlete Development Pathway is abstractly represented in the *Talent Plan 2016–2020* (Sport New Zealand 2015a). Its abstract nature arguably reflects the contested terrain in which athlete development is situated. This contention is supported by the quote in the *TDF*; "[m]ore information regarding this visual will be provided to the sector in 2016/17" (Sport New Zealand 2015a, p.4) and the response I received in January 2020 from SNZ when preparing to write this chapter:

> [u]nfortunately the pathway document was not progressed any further, so there is no further information other than what is in both the Talent Plan and Coaching Plan documents. As we develop a 2020–2024 Sport Plan in the first half of this year it is very likely we will revisit the pathway.
>
> *(personal communication, 8 January 2020)*

Despite the work not having progressed on the Athlete Development Pathway, in the *Talent Plan 2016–2020* (Sport New Zealand 2015a) SNZ still lauds it as the supporting document for its recently developed, evidence-based "Balance is Better" philosophy, which put the needs of the participants first. According to SNZ, the focus of the Balance is Better philosophy is to grow

> the capability of the sporting system to better prepare athletes in their development phase to help them realise their potential. Balance is Better has now become a broader conversation underpinning Sport NZ's overall approach to youth sport that focusses on maximising participation and skill development.
>
> *(Sport New Zealand n.d. b)*

SNZ's Balance is Better philosophy and resources (https://sportnz.org.nz/resources/balance-is-better-philosophy/) consistently and clearly challenge three myths prevalent in youth sport with the following statements:

1   Childhood success is not a reliable predictor of future success
2   Identifying athletes early and specialising early is taking its toll on young people

Sports coaching, education and development **101**

3   A focus on winning rather than development is a problem for young people, because it can have unintended consequences on their wellbeing and affect their motivation to take part (Sport New Zealand n.d. b)

Challenging the orthodoxy results in resistance. This was evident when the North Harbour Rugby Union chose to draw on the Balance is Better philosophy when making the decision not to send an under-13 representative team to a popular tournament. The general manager of the Union said that this decision had been debated for over a year and while he acknowledged that not everyone would agree with the decision he went onto say,

> Harbour Rugby's purpose is improving lives through rugby... and when it comes to our community we want to maximise engagement and grow participation. For us this means... putting the kids at the centre of the experience. The more kids that play, the more they have fun, the longer they will stay in the game.

The decision drew "scathing criticism on social media, with some former members calling it a sad day for the sport" but North Harbour's engagement and participation team leader said "this is not saying performance or representative programs are negative…This is about adjusting our current system and introducing a talent development program at a more appropriate age and stage" (Radio New Zealand 2019, paras. 28–29).

SNZ's sport development team appear to be aware of the contested terrain around the Balance is Better initiative. For example, at the beginning of 2020 when SNZ announced its Balance is Better Regional Forums, they encouraged the Regional Sports Trust to make sure that the forums were

> well supported and ensure the *right people* are in the room within each region. This is a great opportunity for regional and local leaders involved in delivering youth sport and physical activity to *further understand the importance of this work.*
>
> *(personal communication, 20 February 2020, emphasis added)*

The contested nature of New Zealand's sports coaching terrain has not lessened with SNZ releasing its Strategic Direction 2020–2032 entitled "Every Body Active" (Sport New Zealand 2019). The vision and purpose of this Strategic Direction is dramatically different from that articulated in SNZ's previous Strategic Plan 2015–2020. In the latter the vision was for New Zealand to be "the world's most successful sporting nation" (Sport New Zealand n.d. c), whereas in Sport NZ's Strategic Direction 2020–2032 the stated vision is: "Every Body Active" and its purpose is to "contribute to the wellbeing of everybody in Aotearoa New Zealand by leading an enriching and inspiring Play, Active Recreation and Sport system" (Sport New Zealand 2019, p.14). Arguably, the contestation occurs because of the enduring "binary" debates that position elite and community,

102 Tania Cassidy

as well as (elite) performance and wellbeing, as oppositional. Potentially fuelling further contestation in the sports coaching terrain is that in the 45 pages of "Every Body Active" the words "coach", "coaches" and "coaching" were, collectively, mentioned only eight times. That SNZ explicitly reduces the visibility of, and opportunities for, coaches to be key stakeholders in their Strategic Direction 2020–2032 is perplexing because it undermines the potential good coaches have to promote wellbeing for everybody.

To understand possible reasons as to why SNZ's Strategic Direction 2020–2032, and the accompanying Strategic Plan 2020–2024, have dramatically departed from their previous Strategic Plan, it is useful to understand the current social and political environment in Aotearoa New Zealand. In 2017, a finding of research conducted by the Child Poverty Monitor was "that 290,000 NZ children – around 27% of kids – were living in income poverty" (UNICEF n.d a). The definition of income poverty is highly relevant to those working in the sport sector because it means not only

> homelessness, not having access to healthy [or enough] food, …or coming home to a cold damp house to sleep in a shared bed. It can [also] mean missing out on activities like learning a musical instrument or *playing sport*, or even having a birthday party.
>
> *(emphasis added) (UNICEF n.d a)*

Additionally, in 2019 the New Zealand Government released its first Wellbeing Budget. In describing the priorities of the Budget, Prime Minster Ardern said "[o]ur five Wellbeing Budget priorities show how we have broadened our definition of success for our country to one that incorporates not just the health of our finances, but also of our natural resources, people and communities" (New Zealand Treasury 2019). The Minister of Finance went on to say that the Wellbeing Budget "represents a significant departure from the status quo…The old ways have left too many people behind. It is time to change…." (New Zealand Treasury 2019).

The language used in the Strategic Plan 2020–2024, within the Strategic Direction 2020–2032, suggests the authors were aware of the above social and political environments as well as the contestable nature of the terrain they were traversing. When describing the strategies adopted to maintain momentum in sport development, they encouraged national and regional sports organisations to share evidence regarding the "need for change", run courses to upskill sport development leaders, undertake pilot work with partners and support "decision-makers *to stand firm against opposing views*" (Sport New Zealand 2019, p.25, *emphasis added*).

It is too early to tell what the Strategic Direction 2020–2034, and the Strategic Plan 2020–2024, will mean for coaches, especially in light of the current COVID-19 related reorganisation of the sports sector. However, prior to New

Zealand entering a State of National Emergency on 26 March 2020 there were hints of what lay ahead. In an email conversation with a SNZ coaching consultant he stated:

> [T]he release of the Sport NZ strategy (2020–2024) coupled with the re-shaping of the Coaching & Talent Team into the Sport Development team essentially means it would be unlikely that Sport NZ would deliver a stand alone coaching conference in the next 4 years.
>
> *(personal communication, 10 February 2020)*

Part 4: COVID-19

The New Zealand Government committed $265m to assist the sport sector to recover from the impacts of COVID-19. Yet, this support comes with expectations that the sector will achieve the following outcomes: (1) reset and rebuild, (2) strengthen and adapt and, (3) be different and better (Sport New Zealand n.d. d). To achieve these outcomes changes will have to occur, which will inevitably have an impact on coaching and coach development.

At the beginning of the COVID-19 lockdown, the CEO of SNZ encouraged the seven major (team) sporting bodies (netball, rugby league, rugby union, football, cricket, basketball and field hockey) to do things differently and work together to "share, among other things, their experiences and challenges" (George 2020, para. 18). Yet the subsequent actions of SNZ, which saw them fund only the four traditional winter sports (netball, rugby union, rugby league, and football) did little to reflect their edict of doing things differently. The CEO of Basketball NZ challenged SNZ's funding decision saying that it was a "kick in the guts" for the sport and that it "suffered an institutional bias against it" (New Zealand Herald 7 July 2020, para. 4). In response to a public stouch about SNZ's funding decision the government stepped in and subsequently the basketball leagues were funded.

Despite the initial snub Basketball NZ showed itself to be very nimble in face of the COVID-19 adversity and gained considerable plaudits. For Basketball NZ to be so adaptable, the people working in the organisation had to be willing to change. Yet, if it continues to be an innovative organisation, then Basketball NZ will need to support its people, including coaches, further develop skills to successfully work in a changing environment. Historically developing such skills have not been part of orthodox coach development programmes.

Individual sports appear to have had fewer issues with COVID-19 restrictions than team sports, but they have still needed to be adaptable. For example, there was an upsurge of people playing golf post lockdown, with coaches in many clubs having to adapt to accommodate more, and new, playing populations. In the case of the latter, one coach described how she had previously "spent 20 years getting women to come along and get on the range and work with them for five weeks

104 Tania Cassidy

and then never see them again", whereas after introducing a new programme called *She Loves Golf* she has seen a rise in new memberships. (Hepburn 2020, para. 6).

Institutional change is required for sports to successfully negotiate the COVID-19 influenced landscape and coach development has an integral part to play in this success. Already sports organisations are adapting what, and how, they deliver in the name of coach development (see Leaders from Lockdown [https://womeninsport.org.nz/programmes/leadership-from-lockdown/] and Connecting Coaches [https://conference.oas.org.nz/]). This is only the beginning of, what will likely be, a watershed moment for sport and coach development in Aotearoa New Zealand.

Conclusion

The terrain of the sports sector is continuously contested, which inevitably influences what decisions coaches make as to what, how and why they do what they do. This chapter has provided examples of the contestation that has occurred in the sector over the past two decades. Debate has occurred over what philosophies, models and language to use, which has in turn driven the direction of the discussions, and subsequent decisions, around coaching practices. Sport coaches work in a sector that is increasingly complex and dynamic, which has been exacerbated by the COVID-19 pandemic. Coaches will need to be supported to develop practices that align with the Strategic Direction 2020–2034, which arguably represents another paradigmatic shift and risks further contestation. Yet, a degree of contestation supports the agenda of SNZ, and the New Zealand Government, who have made it clear that the status quo is no longer viable, and a "reset" is required.

Notes

1 In October 2011 the then minister of sport, Murray McCully, announced that from February 2012 SPARC would become Sport New Zealand.
2 After the 2017 general election in New Zealand, Grant Robertson was appointed Minister of Finance, Minister for Sport and Recreation, and Associate Minister for Arts, Culture and Heritage.

References

Abbott, A. & Collins, D. 2004, 'Eliminating the dichotomy between theory and practice in talent identification and development: considering the role of psychology', *Journal of Sports Sciences*, Vol. 22, no. 5, pp. 395–408, https://doi.org/10.1080/02640410410 001675324
Bailey, R. & Morley, D. 2006, 'Towards a model of talent development in physical education', *Sport, Education and Society*, Vol. 11, no. 3, pp. 211–230, doi.org/10.1080/ 13573320600813366

Sports coaching, education and development **105**

Balyi, I. & Hamilton A. 2004, *Long-term athlete development: Trainability in childhood and adolescence—windows of opportunity—optimal trainability*, National Coaching Institute British Columbia & Advanced Training and Performance Ltd., Victoria, Canada.

Bergon, M., Mountjoy, M., & Armstrong, N., et al., 2015, 'International Olympic Committee consensus statement on youth athletic development', *British Journal of Sports Medicine*, Vol. 49, pp. 843–851, doi.org/10.1136/bjsports-2015-094962.

Cassidy, T. & Kidman, L. 2010, 'Initiating a national coaching curriculum: a paradigmatic shift?' *Physical Education and Sport Pedagogy*, Vol. 15, no.3, pp. 307–322, doi.org/10.1080/17408980903409907.

Côté, J. & Hancock, D. J. 2016, 'Evidence-based policies for youth sport programmes', *International Journal of Sport Policy and Politics*, Vol. 8, no. 1, pp. 51–65, doi.org/10.1080/19406940.2014.919338.

Côté, J., Murphy-Mills, J. & Abernethy, B. 2012, 'The development of skill in sport', in N. Hodges & A. M. Williams (eds.), *Skill acquisition in sport: Research, theory and practice,* Routledge, New York, pp. 269–286.

Côté, J., Lidor, R. & Hackfort, D. 2009, 'ISSP position stand: to sample or to specialize? Seven postulates about youth sport activities that lead to continued participation and elite performance', *International Journal or Sport and Exercise Psychology*, Vol. 9, pp. 7–17, doi.org/10.1080/1612197X.2009.9671889.

Côté, J. & Vierimaa, M. 2014, 'The developmental model of sport participation: 15 years after its first conceptualisation', *Science and Sports*, pp. 63–69, https://doi.org/10.1016/J.SCISPO.2014.08.133

Day, D. 2011, Craft coaching and the 'discerning eye' of the coach. *International Journal of Sport Science and Coaching*, Vol. 6, no. 1, pp. 179–195, https://doi.org/10.1260/1747-9541.6.1.179

Ford, P., De Ste Croix, M. & Lloyd, R. et al., 2011, 'The long-term athlete development model: Physiological evidence and application', *Journal of Sports Sciences*, Vol. 29, no. 4, pp. 389–402, https://doi.org/10.1080/02640414.2010.536849

George, Z. 2020, *Coronavirus: Major NZ sports working together on a Covid-19 response*, viewed 14 December 2020, https://www.stuff.co.nz/national/health/coronavirus/120330800/coronavirus-major-nz-sports-working-together-on-covid19-response.

Gilbert, W. 2017, *Coaching better every season. A year-round system for athlete development and program auccess*, Human Kinetics, Champaign, IL.

Hepburn, S. 2019, *Sport NZ pledges not to compel changes*, viewed 17 August 2020, https://www.odt.co.nz/sport/other-sport/sport-nz-pledges-not-compel-changes.

Hepburn, S. 2020, *Women playing and staying – Duncan*, viewed 14 December 2020, https://www.odt.co.nz/sport/golf/women-playing-and-staying-%E2%80%94-duncan.

Kidman, L. & Keelty, D. n.d., *Coaching and Coach Development in New Zealand*, viewed 30 October 2020, http://156.62.60.45/bitstream/handle/10292/9510/Coaching%20in%20NZ%20article%204-2-15.pdf?sequence=5&isAllowed=y.

Lloyd, R. S. & Oliver, J. L. 2012, 'The youth physical development model: A new approach to long-term athletic development', *Strength and Conditioning Journal*, Vol. 34, no. 3, pp. 61–72, https://doi.org/10.1519/SSC.0b013e31825760ea

Ministerial Taskforce. 2001, *Getting set for an active nation: Report of the sport, fitness and leisure Ministerial taskforce*, The Taskforce, Wellington.

New Zealand Government. 2000, *Major review into sport, fitness and leisure*, viewed 17 August 2020, https://www.beehive.govt.nz/release/major-review-sport-fitness-and-leisure.

New Zealand Government. 2005, *Press release. The graham report*, viewed 17 August 2020, https://www.scoop.co.nz/stories/PA0505/S00664/the-graham-report.htm.

New Zealand Government. 2012, *SPARC changes to Sport New Zealand*, viewed 17 August 2020, https://mch.govt.nz/sparc-changes-sport-new-zealand.

New Zealand Herald. 2020, *Sport: Basketball the little winner in latest $80m virus handout*, viewed 14 December 2020, https://www.nzherald.co.nz/sport/sport-basketball-the-little-winner-in-latest-80m-virus-handout/77OKT77UXXVVA63IM3RDVH2SHA/.

New Zealand Treasury. 2019, *The wellbeing budget*, viewed 17 August 2020, https://treasury.govt.nz/sites/default/files/2019-06/b19-wellbeing-budget.pdf.

Radio New Zealand. 2019, *Auckland rugby union to can junior rep competition*, viewed 17 August 2020, https://www.rnz.co.nz/news/national/383210/auckland-rugby-union-to-can-junior-rep-competition.

SPARC. 2004, *The New Zealand coaching strategy*, viewed 17 August 2020, https://sportnz.org.nz/assets/Uploads/The-New-Zealand-Coaching-Strategy-2016.pdf.

SPARC. 2006, *Coach development framework*, viewed 17 August 2020, https://sportnz.org.nz/assets/Uploads/attachments/managing-sport/coaching/Coach-Development-Framework.pdf.

Sport New Zealand. n.d. a, *Sport NZ group strategic plan 2015–2020*, viewed 17 August 2020, https://sportnz.org.nz/about-us/our-publications/our-strategies/sport-nz-group-strategic-plan-2015-2020/.

Sport New Zealand. n.d. b, *Balance is Better Philosophy*, viewed 17 August 2020, https://sportnz.org.nz/focus-areas/youth-sport/balance-is-better-philosophy/.

Sport New Zealand, n.d. c, *Sport NZ Group Strategic Plan 2015–2020*, viewed 17 August 2020, https://sportnz.org.nz/assets/Uploads/attachments/About-us/Sport-NZ-Group-Strategic-Plan-2015-2020.pdf.

Sport New Zealand. n.d. d, COVID-19 response, viewed 14 December 2020, https://sportnz.org.nz/covid-19-response/overview/.

Sport New Zealand. 2015a, *Talent Plan 2016–2020*, viewed 8 December 2020, https://sportnz.org.nz/media/1704/sportnz-talentplan-v01.pdf.

Sport New Zealand. 2015b, *New Zealand community sport coaching plan (2016–2020)*, viewed 17 August 2020, https://sportnz.org.nz/assets/Uploads/SportNZ-CommunitySport-CoachingPlan-July2016.pdf.

Sport New Zealand. 2019, *Every body active*, viewed 17 August 2020, https://sportnz.org.nz/assets/Uploads/strategy-doc-18.12.19.pdf.

UNICEF. n.d. a, *A fair childhood*, viewed 17 August 2020, https://www.unicef.org.nz/in-new-zealand/fair-childhood.

UNICEF. n.d. b, *COVID-19: Number of children living in household poverty set to soar*, viewed 17 August 2020, https://www.unicef.org.nz/stories/number-of-children-living-in-household-poverty-set-to-soar.

White, B. 2020, *The COVID-19 pandemic is a unique opportunity for our sector. We are faced with the choice to re-build the sport sector as it was, or to realise the possibilities that lie before us*, viewed 17 August 2020, https://balanceisbetter.org.nz/is-covid-19-the-reset-we-need-to-improve-sport-for-women-and-girls/.

10

THE SPORTING MYTHSCAPES OF AOTEAROA NEW ZEALAND

Mark Falcous and Sebastian Potgieter[1]

Introduction

Popular understandings of the social presence of sport in Aotearoa New Zealand overwhelmingly reflect what Coakley (2015, p. 403) has termed the "great sport myth". This myth reflects "the pervasive and nearly unshakeable belief in the inherent purity and goodness of sport as a social institution", and further, that "the purity and goodness of sport is transmitted to those who participate in or consume it; and [that] sport inevitably leads to individual and community development". This is a view consistently reflected across media, by politicians, sports administrators, educators, athletes and marketeers who promote sport as a unifying, character building, integrative force, and hence a social good. This belief idealises the social presence of sport and hence forestalls critical analysis. As Roland Barthes (1957/2012) notes, myth is not falsehood, nor illusion. Alternatively, myth "hides nothing: its function is to distort, not to make disappear" (p. 231). The great sport myth, however, cannot be understood as monolithic, but operates in nationally specific and nuanced forms, is multi-layered, and shifts over time.

In the case of New Zealand, the construction of sport as a praiseworthy institution intersects numerous themes. First, what Consedine (1989, p. 172) terms "the most fundamental and persistent myth about our society, deeply embedded in the Pakeha [*sic*] psyche"; that the country is egalitarian. In this regard, sport is celebrated as a "level playing field". Second, centring on the unifying role of participation and international competition, sports' mythos are strongly linked with expressions of nationhood. Contra these myths, as Falcous (2007a) argues, selected sports have been historically promoted and given patronage that have entrenched the hegemonic male, white settler/Pākehā, middle classes as central to, first, the colonial and subsequently post-colonial nation. That is, sport is in

DOI: 10.4324/9781003034445-10

108 Mark Falcous and Sebastian Potgieter

fact socially contested as interest groups struggle to impose the selective values, norms and identities that it can (quite literally) embody.

Within this chapter we invoke the notion of *mythscapes* (Bell 2003) to interrogate the narrativisation of the sporting past. Bell (2003, p. 66) defines the mythscape as

> the temporally and spatially extended discursive realm wherein the struggle for control of people's memories and the formation of nationalist narratives are (re)written: it is the perpetually mutating repository for the representation of the past for the purposes of the present.

Thus, how the past is remembered tells us about present day, power-laden narrations of the sporting nation. We develop Falcous and Newman's (2015) use of the term *sporting mythscapes* that captures how sports images and ideas circulate widely: within popular literature, museums, awards, commercial culture (from cereal boxes to TV advertising), and memorials such as statues and trophies to invoke a particular rendition of the sporting nation. Across this sporting mythscape certain codes, events, figures and achievements are remembered, memorialised, highlighted and celebrated. Others meanwhile are forgotten, ignored or obscured. Our focus in this chapter is one feature of the national sporting mythscape – historical representation. Following Bell (2003, p. 69), we explore the "everyday actualization and propagation" of a selective national imagination in and through narratives of the sporting past. In this regard, there are questions around which versions of the sporting past predominate, and how these are entangled with the wider identity politics of the nation. We explore three cases to consider how the representation of past events constitutes a national sporting mythscape: the 1976 Montreal Olympic boycott; the 1981 Springbok tour; and the 1907–1908 All Golds.

1976 Montreal Olympic Boycott

In 1976 New Zealand sport was at the centre of a boycott of the Montreal Olympic Games due to an All Blacks rugby tour of apartheid South Africa, in defiance of a United Nations' sporting embargo (see Mason 2007). The tour commenced shortly after the Soweto uprising in which 176 school children protesting against compulsory Afrikaans tuition (the language of the apartheid state) were killed by police. O'Meara (1996) maintains that Soweto was "[the] worst public relations disaster in the history of apartheid" (p. 223) and was "perceived internationally as a problem created by a recalcitrant, ethnic Afrikaner government" (p. 422). This was the second time the All Blacks had toured South Africa shortly after a massacre, the first being in March 1960 when police in Sharpeville shot and killed 69 protestors. The 1976 tour led to largely African nations calling on the International Olympic Committee (IOC) to exclude New Zealand from the Montreal games. After the IOC refused, 28 nations responded with a boycott and others followed. The IOC position was that South Africa was already excluded from Olympic competition, and that it did not have jurisdiction over rugby so it could not force New Zealand out; nor did the New Zealand Olympic Committee (NZOC) volunteer to withdraw. The IOC and NZOC subsequently declined a compromise option to issue a joint statement condemning apartheid and the rugby tour (Romanos 2008). The boycott highlighted New Zealand rugby's obstinate determination to maintain ties with South Africa in defiance of international consensus.

Within New Zealand, popular accounts of the 1976 Olympics principally emphasise John Walker's 1,500 m gold medal success. Palenski and Romanos (2000) award Walker the title of champion athlete of the decade. He was also recently celebrated in a life-sized bronze statue in Manurewa, south Auckland, which depicts him crossing the finish line at the 1976 Olympics. Such remembrances situate Walker as an icon of New Zealand sport, celebrated and revered. Accounts of the boycott and its contexts, and his success, however, are highly selective.

Romanos (2008) presents an account of the boycott, ignoring the broader context of ties to apartheid South Africa, is sceptical of boycotters' motives, frames the boycott as a failure, and suggests the episode saw New Zealand vindicated. He frames boycott organisers Abraham Ordia and Jean-Claude Ganga of the Supreme Council for Sport in Africa as "mak[ing] threatening noises about the Montreal Olympics" (p. 126). Ordia's accompanying photograph is captioned as having "New Zealand in his sights" (p. 136). The subsequent boycott Romanos labels "inevitable" (not contingent or preventable), and he contrasts "little New Zealand" with the "combined strength" of the multilateral boycott movement. He praises the IOC for not excluding New Zealand, as "[having] stood firm on a principle" (p. 137). He also frames the disappointment of African athletes as "show[ing] up the boycott for what it was really worth". Romanos summarises that "the New Zealanders won in 1976" but concedes "it cost them in terms of popularity" (p. 137). Romanos ultimately characterises the event as "the disappointing boycott by the black African nations" (p. 150), conveying it as "unsuccessful, ill-advised and, indeed, harming African athletes: the losers were the black African athletes" (p. 137). Indeed, a footnote to Romanos' (2008) account details Ganga's involvement in IOC corruption some 26 years later, reinforcing the framing of the boycott leaders as nefarious. Palenski (2015) offers a similar framing of the boycott: not only was the New Zealand team in Montreal "blameless" but most of the boycotting nations were "undemocratic [in] nature" (p. 346). Ultimately, both Romanos (2008) and Palenski's (2015) accounts ignore the role of sport in consolidating apartheid, assert the virtues of New Zealand sport, and represent New Zealand as the innocent victim of naïve African maleficence led by provocateurs.

Remembrances of 1976 through John Walker are selective and ignore the broader contexts of his success. Notably, Walker's key rival, Tanzanian Flibert Bayi, who had defeated Walker at the 1974 Christchurch Commonwealth Games, and was then world record holder, did not compete due to the boycott.

110 Mark Falcous and Sebastian Potgieter

Palenski and Romanos (2000, p. 117) recount that "Walker caused some flutters when he was eliminated early from the 800m, but in the 1500m – in a final weakened by an African boycott – he was always the man to watch". In this de-contextualised framing, Palenski and Romanos (2000) effectively blame Bayi's absence on "an African Boycott" and forget that New Zealand was the source of the boycott. Romanos (2006) subsequently regurgitates the same text with a minor addition: "in a final weakened by an African Boycott, which prevented the showdown with Bayi – he [Walker] was always the man to watch" (p. 22).

Palenski and Romanos' framing of the 1976 Olympics ignores New Zealand's role in the perpetuation of apartheid through sport and especially rugby, decisions made by the IOC, and offers no explanation as to why the NZOC decided to compete in the games. Instead, the focus is on Walker's success, and even where mention of the broader contexts is made (i.e., the absence of Bayi), it is minimised. It is also notable that at the time Ces Blazey was chairman of both the New Zealand Rugby Football Union (NZRFU) and the New Zealand Amateur Athletics Association, thus blurring the boundary between the administration of Olympic sports and rugby (Thompson 1975). Moreover, within these accounts, New Zealand is a virtuous "small player", "punching above its weight". Critics are dismissed as nefarious and wider implications and moral questions of linkages with apartheid South Africa are ignored.

1981 Springbok tour: The mythos of anti-racist tolerance?

Opposition to rugby ties with apartheid South Africa reached a peak in 1981. In defiance of the 1977 Gleneagles Agreement (catalysed by the 1976 Montreal boycott) which urged Commonwealth nations to dissuade their sporting bodies from playing against South Africa, the NZRFU invited the Springboks to tour New Zealand. For its 16-match (only 14 were played), 56-day duration thousands of citizens publicly, and sometimes violently, demonstrated against the tour. Others mobilised in support. Stadiums came to resemble fortresses barricaded with barbed-wire and were guarded by riot police specially trained for the tour. Richards (1996) estimates that by the end of the tour, more than 150,000 New Zealanders had protested in 28 centres across the country, with around 2,000 arrests for tour-related offences. Accounts of the tumultuous events of the 1981 tour have been subject to numerous literary and television documentary accounts, many of which frame the events as nation defining.

The accounts of anti-tour demonstrations highlight that the protesters opposed more than apartheid (see Chapple 1984; Freeman & Hollins 1982; MacLean, 2000, 2001, 2010; Newnham 1981; Phillips, 1987; Richards, 1999). The protests also encompassed domestic issues: "internal" racism obscured by the myth of egalitarianism, Māori liberation, patriarchal masculinity embodied in rugby culture, and a conservative and increasingly racist government that endorsed and enabled the tour. For Chapple (1984), resistance to the tour had "grown far beyond the original anti-apartheid issue" (p. 186) and exposed "New

Zealand's own racism, its intolerance, its easily sanctioned violence" (p. 277). Male rugby culture was targeted by the anti-tour campaign for its "intolerance", "racism" and general "ignorance" of the world (p. 241). MacLean (2012) summarises the anti-tour campaign as "the culmination of a series of post-1968 protest actions that had a significant focus on issues 'abroad', but also drew on 'domestic' issues including Māori land and sociocultural rights, feminist causes, and trade union campaigns" (p. 455). "There was nothing simple about this campaign", he concludes (MacLean 2010, p. 72).

Ignoring and silencing the wider critiques of rugby voiced by protestors, popular accounts of the tour in subsequent decades have instead emphasised the anti-racist and anti-apartheid elements of resistance to the tour. Rather than viewing rugby as consolidating racism, they valorise it as aiding the dismantling of apartheid. For example, Chester and McMillan (1990, p. 566) refer to anti-tour protests in 1981 as expressions of "opposition to the South African Government's racial policies". While recognising the evils of apartheid, they maintain that the Springboks could "help bring [about] change". This framing disregards the fact that in 1981 the side was still racially selected (one "coloured" player joined the team) and that rugby continued to prop up Afrikaner nationalism. For Barrow (1992, p. 181), the "allegations that playing with the Springboks was 'playing with apartheid'" and tantamount to "endorsement and approval… was obviously nonsensical". Rather, he represents New Zealand as an egalitarian nation "which prides itself on its racial tolerance", whose philosophies "contradict" and are "diametrically opposed" to apartheid (p. 162), and where "Māori… enjoyed equal rights on the rugby field" (p. 180). Contrary to overwhelming international opinion at that time, Barrow argued that sporting contact with South Africa "should be encouraged" because "sport, and particularly rugby, has done more than anything to break down apartheid" (p. 171).

Similarly, Macdonald and Connew (1996, p. 110) contextualise the tour as part of the "struggle for justice in a foreign land". In so doing they relocate events *outside* New Zealand. Quinn (2002, p. 144) likewise emphasises that "protestors were appalled at the apartheid laws in South Africa". Palenski (2015, p. 366), meanwhile, is sceptical of activist accounts, writing that there "were *suggestions* that some of the protesters were motivated for *other* reasons [emphasis added]". He never elaborates on what these "other" reasons were, nor does he refer to any activist accounts to inform his interpretation of the anti-tour campaign. In so doing, Palenski diminishes the complexity of the tour, omitting anything which may cloud the view that the issue was simply South African apartheid. Despite the fact that the NZRFU continued to play against South Africa in violation of UN resolutions and a Commonwealth agreement, Palenski (2015, p. 319) maintains that New Zealand rugby had contributed to the collapse of apartheid: "rugby people themselves initiated the small dent in apartheid (because of the protests preceding the 1928, 1949 and 1960 tours), something for which they have never been given credit". Notably though, he does not lend the same status to anti-tour protestors in 1981.

112 Mark Falcous and Sebastian Potgieter

These popular representations of the tour both conceal the complexity of the anti-tour campaign and obscure critiques of New Zealand society, while consolidating the apparent social virtue of rugby. These rugby advocates have constructed their narratives according to the myth which presents rugby within New Zealand as inclusive, harmonious, egalitarian and an anti-apartheid force. What rarely (if ever) makes it into these narratives is that throughout the tour stadiums were sold out (indicating substantial support); that the Springboks were inundated with letters of support from New Zealanders upon their arrival; that 46% of potential viewers watched the final test match on television (Ryan & Watson 2018); that playing sport against South Africa (particularly rugby) consolidated white confidence in apartheid; or that Prime Minister Robert Muldoon, who had staunchly defended the tour, won the subsequent general election in November 1981. These facts demonstrate the level of support for the tour games, the Springboks, and the key political architects of the event. Popular remembrances of 1981 romanticise rugby as an anti-apartheid lever whilst silencing the critiques of racism, patriarchal gender relations, rugby culture, and intolerant and conservative government identified by activists. These are highly selective representations of the tour which ignore New Zealand's own social complexion including critiques of rugby's policies, its place within the national culture, or the disunity it catalysed in 1981.

Forgetting the 1907–1908 All Golds and the suppression of Rugby League

As we have noted above, one feature of the sporting mythscape is that particular figures, events and sporting codes are forgotten, ignored or obscured compared to others. A potent example is the 1907–1908 *professional*, player-led, rugby tour to Britain which receives scant attention relative to other pioneering tours playing *amateur* rugby under the control of the NZRFU. As Falcous (2007b) details, the touring team, popularly known as the "All Golds", provided the genesis of rugby league in New Zealand. Which historical teams and figures are forgotten or ignored tells us much about how they work as embodiments of particular interests, cultural values and identities. The relative absence of the All Golds from the nation's sporting pantheon, and silences about their legacy, affirms sporting hierarchies in the present.

The recent centenaries of foundational rugby tours was revealing in terms of uneven commemorations. For example, the 1907–1908 All Golds are largely forgotten, the exception being a solitary, self-published account (Haynes 1996) and no books were published to mark their centenary. There was a muted attempt to commemorate the team with a New Zealand Rugby League (NZRL) centenary tour which matched some themes of the original, but this proceeded with no lasting commemoration within New Zealand. By contrast, the 1905 "originals" amateur rugby union tour stimulated multiple popular centennial recollections (see Howitt & Haworth 2005; McCrystal 2005; Tobin 2005). The captain of

Sporting mythscapes **113**

that team, Dave Gallaher, is liturgised in the naming of the trophy awarded in the Auckland premier men's club competition (since 1922) and in international games between France and New Zealand (since 2000). Furthermore, in 2011 an imposing 2.7 m high statue of Gallaher was unveiled outside Eden Park in Auckland. This liturgisation entangles Gallaher's service (and ultimately his death) in war, and his role as a pioneering All Black. Such representations reassert the centrality of amateur rugby union, and hence Pākehā masculinity and middle-class patronage.

In contrast, there is an absence of commemoration of the All Golds or their chief impetus Albert Baskerville, who at aged 26 was a prodigious entrepreneur, negotiator, and administrator who also, remarkably, played on the tour (see Haynes 1996). Indeed, the 1907–1908 tour was a notable pioneering feat on several counts in that it was player-organised, financed and led, overcame vicious resistance; the team embarked to play a code they had never seen before; and they won test series' against both Australia and Great Britain. Furthermore, they played against the strength of professional English rugby (which Gallaher's 1905 team did not) due to the 1895 amateur-professional split which originated northern union/rugby league. The players' collectivism in each investing £50 and receiving back an equal share of the tour's profits represented an audacious entrepreneurial approach, defying convention that would seemingly accord with the "against the odds battler" mythos noted above. There is, however, relatively little remembrance of the team, Baskerville, and especially the subsequent suppression of rugby league.

Like Baskerville, other pioneering All Golds are largely forgotten. Lance Todd, for example, was a prolific tourist, and enjoyed a subsequent career playing, managing and administering in the British game, commentating on BBC radio, and relinquishing his professional career to serve with the ANZACs during World War I. This professional path was not available in his homeland due to the suppression of rugby league, and even his military service (akin to Gallaher) did not stimulate memorialisation. Similarly, George W. Smith helped to select the All Golds touring party and at the time was the best known athlete in the country. He had been the winning jockey in the 1884 New Zealand cup, had 15 national titles in athletics, as well as multiple Australasian championships and the 1902 British AAA quarter-mile hurdles in an unofficial world record time of 58.5s, and had represented New Zealand in amateur rugby (as a 1905 "original"). He represented the 1907–1908 professional team as vice captain and later played professionally and coached in England. This staggering pedigree across multiple sports saw Smith inducted into the New Zealand Sports Hall of Fame in 1995, but no commemorations akin to Gallaher exist in his name.

Whilst the All Golds tour receives brief mention in several books (e.g., Palenski 2015; Quinn 1986), their significance as a challenge to a dominant rugby ethos, and the suppression that surrounded their endeavour is largely ignored. For example, there is little mention of the backlash whereby the NZRFU, local councils, and the press tried to "scupper" the tour, and pressured players to sign

114 Mark Falcous and Sebastian Potgieter

a declaration of loyalty to amateur rugby union. Furthermore, Baskerville was threatened by the NZRFU and banned from all Wellington grounds, whilst Petone borough council banned him from their recreation ground. The national press, meanwhile, portrayed him as "[a] secretive organiser of a tour disloyal to the rugby union" (Haynes 1996, p. 21). Conflicts surrounding the emergence of a rival professional rugby ethos also receive scant attention. Indeed, attempts to establish rugby league (then known as "Northern Union") in New Zealand by returning All Golds players met with similar resistance to the tour itself (see Falcous 2007b; Haynes 1996). Attempts to establish rugby league in New Zealand occurred against attempts to inhibit the game. These included, denying access to municipal grounds and keeping the game out of schools, a campaign to (incorrectly) brand league players as professionals, flouting of amateur rules to pay players either to keep them in union or lure them back from league and media hostility (Greenwood 2007). For instance, players who "professionalised" themselves were banned by rugby union authorities. These formal regulations were complimented by ostracism, stigmatisation and distain for rugby league (see Greenwood & Watson 2001). As Falcous (2007b, p. 437) has argued "the campaign against rugby league and the hypocritical application of amateurism regulations shatter the myth of the nationally unifying role of amateur rugby union in New Zealand".

Yet this conflict is largely omitted from popular sports history writing and commemorations. Quinn (1986), for example, suggests that "the 'All Golds' came home ... and rugby league flourished as a result of their success on tour" (p. 121). This assessment ignores the conflict of values that the tour symbolised, the threat to the dominant position of amateur rugby (which was becoming entrenched as a key pillar of colonial nationalism), and the subsequent century-long suppression of rugby league. These silences are reflected at numerous points such as the selective commemoration of George Nepia. A star of the 1924–1925 "invincibles" All Black team, Nepia is hailed as a national rugby union icon and is an inductee of the New Zealand Sports Hall of Fame. His 1990 induction was commemorated with a stamp featuring Nepia in an All Black jersey. What is largely forgotten in accounts of Nepia is his switch to rugby league. Playing league, however, his biography reveals, saw him treated "little better than a criminal" and painted as "disloyal to the game which had done so much for [him]" (Nepia & McLean 1963, p. 181). By Nepia's own account, playing rugby league was a means to alleviate financial hardship. Yet this seems the primary point emphasised about his code-switch. Howitt & Haworth (2003) elevate Nepia to "Player of the Decade" for 1920–1930 and detail his rugby success but emphasise that due to "considerable financial hardship...[Nepia] accepted an offer to play rugby league in Britain" (p. 62). So too, Palenski (2015, p. 250) writes that "it was money rather than the game that attracted Nepia". Emphasising financial benefit is recurrent in accounts of union players switching to league. McCarthy (1968) reminds readers that "in the majority of cases" it was financial incentive "rather than League's attractions or discontent with Rugby Union that caused players to make the change" (p. 54). This appears at odds with Nepia's recollection that: "I found it, to play, fast and exhilarating" (Nepia & McLean 1963, p. 182) and "compared with Rugby Union...I found this new game fast and open" (p. 183). Nevertheless, the commemoration of Nepia means it is his stature in amateur rugby union which is elevated while his ostracism, and exploits in rugby league remain obscured.

Imbalanced and selective commemorations brush over histories which would challenge governing myths by highlighting the suppression of rugby league. Instead, this is silenced within accounts which liturgise amateur rugby as nationally unifying. Indeed, contemporary debates around the effects of "professionalism" in rugby apparently commencing in 1995 ignore the debate and circumstances of 90 years previously and the subsequent suppression of rugby league in defence of amateurism as a pillar of a particular set of identity politics.

Conclusions

In this chapter we have explored the popular narrativisation of the past as a feature of New Zealand's sporting mythscape. Across this mythscape representations range from piecemeal, romanticised accounts that emphasise the virtuousness of New Zealand sport, memorialisations of selective figures and events, to silences and omissions regarding others. The three cases we have presented illustrate how the construction of past sporting contexts, events and figures inform broader notions of identity, origins and community. The first two cases reflect the assertion of what Bell (2003) terms "governing mythology"; that is, "the attempt to impose a definite meaning on the past, on the nation and its history" (p. 74). Here, popular representations (trophies, literature and statues) present a dramatised yet simplified story that selectively narrates the sporting past in a romanticised and uni-vocal way. This reflects a narcissistic nationalism; a defensive, idealising version of the sporting nation, unreflexive to flaws and contestedness. The result is the assertion that New Zealand is characterised by tough, hard-working, and honorable (male) athletes who battle against the odds on the world sporting stage. Selected male athletes beyond the cases we have observed are valorised as embodying this essence: Gallaher, Nepia, Lovelock, Snell, Lydiard, Charles, Meads, Walker, Hadlee, Blake, Bourne, Carter, McCaw. Certain moments/events: the "originals", the "invincibles", 1982 All Whites, Rugby World Cup 1987, 1995 Americas Cup meanwhile are recounted as great collective triumphs. This representation overwhelmingly reinforces sporting hierarchies, but most obviously (mostly) Pākehā men as key embodiments of "national" values; asserting the prowess of New Zealanders within global affairs in a continuous linear progression.[2] The resourceful-battler archetype draws upon long-standing white-settler, masculine-centric values valorising hard-work and resilience in tough circumstances. The recurrent invocation of these "legends" and events act as "resonant rituals and symbols" (Bell 2003, p. 70) through which a selective version of the nation is reaffirmed through the telling of its sporting

116 Mark Falcous and Sebastian Potgieter

history. At times, female achievements are briefly referenced at the fringes of this pantheon: Yvette Williams, Susan Devoy, Barbara Kendall, Sarah Ulmer, Valerie Adams, Lisa Carrington may receive brief mention. But it is worth noting that of the 11 sports statues in the country nine are men and the remaining two are racehorses, perfectly revealing the self-fulfilling patriarchal nature of sporting commemoration.

Controversies or defeats (Montreal 1976, the 1981 Springbok tour, the 1981 underarm bowling incident) are cast in line with this narrative; framed to emphasise national virtue and presented in selective, piecemeal ways that diminish or ignore sport as contested and power laden (and hence exclusionary). Within this skewed narrative New Zealand sport is framed as morally virtuous. For instance, the first two cases we explored ignore decades of support of apartheid South Africa, instead presenting the nation in this regard as blameless victim of unjustified politicisation, or in fact as an unmitigated anti-apartheid force.

The final case of the 1907–1908 All Golds and rugby league demonstrates how silences also characterise the sporting mythscape. Sporting figures and deeds which provide an alternative narrative of the sporting nation, as exclusionary and class ridden, are hidden at the margins. Thus, Baskerville, Todd and Smith are largely forgotten, just as the likes of Houweta, the 1888 "Natives" tour, Yvette Williams, or the 1986 Cavaliers tour do not make it into the sporting pantheon. As Bell (2003) notes, "There will always be dissent and the story will never be accepted consistently and universally" (p. 74). In this sense, governing myths are "constantly contested by subaltern myths ... as likely to be concerned with past oppression and suffering as the hands of dominant groups as by tales of national glory" (p. 74). Thus, there is always the scope for accounts outside of the nationally revered and alternative interpretations and recollections.

Notes

1 Thanks are extended to the editors and to Douglas Booth for feedback on this chapter.
2 Sports statues in New Zealand reflect this: Boxer: Bob Fitsimmons (Timaru, 1987), runners: Jack Lovelock (Timaru, 2002), Peter Snell (Opunake, 2007), John Walker (Manurewa, 2018) and Arthur Lydiard (Auckland), rugby: Dave Gallaher (2011) and Michael Jones (Auckland, 2011), Colin Meads (Te Kuiti, 2017), Rallying: Possum Bourne (Pukekohe, 2012), and racehorses: Bonecrusher (Ellerslie, 2018) and Phar Lap (Timaru, 2009). In the present, such sports heritage is seen as a way of offering a positive view of a town's heritage and to show that it can produce heroes. In the context of the mythscape it is a powerful measure of selective representation. Furthermore, the relative recency of the proliferation of these statues demonstrates a burgeoning tendency and interest in commemoration.

References

Barthes, R. 1957/2012, *Mythologies*, Hill & Wang, New York.
Barrow, G. 1992, *All Blacks versus springboks: A century of rugby rivalry*, Penguin, Auckland.
Bell, D. S. 2003, 'Mythscapes: memory, mythology, and national identity', *The British Journal of Sociology*, Vol. 54, no. 1, pp. 63–68.

Chapple, G. 1984, *1981: The tour*, Reed, Wellington.

Chester, R. H. & McMillan, N. A. C. 1990, *The visitors: A history of international Rugby teams in New Zealand*, Moa Publications, Wellington.

Coakley, J. 2015, 'Assessing the sociology of sport: on cultural sensibilities and the great sport myth', *International Review for the Sociology of Sport*, Vol. 50, no. 4–5, pp. 402–406.

Consedine, R. 1989, 'Inequality and the Egalitarian myth', in D. Novitz, & B. Willmott (eds.), *Cultural identity in New Zealand*, G. P. Books, Wellington, pp. 172–186.

Falcous, M. 2007a, 'The decolonizing national imaginary: promotional media constructions during the 2005 Lions tour of Aotearoa New Zealand', *Journal of Sport and Social Issues*, Vol. 31, no. 4, pp. 374–393.

Falcous, M. 2007b, 'Rugby league in the national imaginary of New Zealand Aotearoa', *Sport in History*, Vol. 27, no. 3, pp. 423–446.

Falcous, M. & Newman, J. 2015, 'Sporting mythscapes, neo-liberal histories, and post-colonial amnesia in Aotearoa/New Zealand', *International Review for the Sociology of Sport*, Vol. 51, no. 1, pp. 61–77.

Freeman, M. & Hollins, R. (eds.) 1982, *Arms linked: Women against the tour*, MOST, Auckland.

Greenwood, B. 2007, '1908: The Year Rugby League Came to New Zealand', *Sport in History*, Vol. 27, no. 3, pp. 343–363.

Greenwood, B., & Watson, J. 2001. 'The "famous northern union game": The rise and fall of rugby league in Wanganui, 1910-15', *Sporting Traditions*, Vol. 18, no. 1, pp. 33–41.

Haynes, J. 1996, *From All Blacks to All Golds*, Self published, Christchurch.

Howitt, B. & Haworth, D. 2003, *All Black magic: 100 years of New Zealand test Rugby*, Harper Sports, Auckland.

Howitt B. & Haworth, D. 2005, *The 1905 originals*, Harper Collins, Auckland.

Macdonald, F. & Connew, B. 1996, *The game of our lives: The story of rugby and New Zealand and how they've shaped each other*, Viking, Auckland.

MacLean, M. 2000, 'Football as social critique: protest movements, rugby and history in Aotearoa, New Zealand', *International Journal of the History of Sport*, Vol. 17, no. 2–3, pp. 255–277.

MacLean, M. 2001, 'Almost the same, but not quite…almost the same, but not white': Māori and Aotearoa/New Zealand's 1981 Springbok Tour', *Kunapipi: Journal of Postcolonial Writing,* Vol. 23, no. 1, pp. 69–82.

MacLean, M. 2010, 'Anti-Apartheid boycotts and the affective economies of struggle: the case of Aotearoa New Zealand', *Sport in Society*, Vol. 13, no. 1, pp. 72–91.

MacLean, M. 2012, 'Springbok tour of New Zealand (1981) (South African Rugby Tour)', in J. Nauright & C. Parish, (eds.), *Sport around the world: History, culture and practice*, ABC-Clio, Santa Barbara, CA, pp. 454–456.

Mason, C. W. 2007, 'The bridge to change: the 1976 Montreal Olympic Games, South African Apartheid policy, and the Olympic boycott paradigm', in G. P. Schau & S. R. Wenn (eds.), *Onward to the Olympics: Historical perspectives on the Olympic games*, Wilfrid Laurier University Press, Canada, pp. 285–297.

McCarthy, W. 1968, *Haka! The All Black story*, Pelham Books, London.

McCrystal, J. 2005, *The originals: 1905 All Black Rugby Odyssey*, Random House, Auckland.

Nepia, G. & McLean, T. 1963, *I, George Nepia: The golden years of Rugby football*, Reed, Wellington.

Newnham, T. 1981, *By batons and barbed wire: A response to the 1981 springbok tour of New Zealand*, Real Pictures, Auckland.

O'Meara, D. 1996, *Forty Lost Years: The Apartheid State and the Politics of the National Party, 1948–1994*, Ravan Press, Randburg.

Palenski, R. 2015, *Rugby: A New Zealand history*, Auckland University Press, Auckland.

Palenski, R. & Romanos, J. (eds.). 2000, *Champions. New Zealand Sports greats of the 20th century*, Hodder Moa Beckett, Auckland.

Phillips, J. 1987, *A man's country? The image of the Pākehā male: A history*, Penguin, Auckland.

Quinn, K. 1986, *New Zealand sporting disasters, disappointments and curiosities*, Random House, Auckland.

Quinn, K. 2002, *Outrageous Rugby moments: Stories of controversy, humour, scandal and disgrace*, Hodder Moa Beckett, Auckland.

Richards, T. 1996, 'Thou shalt play! What 60 Years of controversy over New Zealand's sporting contact with South Africa tell us about ourselves', *New Zealand Studies*, Vol. 6, no. 2, pp. 26–32.

Richards, T. 1999, *Dancing on our bones: New Zealand, South Africa, Rugby and racism*, Bridget Williams Books, Wellington.

Romanos, J. 2006, *New Zealand's 100 sports history makers*, Printlink, Wellington.

Romanos, J. 2008, *Our Olympic century*, Trio Books, Wellington.

Ryan, G. & Watson, G. 2018, *Sport and the New Zealanders: A history*, Auckland University Press, Auckland.

Thompson, R. 1975, *Retreat from Apartheid. New Zealand sporting contacts with South Africa*, Oxford University Press, London.

Tobin, C. 2005, *The original All Blacks*, Hodder Moa Beckett, Auckland.

11

GLOBAL/LOCAL CELEBRITY AND NATIONAL SPORT STARDOM

Examining Sonny Bill Williams, Brendon McCullum and Lydia Ko

Damion Sturm and Koji Kobayashi

Introduction

For a nation accustomed to "punching above its weight" on the global sporting stage, Aotearoa New Zealand has a large pool of potential star athletes ripe for lionising, celebrating and analysing. In this chapter, our interest extends beyond the mere "celebrification" of individuals who have risen to prominence through sporting deeds. Rather, we assert that the case studies of Sonny Bill Williams, Brendon McCullum and Lydia Ko illuminate a contested terrain for how national sport stardom can be articulated, affixed and displayed with respect to the local and global significance of their sporting achievements. Indeed, questions pertaining to their national allegiances persist, with both Williams and McCullum perceived as "mercurial" sporting mercenaries who potentially choose franchises and finances over national representation, while Ko's "New Zealandness" and potential "re-claiming" by Korea is also scrutinised. More broadly, we will probe some of the challenges and contestations surrounding global/local celebrity and national sport stardom in this chapter.

Sport celebrity, global-local fluidity and Aotearoa New Zealand

Modern celebrityhood emerged out of the cinema industry in the early twentieth century as star actors' images and stories were produced and disseminated via the print media and newsreels, serving as "a forum for the general public to develop more intimate, visually informed, relationships with an array of public personalities" (Andrews & Jackson 2001, p. 3). The phenomenal growth of mass media technologies from newspapers and radio to television and personalised social, digital and mobile media has only expanded the scale and scope of opportunities for the wider public to instantaneously and voraciously consume familiar

DOI: 10.4324/9781003034445-11

personalities and figures. Consequently, celebrities came to function as a potent signifier of particular values, styles or identities that were desired, admired or even consecrated by their fans and followers alike. Turner (2014) argues that celebrity can be understood as a semiotic regime that sustains and reinforces the discursive linkages between individualism, material wealth and conspicuous consumption, which is central to the prosperity and legitimacy of the culture industry, and capitalist accumulation more generally. Moreover, Redmond (2014, 2018) asserts that celebrity can be conceived to operate in and as a realm that is affective, sensory, aesthetic, liquid and "to be experienced".

While celebrity may offer a reflection of societal values and norms, celebrity studies also consider celebrity as "an embodiment of a discursive battleground" (Marshall 1997, p. 65) through which such values and norms are constantly re-affirmed, contested or negotiated. In the same vein, Rowe (2004, p. 7) asserts that the relationships among celebrity, sport, and media are "always everywhere in process, influencing and being influenced by each other in a perpetual dance of assertion and counter-assertion". This perpetual exchange of articulation and re-articulation is considered even more prominent in the age of social media through which voices of celebrities can be heard directly – without filters of the traditional mass media – in the forms of, for instance, protest or activism (Galily 2019), and self-branding or self-promotion (Sturm 2019). It is within this context of contemporary cultural production that celebrity is circulated, consumed and articulated globally across a variety of traditional and more "participatory" media outlets.

Turning our attention to sport, unlike the often fictional character or creation portrayed and performed within other mass entertainment realms, there is the sense of a "real person" and an "unrivalled quality of authenticity" (Smart 2005, p. 194) that surrounds the sport star. In many respects, sport stardom can also be viewed as meritocratic, earned and measured primarily through sporting achievement, excellence, elite competitions and physical capital (Andrews & Jackson 2001; Shilling 1991; Whannel 2002). Smart (2005, p. 194) observes, "it is through the exceptional quality of their sport performances, and media coverage of the same, that individual athletes and players generally become widely known and acquire star status". Conversely, sport stardom is also constructed and constrained by other influences. For example, an elevated media profile, presence and the ability to cultivate and perform a charismatic media personality helps to grow local/global audiences and endear sport celebrities to fans (Sturm 2019; Whannel 2002).

Moreover, the potential blurring of on-field stardom and off-field persona may refocus attention towards (a) celebrity lifestyles and private lives (Turner 2014); (b) representation of cultural identities in relation to, for instance, gender, sexuality, race and ethnicity (Andrews & Jackson 2001); and (c) a subsequent interest in salaciousness, transgressions and scandals (Wenner 2013; Whannel 1999). Finally, when ascribing stardom, the cultural value and global visibility of select sports "matters" in different local and global contexts (Sandvoss 2012).

Andrews and Jackson (2001) note that sport celebrities are commonly associated with collective sensibilities and identities through representation of a team, a city or a nation in sporting contests – hence the elevation of select individuals as national "stars", ambassadors or even evocations as heroic, dependent on the scope and scale of achievements, the national significance of the sport, and the symbolic embodiment of particular cultural identity with respect to gender, sexuality, race, ethnicity, religion and so forth.

In this chapter, we pay special attention to the interface between the global and the local for representations of sport celebrities. Andrews et al. (1996) provided a seminal account on Michael Jordan as a global sporting icon located and examined within specific localities, media environments and political discourses of different nations such as Britain, New Zealand and Poland. In turn, the authors proposed that global sport celebrity, as a cultural artefact, "is simultaneously homogeneous in terms of the commodity signs being circulated, and heterogeneous in terms of the ways in which these commodity signs are consumed" (Andrews et al. 1996, p. 453). Much of the subsequent sport celebrity works principally supported this assertion and offered further evidence of, and limitations to, it. For instance, Giardina (2001) situated Martina Hingis as a cosmopolitan and flexible citizen whose images and stories were malleable across a variety of localised representations and argued for a nuanced difference between her and other star tennis figures, such as Venus Williams and Anna Kournikova, who were represented more consistently across the globe.

Similarly, Grainger et al. (2005) classified sport celebrities in terms of their marketability on the global-local continuum with David Beckham being "transnational", Australian Olympic swimmer Ian Thorpe being "global-local", and New Zealand rugby (NZR) legend Johan Lomu being "exotic local". In short, global or transnational sport celebrity is inevitably subjected to "collective configurations" (Marshall 1997) such as local/national sensibility, gender, sexuality, race and ethnicity. Additionally, the ubiquity of contemporary digital media seems to have only facilitated the global-local simultaneity, intercultural dialogues and fluid forms of identity politics (Kobayashi & Cho 2019). Of course, the appeal and marketability of sport stars are, in any case, vexed due to the wide-ranging constraints that impact on aspects of sport star construction, circulation and consumption. Hence, simultaneously, the star's situatedness in a specific sport and location influences the nationalistic/international lens and local or global appeal for those who are/are not in widely disseminated sports that garner larger attention. Such parameters also carry media and commercial value, with Kellner (1996) conceiving of a marketable difference shaped around perceived moral, social and cultural values, and often laced with inherent racial connotations in which sport stars ideally are compliant and malleable commodities for corporations (Sandvoss 2012; Wenner 2013). Moreover, while charismatic media performances and personalities can bolster the marketability of stars (Whannel 2002), this too is tempered by an inherent gender bias that privileges high-profile males, with female stars primarily constructed and consumed around narrow versions of beauty and appearance (Sturm 2019; Toffoletti 2016).

While much scholarly attention has been given to sport celebrities in the Global North, less is written about New Zealand sport stars despite the nation's history of producing world-class athletes across a range of sporting disciplines (see Ryan & Watson 2018). We now turn our attention to three case studies that illustrate articulations of global/local celebrity, albeit with contestations, and a blurring of their status as national sport stars. Specifically, our chapter scrutinises the dominant media representations, narratives and key career junctures for these three stars. Privileging a representational framework that focuses on traditional texts produced by the media industry, insights are primarily drawn from media sources that include the mainstream press, televised coverage and other sport-specific cultural intermediaries, buttressed by public perceptions elicited and evoked via responses to such media content (e.g., online newspaper commentary and across social media platforms).

Liquid and agential celebrity: Sonny Bill Williams

With his ability to play more than one sport at the elite level (having representative honours and national/global accomplishments in the codes of rugby, rugby league, sevens and boxing)[1], Sonny Bill Williams (SBW) is an enigmatic and rare breed of contemporary star athlete. Moreover, Williams is astutely aware of the high demand for his services, often only signing short-term contracts that increasingly operate on his own terms (Kent 2015). Williams offers an intriguing insight into a version of contemporary stardom that, arguably, literally embodies liquid and "agential" stardom, while largely being reduced to oscillating binary narratives that project Williams as either a "mercurial" star athlete or, notably via his SBW brand and image, as a sporting "mercenary".

Williams was born to, and raised by, a Samoan father and a Pākehā mother in Auckland. With his Samoan heritage and citizenship, Williams can be readily located within wider discourses of the "browning" (Grainger et al. 2012) or "Polynesianisation" (Ryan 2007) of rugby through which a Pākehā-dominated "national" sport was diversified and transformed by the rise of Māori and Polynesian players and mobilised to support the discursive formation of, otherwise contested, inter-racial harmony in Aotearoa New Zealand. Despite his notable sporting talents and achievements – and perhaps because of the postcolonial racialisation still at play, many public and mainstream media aspersions have centred around SBW "mercenary" narratives, particularly via money-orientated barbs (i.e., "Money Bill Williams"). Nevertheless, such critiques are highly contestable. For example, returning to a polarising thread of fanfare and disdain in New Zealand in 2010, Williams had reputedly rejected $2m per season from Toulon in French rugby to sign with NZR for $500,000 (Kent 2015). Additionally, derogatory remarks around an assumed "code-hopping" propensity saw Williams branded as national "traitor", despite annually making New Zealand

National sport stardom **123**

representative teams in different sports (e.g., the Rugby League World Cup in 2013, or in sevens at the 2016 Rio Olympics). Through a flexible approach seemingly centred around challenges, titles and legacies rather than a long-term commitment to NZR, perhaps the dismissive mass media representations and public perceptions of SBW as a "mercenary" can be interpreted by some as emancipatory and agential. Indeed, Kent (2015) argues that the various football codes were essentially reshaped around and by Williams to accommodate his star power, such as Williams' seasons with NZR (2010–2012; 2014–2015; 2017–2019) primarily structured around World Cup campaigns.

Williams' flexible approach to contractual arrangements arguably would not have emerged if not for initially breaking a five-year National Rugby League (NRL) contract with the Sydney-based Canterbury Bulldogs in 2008, when he absconded over night to France and subsequently was banned from the NRL for five years. The ban prompted Williams to pursue rugby union, ultimately achieving two World Cup victories, one Super Rugby and one provincial championship in New Zealand, interspersed with being crowned the New Zealand heavyweight boxing champion in 2011. Williams also won two NRL titles across his career, with Canterbury in 2004 and the Sydney Roosters in 2013.

Williams' approach to contemporary sporting disciplines and contracts seemingly points to an agential capacity to fluidly and seamlessly cross sporting codes as both a symbolic and physical embodiment of liquid celebrity (Redmond 2014, 2018). On the one hand, his liquid capacities are connected to forms of global, commercial and media malleability, with Sandvoss (2012, p. 183) noting liquid sport stars are "public texts whose significance and popularity derive from their ability to accommodate individual and flexible discourses of contemporary identities and citizenship". This also encompasses the crafting of a publicly presented "SBW" persona, as both the self-managed display of a public self (Marshall 2016) and careful cultivation by cultural intermediaries to maximise SBW's value and appeal as an image, brand and celebrity (Whannel 2002). Thus, the SBW persona projects, reinforces and playfully blurs transnational, transcultural and polysemic renderings of 'national' sport stardom via his dual Samoan heritage and New Zealand citizenship, his Muslim faith, as well as his glocal branding, commodification and circulation in various leagues and competitions.

On the other hand, SBW's liquid celebrity is seemingly also individuated and agential (York 2013), pro-offering "physical capital" (Shilling 1991) that is talent-laden and highly malleable via an adaptable skillset fluidly transferred to different elite sports. York (2013) ponders, outside of mere incorporation versus resistance, whether forms of celebrity agency potentially enable stars to rework their own commodification on their own terms. Williams' fluidity across sporting codes and flexibility within contractual arrangements arguably caters to exploiting his star power in a "mercenary-like" capacity that increasingly seems to be on his terms. For example, despite never having been an All Black, Williams' various demands for flexible contractual arrangements since 2010 were unique within a NZR setting where old traditions of pride in the jersey, and All Black

124 Damion Sturm and Koji Kobayashi

selection as an honour and a privilege were seemingly sacrosanct, not something to be negotiated (Kent 2015).[2]

Additionally, SBW operates and circulates as a glocal commodity, endorsing numerous products, companies and All Black associated brands to New Zealand audiences while also negotiating space for his personal sponsors. More specifically, while he is readily commodified to suit the specific sport and contract in place, Williams still exercises selectivity and fluidity around his co-option. For example, during his first NZR contract, he allegedly turned down a rival energy drink sponsor given his relationship with Powerade. Moreover, Williams' deferred becoming a global ambassador for Adidas until 2014 to circumvent any initial long-term commitment to NZR (Kent 2015). More recently, he negotiated the removal of sponsors on his jersey, including the BNZ bank in 2017 and gambling firms Betfair and Unibet in 2020, citing his Muslim faith.

SBW as a brand has glocal appeal, operating within what Whannel (2002) labels a "media vortex" due to the intense media scrutiny, hype and coverage he is accorded. His on-field sport star performances make him bankable and ensure audiences pay to watch him play, such as via previous "pay per view" boxing matches, while his returns to the NRL in both 2013 and 2020, as well as 2020 debut in the Super League, dominated media coverage. Williams' "mercenary-like" fluid contracts and ever-changing sports serve to frustrate some sections of the press or social media users, although, generally, Williams is accorded critical recognition for his extraordinary talent, exceptional athleticism, impressive physique and sustained performances at the elite level (i.e., the mercurial star with the rare ability to "code-hop" so effectively).

Of course, there is also intense scrutiny of SBW's "private" life, an intrigue no doubt piqued by his Muslim beliefs and apparently "family-focused" lifestyle, spliced with the occasional celebrity relationship or scandal from the past, such as his "hotel toilet tryst" with Australian triathlete Candace Falzon in Sydney in 2007 (Bednall 2020). Finally, Williams is subjected to an overwhelming interest in and eroticisation of his hypermuscular physique. Through sporting performances and promotional regimes, SBW's projection of a fetishised, commodified and idealised body seemingly places an inordinate emphasis on his appearance that, arguably, is more commonplace to female sport star (re)presentations (Sturm 2019).

Collectively, Williams relies upon a risky agential strategy of being able to interchange, adapt and play different elite sports on a series of short-term contracts, while avoiding any performative decline or injury that may negate his future participation. Arguably, he has an agential capacity in taking some of the power away from clubs and codes by dictating his own terms and not being bound by unfavourable conditions (Kent 2015). Of course, this frequent code-hopping ensures a polarising reception from governing bodies, fans and the press who may consider his conduct and approach "mercenary like", potentially treating elite sport as his playground and the various codes as sites for financial exploitation.

The Brazen hero: Brendon McCullum

Brendon McCullum offers another intriguing case study for New Zealand sport stardom who, like Williams, largely polarised national audiences via a similarly conceived star narrative of mercurial talent versus perceived sporting mercenary. Fundamental to McCullum's late-career transformation were a series of "exceptional" international sporting performances that set New Zealand Cricket (NZC) records, alongside the cultivation of a charismatic personality that resonated with nationalistic discourses of Pākehā manhood.

Unlike rugby which was fervently embraced by Māori and Polynesian populations, cricket has largely remained a Pākehā-dominated sport due to, according to Ryan (2007), its development centred on the urban middle-class and its requirements of lengthy playing time and expenses for both equipment and facility, with the latter serving as obstacles to the participation of Māori and Polynesian populations who were proportionally over-represented in lower socio-economic areas (see also chapter 4). Although cricket might be considered as a site where Pākehā privileges have been upheld and reproduced, the Pākehā manhood represented by McCullum cannot merely be reduced to a unilinear, uncontested narrative of "white masculinity". Rather, McCullum's career arc adheres to elements of Whannel's (1999, 2002) narrative cycle of "celebration, transgression, punishment and redemption" through which his gentlemanhood, discipline and loyalty to the nation were questioned and scrutinised. McCullum's early years reflect a rise motif that recognised and elevated initial successes but, arguably, was also thwarted by aspersions of arrogance, aloofness or abrasiveness that persisted across his career. Alderson (2015, para.23) notes, "rarely have perceptions around a New Zealand sportsman generated such a spectrum of applause and derision. Across McCullum's career, opinion tended to be compartmentalised into phrases like 'brash maverick', 'cocky mercenary', 'generous benefactor' and 'loyal mate'".

In this vein, McCullum may adhere to Whannel's (2002, p. 195) notion of "maverick individualism", as "audiences want entertainment and charismatic stars provide a break from the mundane". McCullum potentially projected maverick individualism via a heavily tattooed arm, occasionally bleached hair and flamboyant, mercurial batting displays that destabilised the veil of conservatism generally shrouding cricket and its traditions (Malcolm 2013). Hence, "swashbuckling" and brazen batting displays can also be interpreted as brash, aloof and arrogant, particularly as high-risk plays offer spectacular and exceptional performances tempered with recklessness, inconsistencies, failures and "soft" dismissals. In reality, McCullum's "maverick" qualities were negligible and paled in comparison to the unruly behaviours, undisciplined bodies and transgressions of former players such as Ian Botham or Shane Warne who were "defying constraints, rebelling against regulation, whilst still performing" (Whannel 1999, p. 262) through their numerous on- and off-field exploits.

McCullum maintained longevity and stability to his career, representing NZC in all international forms between 2002 and 2016 (including an NZC record 101 consecutive tests) while avoiding any notable transgressions or elongated form slumps (i.e., there was no significant "fall" arc to the narrative). His on-field displays can be substantiated through cricket's veneration of statistics (Malcolm 2013), with regular strong performances discernible and noteworthy across his career.[3] Significantly, McCullum became one of the most successful batsmen in T20 cricket, including a "mercurial" 158 off 73 balls in the inaugural match of the Indian Premier League in 2008. McCullum's record-setting individual score was previously considered unfathomable and unattainable in what subsequently became the most powerful global cricket league (Wigmore 2020) which, in turn, afforded McCullum opportunities to "cash in" on other global T20 leagues as a marauding cricket mercenary.

Intriguingly, through a set of "extraordinary" achievements, coupled with the renewed projection of a charismatic and endearing personality that, collectively, reduced the negative perceptions of and reception to his "maverick" displays, McCullum underwent elements of Whannel's (1999, 2002) "redemption phase" in his final three years (2014 to 2016). Various accolades, records and milestones were achieved by or bestowed upon McCullum, including an "exceptional" 2014 test season where he became the first New Zealander to score a 300, as well as 1,000 Test runs in a calendar year (with notable scores of 302, 225, 224 and 195). McCullum was also honoured with national and international awards, while NZC saw an upturn in its rankings, records and successes. NZC co-hosting the 2015 Cricket World Cup was arguably most significant for the public perception of McCullum, who projected a charismatic persona that became a focal point for many nationalistic outpourings of affection (Alderson 2015). McCullum spoke of his pride and privilege in representing New Zealand while being lionised for embodying heroic qualities through his acrobatic fielding, tactical acumen and big-hitting that orchestrated many of NZC's victories and their first finals appearance. That McCullum scored the fastest test 100 (and hit the most test sixes) in his final match to retire from international cricket in 2016 seemingly emboldened and endorsed his brazen "mercurial" batting displays.

To make sense of McCullum's stardom requires the recognition and reassemblage of a set of heroic representations linked to the nation and national identity. McCullum's fluid transnational performances and following can be understood via his circulation, mediatisation and commodification as a star performer in different international cricket events and global T20 franchise leagues. However, most prominently through his "redemption" phase, McCullum's image was ascribed with "New Zealand" traits, with his leadership, morality and character assumed as nationalistic attributes that are both aligned to and reinforced by the heroic and ambassadorial functioning of sport stardom (Sandvoss 2012; Turner 2014; Whannel 2002). Consequently, the overarching narrative – though contested at times – of McCullum engenders the hegemonic "kiwi bloke" masculine ideal via bravado, stoicism and clichés associated with "punching above

National sport stardom **127**

his weight" and "playing through pain" (Phillips 1996), while being projected as a devoted family man, who values mateship while retaining an interest in rugby, beer and racing (McGee 2016).

A proud "Kowi"? Locating Lydia Ko

As a golf prodigy and teen sensation, Lydia Ko garnered unusual attention for a New Zealand athlete from every corner of the global sport media industry largely due to the global appeal and status of golf. In comparison to Williams and McCullum, Ko more vividly reinforces Whannel's (2002) "rise and fall" sport star narrative, having a rapid rise and phenomenal career success alongside a more recent dramatic decline. In addition, Ko's narrative reflects a "postfeminist sensibility" (Toffoletti 2016) as she has been celebrated as a more successful Kiwi golfer on the global stage than her male counterparts, while being mobilised as a symbol of twenty-first-century New Zealand that is projected as young, multicultural and inclusive. We will return to this career overview shortly. More intriguing is the fluidity and contestability of national identity and local/global articulations of celebrity that circulate around Ko. Born in South Korea, Ko migrated to New Zealand as an infant in the late 1990s. Due to her ancestry and global profile, elements of "othering" potentially play out around her identity, with re-appropriations and re-assertions of Ko's claims to "New Zealandness" commonplace in the popular imagination and press. Collectively, however, this is largely tempered by Ko's global/local stardom and phenomenal golf successes.

Ko immediately showed signs of exceptional talent by entering the New Zealand national amateur championship as a seven-year-old. Subsequently, her rise narrative becomes more pronounced, with Ko becoming the youngest player to win both a professional event in Australia at the age of 14 and a Ladies Professional Golf Association (LPGA) event at 15, before turning professional at 16. On the global golf circuit, world rankings, tournament victories and career earnings offer the essential parameters to evaluate the attributes of meritocracy and achievement fundamental to sport stardom (Andrews & Jackson 2001: Smart 2005). Ko became the no.1 ranked player in 2015, maintaining the top ranking for 84 weeks, won 15 LPGA tournaments including two major titles, and earnt approximately (US)\$10.5m across her career.[4] Unsurprisingly, Ko was also bestowed with numerous golf and New Zealand sporting awards and accolades, further reifying her status as a nationally and globally celebrated sport star. However, since 2017 Ko's career had seemingly been in decline, with only one LPGA victory (2018) and a significant drop in her earnings, placings and ranking (ranked 40th in 2020). Nevertheless, in 2021 Ko secured another LPGA victory while winning a silver medal at the Tokyo Olympics to improve her earnings and rankings (currently ranked 9th in 2021).

In addition to this unparalleled success as a global/local star, Ko affords an illuminating case of how contemporary national identity within Aotearoa New Zealand is affirmed, contested and renewed. On the one hand, given her Korean roots and racial or phenotypical attributes, Ko has been celebrated as a face of multicultural narratives and inclusion of immigrants, especially those from Asia. According to the New Zealand census, the number of those who identified ethnically as "Asian" (e.g., Chinese, Indian and Korean) rapidly increased from 46,035 in 1986 to 540,000 in 2013, while 2013's number accounted for 12% of the total population (Chang et al. 2019). Moreover, Larner (2006) observes that contemporary economic and social activities, relations and experiences are increasingly characterised by "multiculturalism in everyday life" within Aotearoa New Zealand.

It is within this context that Alderson (2013) suggested that Lydia Ko "has become a poster child for multiculturalism in sport" (para. 2) and "can play a pivotal role in New Zealand society" (para. 1). In this sense, Ko can be considered as one of "those with 'hybrid' identities in the processes associated with cultural re-visioning" (Larner 2006, p. 142). The hybrid identification is perhaps most clearly manifested in the colloquial reference "Kowi" – a combination of Korean and Kiwi – and her embodiment of it. As Ko responded in an interview,

> Obviously, when someone looks at me, they see a Korean face. I'm proud to be born in Korea and to represent New Zealand. That's something I'm fortunate to have: support from two amazing countries. I'm a Korean Kiwi, or as we say it, Kowi.
>
> *(Mell 2016, para. 4)*

On the other hand, the combination of Korean roots and the global fame of Ko was also viewed as a risk to New Zealand, as she could be "reclaimed" by South Korea. New Zealand Golf had experienced cases of Korean players who were trained and supported as amateurs only then to return to Korea upon turning professional. Most notable was the example of Shin-Ae Ahn in 2008, who had previously trained in her teens and represented New Zealand for four years as Sharon Ahn (Chang et al. 2019). More broadly, the trend of claiming Korean-ness became prevalent when female golfers of Korean descent emerged as rising global stars – most famously Christina Kim and Michelle Wie. As Chang et al. (2019) note, the Korean media accused Kim and Wie of opportunistically performing, and capitalising on, their Korean-ness for their own benefits (e.g., sponsorship, media coverage and attention from Korean companies and fans) without changing their allegiance from the United States as their nation of citizenship, representation and residence.

In contrast, Ko has been consistent in proclaiming herself as a New Zealander since obtaining citizenship at the age of 12. Although her decision to study at Korea University – though mostly by distance – raised some questions about her motives, Ko maintained that such a choice was simply logistical, enabling her to continue playing (Chang et al. 2019). Ko further reiterated her commitment to New Zealand at the 2016 Olympics, noting "there have been questions to me about changing my nationality back to Korea, but, at the end of the day, …I'm proud to have the [New Zealand] flag on my bag" (Mell 2016, para. 3). Consequently, the Korean-ness of Ko initially fueled public anxiety about a potential change of allegiance, yet, through constant public reassurances, Ko's Korean-ness has been largely mobilised in a New Zealand context to promote a national vision of being young, female, inclusive and ethnically diverse.

Conclusion

Our case studies have highlighted the contestable nature of assigning, affixing and renewing national sport stardom. The very frameworks and fluidity of global sport can, at one and the same time, serve to ascribe, reinforce and disrupt global/local celebrityhood, particularly as many outwardly "global" sporting competitions retain linkages to the local and the nation. In turn, sport stardom can operate across this terrain in a manner that is representative, aspirational and potentially heroic, notably by drawing upon sporting achievements to symbolically evoke and mobilise forms of national identity and nationalism. Nevertheless, despite indelible links back to the nation, precisely how global/local celebrity gets articulated, coupled with the discursive battleground that can erupt around identity politics, potentially leaves the very "New Zealandness" of sport stars in flux.

Intriguingly, cultural and gendered identities come to the fore amongst the nationalistic articulations that entangle our case studies. Brendon McCullum is arguably, at face value, the least complicated of the three stars, reproducing elements of the dominant and long-standing white-settler/Pākehā, middle-class and masculine-centric values that are most closely aligned to an assumed "traditional" set of nationalistic values, norms and identities. Hence, McCullum's long-established NZC career reinforces and is re-inscribed with assumed nationalistic traits around hard work, toughness and resilience, especially during his final "redemption" years. In contrast, SBW and Lydia Ko furnish a post-colonial refashioning of New Zealand national identity. Williams' own mixed background, as well as his propensity for "code-hopping" further re-affirm the "Polynesianisation" transformations taking place within New Zealand sports, alongside his Muslim faith evincing broader societal changes. Finally, despite the nation's rapidly changing ethnic make-up, Lydia Ko remains perpetually ensnared in identity politics. Pitting her Korean origins against proclamations of "New Zealandness", Ko is often under public pressure to renew, reconfirm and recommit her national allegiance.

Collectively, while each star is globally connected, celebrated and accomplished in elite competitions, representative regimes re-align and re-connect Ko, Williams and McCullum to the nation, playing, performing and achieving for New Zealand, often in nation-based competitions, even if clouded by "mercenary" (Williams and McCullum) or "othering" (Ko) narratives. For Ko, despite being one of New Zealand's most significant global celebrities in terms of sporting achievements, there is an expectation to reassert her national stardom

130 Damion Sturm and Koji Kobayashi

above and beyond the representational realm of elite global golf while, ironically, proffering a "new" New Zealand ideal that is feminine, young and multicultural. McCullum's stardom blended projections and performances of a "mercurial" (trans)national heroic figure, both lauded and maligned as global T20 mercenary, but ultimately redeemed and recognised through nationalistic performances and leadership. Finally, Williams' approach to sport stardom uprooted its traditional stable pathways, fluidly navigating challenges and negotiating contracts that maximised the appeal, currency and power of the SBW brand in various sporting fields. While "mercenary" narratives called his national allegiance into question, especially by dipping in and out of All Blacks contracts, such narratives overlook the agential and liquid opportunities that contemporary sport can afford and that Williams had the rare "mercurial" athletic talents to exploit.

Notes

1 Rugby (Union) and Rugby League offer similar but distinctive variations of rugby football; for example, rugby union comprises 15 players per team and is more international in its scope when compared to rugby league, with 13 players and largely confined to parts of England, Australia, New Zealand, France and the Pacific Island nations. For more details on the history and significance of rugby and rugby league in New Zealand, see Chapters 2, 3 and 10. Sevens is an abbreviated version of rugby, played with seven players across 2 × 7 minute halves (extended for finals) and became an Olympic sport in 2016.
2 Perhaps the only notable equivalent was granting sabbaticals to long-established stars, such as Dan Carter and Conrad Smith in 2013, to allow them to play (and earn) in the Northern Hemisphere in between World Cups.
3 McCullum's career statistics can be accessed via CricInfo: https://www.espncricinfo.com/newzealand/content/player/37737.html
4 Ko's career statistics can be accessed via the LPGA website: https://www.lpga.com/players/lydia-ko/98109/overview

References

Alderson, A. 2013, *Charming Ko a Kiwi treasure*, Otago Daily Times, viewed 24 August 2020, https://www.odt.co.nz/sport/golf/golf-charming-ko-kiwi-treasure
Alderson, A. 2015, *A brilliant leader in his field*. Otago Daily Times, viewed 18 August 2020, https://www.odt.co.nz/sport/cricket/cricket-brilliant-leader-his-field
Andrews, D., Carrington, B., Jackson, S. & Mazur, Z. 1996, 'Jordanscapes: a preliminary analysis of the global popular', *Sociology of Sport Journal,* Vol. 13, no. 4, pp. 428–457, https://doi.org/10.1123/ssj.13.4.428
Andrews, D. & Jackson, S. (eds.). 2001, *Sport stars: The cultural politics of sporting celebrity,* Routledge, London.
Bednall, J. 2020, *Candice Warner confronts Sonny Bill Williams toilet tryst in reality TV show,* New Zealand Herald, viewed 29 January 2021, https://www.nzherald.co.nz/sport/candice-warner-confronts-sonny-bill-williams-toilet-tryst-in-reality-tv-show/563Z6NQBPZSQQ5XDCSGBFVPWPY/
Chang, I., Jackson, S. & Tak, M. 2019, 'Globalization, migration, citizenship, and sport celebrity: locating Lydia Ko between and beyond New Zealand and South Korea', *The International Journal of the History of Sport,* Vol. 36, no. 7–8, pp. 643–659, https://doi.org/10.1080/09523367.2019.1675644

Galily, Y. 2019, '"Shut up and dribble!"? Athletes activism in the age of twittersphere: the case of LeBron James', *Technology in Society*, Vol. 58, no. 101109, pp. 1–4, https://doi.org/10.1016/j.techsoc.2019.01.002

Giardina, M. 2001, 'Global Hingis: flexible citizenship and the transnational celebrity', in D. Andrews & S. Jackson (eds.), *Sport stars: The cultural politics of sporting celebrity*, Routledge, London, pp. 201–217.

Grainger, A. D., Falcous, M. & Newman, J. I. 2012, Postcolonial anxieties and the browning of New Zealand rugby, *The Contemporary Pacific*, Vol. 24, no. 2, pp. 267–295, https://doi.org/10.1353/cp.2012.0029

Grainger, A., Newman, J. & Andrews, D. 2005, 'Global adidas: sport, celebrity and the marketing of difference', in J. Amis & T. Cornwell (eds.), *Global sport sponsorship*, Berg, Oxford, pp. 89–105.

Kellner, D. 1996, 'Sports, media culture, and race – some reflections on Michael Jordan', *Sociology of Sport Journal*, Vol. 13, no. 4, pp. 458–467, https://doi.org/10.1123/ssj.13.4.458

Kent, P. 2015, *Sonny ball: The legend of Sonny Bill Williams*, Pan MacMillan, Sydney.

Kobayashi, K. & Cho, Y. 2019, 'Asian sport celebrity: the nexus of race, ethnicity, and regionality', *The International Journal of the History of Sport*, Vol. 36, no. 7–8, pp. 611–625, https://doi.org/10.1080/09523367.2019.1675410

Larner, W. 2006, 'Brokering citizenship claims: neo-liberalism, biculturalism and multiculturalism in Aotearoa New Zealand', in E. Tastsoglou & A. Dobrowolsky (eds), *Women, migration and citizenship: Making local, national and transnational connections*, Ashgate, Farnham, pp. 131–148.

Malcolm, D. 2013, *Globalizing cricket: Englishness, empire and identity*, Bloomsbury, London.

Marshall, P. 1997, *Celebrity and power: Fame in contemporary culture*, University of Minnesota Press, Minneapolis.

Marshall, P. 2016, *The celebrity persona pandemic*, University of Minnesota Press, Minneapolis.

Mell, R. 2016, *"Korean Kiwi" Ko ready to represent N. Zealand in Olympics*. NBC Sports Group's Golf, viewed 26 August 2020, https://www.golfchannel.com/article/golf-central-blog/proud-korean-kiwi-ko-will-play-olympics-n-zealand

McGee, G. 2016, *Brendon McCullum: Declared*, Upstart Press, Auckland.

Phillips, J. 1996, *A man's country? The image of the pakeha male - A history*, Penguin, Auckland.

Redmond, S. 2014, *Celebrity and the media*, Palgrave Macmillan, London.

Redmond, S. 2018, *Celebrity*, Routledge, London.

Rowe, D. 2004, *Sport, culture and the media: The unruly trinity*, 2nd edn., Open University Press, Buckingham.

Ryan, G. 2007, Few and far between: Māori and Pacific contributions to New Zealand cricket, *Sport in Society*, Vol. 10, no. 1, pp. 71–87, https://doi.org/10.1080/17430430600989167

Ryan, G. & Watson, G. 2018, *Sport and the New Zealanders: A history*, Auckland University Press, Auckland.

Sandvoss, C. 2012, 'From national hero to liquid star: identity and discourse in transnational sports consumption', in C. Sandvoss, M. Real, & A. Bernstein (eds), *Bodies of discourse: Sports stars, media, and the global public*, Peter Lang, London, pp. 171–192.

Shilling, C. 1991, 'Educating the body: physical capital and the production of social inequalities', *Sociology*, Vol. 25, no. 4, pp. 653–672, https://doi.org/10.1177/0038038591025004006

Smart, B. 2005, *The Sport star: Modern sport and the cultural economy of sporting celebrity*, Sage, London.

Sturm, D. 2019, '"I dream of Genie": Eugenie Bouchard's "body" of work on *Facebook*', *Celebrity Studies*, Vol. 10, no. 4, pp. 583–587, https://doi.org/10.1080/19392397.2019.1601808

Toffoletti, K. 2016, 'Analyzing media representations of sportswomen—expanding the conceptual boundaries using a postfeminist sensibility', *Sociology of Sport Journal*, Vol. 33, no. 3, pp. 199–207, https://doi.org/10.1123/ssj.2015-0136

Turner, G. 2014, *Understanding celebrity*, 2nd edn., Sage, London.

Wenner, L. (ed.). 2013, *Fallen sports heroes: Media, and celebrity culture*, Peter Lang, New York:

Whannel, G. 1999, 'Sport stars, narrativization and masculinities', *Leisure Studies*, Vol. 18, no. 3, pp. 249–265, https://doi.org/10.1080/026143699374952

Whannel, G. 2002, *Media sport stars: Masculinities and moralities*, Routledge, London.

Wigmore, T. 2020, *Cricket 2.0: Inside the T20 revolution*, Polaris, Edinburgh.

York, L. 2013, 'Star turn: the challenges of theorizing celebrity agency', *The Journal of Popular Culture*, Vol. 46, no. 6, pp. 1330–1347, https://doi.org/10.1111/jpcu.12091

12

OUTDOOR RECREATION IN AN AGE OF DISRUPTION

Change, challenge and opportunity

Stephen Espiner, Emma J. Stewart and Megan Apse

Introduction

Outdoor recreation has long been a part of the New Zealand psyche, forged through the deep connections to place among both the nation's indigenous people and its more recent settlers, whose associations with the vast, dynamic and largely uninhabited remote landscapes over time nurtured self-reliance, physical and intellectual challenge and a reverence for nature (Devlin 1993). Tangata whenua ways of living with the land, embedded in the concepts of tikanga, kaitiakitanga and tūrangawaewae, are tied to historic practices relating to food gathering and harvesting, spirituality, and exploration (Smith 2004). While early European settlers' relationship with the land was often one of domination based on "breaking in" or "taming" the land for farming (Ross 2008), subsequent generations augmented these characteristics towards the satisfaction of conquering physical challenges in recreation (Barnett & Maclean 2014). Some of these values helped form the foundation of backcountry and wilderness pursuits for particular sectors of New Zealand society in the latter half of the nineteenth and early twentieth centuries, alongside a burgeoning system of national parks and protected area, and the facilitation of recreation experiences by government agencies. As population, personal mobility and tourism increase, education levels rise, and recreation options abound, the number of people participating in outdoor recreation has grown (Sport New Zealand 2019), and recreation has become recognised as one of the aspects of life most valued by New Zealanders (Ministry for the Environment and Statistics New Zealand 2019).

While historical threads continue to influence New Zealanders' recreational engagements with the outdoors, developments are constantly evolving in response to new social, cultural and environmental factors. The pace and scale of these changes varies, as do the implications for current and future governance,

DOI: 10.4324/9781003034445-12

management and participation. The third millennium is sometimes referred to as the "age of disruption" (Stiegler 2019) – an era prefaced (and popularised) by Alvin Toffler's *Future Shock* – in which the effects of rapid or profound environmental, technological and socio-political change result in a future characterised by uncertainty. Against this backdrop of omnipresent change, this chapter examines a range of current and potential "disrupters" and explores the contemporary and future implications for outdoor recreation in Aotearoa New Zealand. The chapter concludes with a research agenda aimed to focus scholarly attention on understanding the nature, scale and scope of these disruptions which arguably represent some of the biggest challenges for researchers in this field.

Multiple signals of change and disruption

Sport and recreation have always been subject to various historic, socio-cultural, political, economic and environmental forces which shape community investment, as well as individual engagement, in specific pursuits. In this section we consider multiple phenomena operating at different spatio-temporal scales, with the potential to disrupt existing outdoor recreation practices. An illustration of selected disruptive forces shaping outdoor recreation practices is depicted in Figure 12.1. These include examples of forces operating at local, national and transnational scales, each of which interacts and intersects in myriad ways. The pace at which disruption occurs also varies, resulting in very different experiences of change and responses to it. The immediacy of a natural disaster or pandemic, for instance, has very different implications for the outdoor recreation sector compared with the incremental and slow-burning character of social or environmental change. The effects of these disrupters are not isolated nor independent; rather, they are interconnected and interactive. The combined effects of

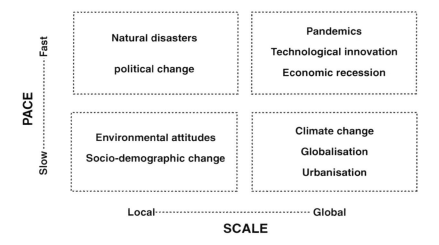

FIGURE 12.1 Disrupters facing the outdoor recreation sector.

such forces of change are characteristic of the age of disruption: that is, an era in which the nature and pace of change points to a future which is less certain than ever before (Stiegler 2019).

Examples are selected from each of the four quadrants in Figure 12.1 to illustrate how these disruptive forces influence outdoor recreation in Aotearoa New Zealand. Moving from the local to the global scale, we start with the fast disrupters, highlighting natural disasters, followed by technological innovation. Attention is then given to the slower burning disrupters, namely sociodemographic change and climate change.

Natural disasters

The upheaval created by natural disasters is an illustration of rapid disruption for the outdoor recreation sector where effects are often manifested at the local level and particularly relevant for Aotearoa New Zealand. Straddling the Pacific and Australian tectonic plates, Aotearoa New Zealand is susceptible to a range of natural hazards such as earthquakes, volcanoes, tsunamis and events linked to extreme weather such as landslides, erosion and flooding (Kilgour et al. 2010; Potter et al. 2015).

In recent years, natural disasters have been the basis of a series of disruptions to outdoor recreation across Aotearoa New Zealand. Canterbury's Port Hills represent an example of a popular recreation resource rendered inaccessible for a significant period due to the 2010/2011 Christchurch earthquake sequence (Christchurch City Council 2020). Earthquake damage to the Port Hills in the form of cliff collapse, rockfall and slope movement in some cases completely engulfed walking and mountain biking tracks and resulted in large areas being closed to the public (Potter et al. 2015). In the decade following the earthquakes, extensive remedial work was undertaken to increase safety, and most tracks were eventually reopened for recreation. However, due to prohibitive repair costs, sections of the Summit Road remain unsuitable for vehicular traffic but are open for cyclists and walkers, an unanticipated bonus for some recreation users in this post–disaster setting (Christchurch City Council 2020).

A further reminder of the geologically active land on which Aotearoa New Zealand sits was the 2019 Whakaari/White Island eruption. The Whakaari volcanic event killed 20 visitors to the island, and injured many more (New Zealand Police 2020), most of whom were international tourists. Several other active volcanoes are settings for a variety of outdoor recreation activities, including the popular Tongariro Crossing adjacent to the frequently active, Mount Ngauruhoe and Mount Ruapehu (Kilgour et al. 2010). During the September 2007 eruption of Mount Ruapehu, two climbers in a hut 600m from the vent were caught in the blast, sustaining serious injuries (Kilgour et al. 2010). Similarly, a storm event in February 2020 caused damage to over 78 tracks on public conservation land in the south of the South Island, closing the Milford Track and the Routeburn Track – two of the nation's premier outdoor recreation products (DOC 2020).

FIGURE 12.2 Closure of a section of the Summit Road to vehicle traffic has resulted in increased access for recreationists undertaking non-motorised pursuits (Photo Credit: E.J. Stewart).

During the same weather event, Fiordland trampers were air-lifted to safety when a slip caused by heavy rains partially destroyed a tramping hut, and high rivers trapped them (Harding & Kelly 2020).

In response to the range of natural hazards disrupting activities in Aotearoa New Zealand in often unexpected and abrupt ways, planners have tried to shift their attention from a "reactive" to a "proactive" risk reduction approach by trying to reduce vulnerability and to building resilience (Orchiston et al. 2013). As an example, the New Zealand Cycle Trail (a network of linked cycle trails throughout the country) states that "bridges are now being built to allow for flood levels 500mm (or more) higher than in the past. Culverts are being enlarged, more are being installed, trails are being raised and some sections chip-sealed or concreted" (MBIE 2019a, p. 10). Similarly, through the collaborative AF8 project (Alpine Fault magnitude 8), work is underway to ensure that Aotearoa New Zealand is prepared for the anticipated rupture of the Alpine Fault (AF8 2020) the consequences of which are likely to be significant for outdoor recreation (and tourism) settings across the South Island.

Technological innovation

The transformational power of technological change is another useful illustration of a relatively rapid disrupter impacting outdoor recreation, with effects experienced both locally and more globally (Martin 2017). First identified in the 1990s (Devlin 1993), technological developments have only amplified in the twenty-first century, with continued advances in light-weight and durable recreation gear, personal safety equipment and the increased accuracy and availability of GPS/location devices. This has occurred alongside an increase in functional technology that comes embedded within everyday personal hand-held devices (Dépatie et al. 2016). The rapid development of Web 2.0, social media platforms and widespread adoption of mobile digital (and communication) devices and their associated applications in society, including by outdoor recreationists, has shaped outdoor recreation in a number of important ways, many of which represent significant challenges and opportunities for the sector.

The power of digital technology to disrupt the outdoor recreation experience is evidenced by the capacity of the smartphone to increase perceptions of safety among recreationists – a function of the communication and information services it provides, such as weather forecasting, map and internet search functions (Dépatie et al. 2016). Notwithstanding Shultis' (2015) finding that technology embedded within all types of recreation equipment is largely perceived to be *positive* for New Zealand outdoor recreationists (due to increased comfort, safety and access), the ubiquity of, and potential reliance on technology should also be viewed with some caution. The signal range and battery life of digital devices, for instance, can impact their effectiveness as safety equipment, and recreationists may not necessarily recognise these limitations until it's too late (Dépatie et al. 2016).

Technological innovation is also disrupting how and where New Zealanders travel for recreation. This is particularly the case with emergent electrified modes of transport, such as electric vehicles (EVs) and e-bike technology, including e-mountain bikes (e-MTBs). While uptake of electrified modes is increasing, the impact these technologies may have on recreation practices is yet to be fully explored. Opportunity undoubtedly exists to increase access and inclusion for groups that are less fit or able (such as those with reduced mobility), thus allowing them access to at least some of the benefits that outdoor recreation affords. However, developments in technology also raise issues around what changes in access might mean for the recreation resource and its existing users. Studies show that traditional mountain-bike riders are wary of e-MTBs, fearing increased trail degradation (from rapid acceleration and speed), increased noise, and an increase in the number of less experienced riders on trails, and, while no evidence has yet been published, the issue of safety and recreation conflict remains (MBIE 2019a, Nielsen et al. 2019).

While technology's well-documented transformative power (Kerr 2016) creates extensive possibilities for the future of outdoor recreation, the use of technology in outdoor recreation will, no doubt, remain contentious. Those resistant to the introduction of new technology in these settings cite its perceived potential to erode traditional skills (including survival skills such as map reading or wayfinding), and its impingement on an outdoor experience that is predicated on removing oneself from the pervasive aspects of modern life (Nielsen et al. 2019). By contrast, some of the benefits of technology in outdoor recreation use are hard to dispute, the most obvious being the issue of safety. Research has shown that the safety benefits of technology (mainly those associated with smart phones) are overestimated by outdoor recreationists (Dépatie et al. 2016), and that mobile

138 Stephen Espiner et al.

coverage encourages less experienced users to go further into the backcountry than they might otherwise go (Nielsen et al. 2019). Given the rapid evolution of technological advances, the likelihood of developments being a catalyst for further, as yet unknown, changes to the outdoor recreation sector is high. These include, for example, the impact that artificial intelligence (AI), augmented reality (AR), virtual reality (VR) and the internet of things (IoT) may have on outdoor recreation practices.

Socio-demographic change

Where technological change can create disruption over very short timescales with wide geographic reach, changes in social values and population dynamics occur slowly and are experienced locally. Nonetheless, socio-demographic change has the potential to transform many aspects of social life. Aotearoa New Zealand is currently in the midst of unprecedented social and demographic change (Spoonley 2020). The population's age structure, ethnic composition, geographic concentration and income distribution are transitioning from one state to another at a rate not previously experienced. The Aotearoa New Zealand of the late 2030s is forecast to be more populous, older, more ethnically diverse, more urban and more mobile than today (Spoonley 2020). These demographic changes will re-make New Zealand, and as such, will have significant impacts on outdoor recreation participation and management.

In recent years, Aotearoa New Zealand has experienced growth in demographic segments that are the least active in outdoor recreation (Sport New Zealand 2015). These social shifts contain the potential to undermine previously held stereotypes of the outdoors as the domain of middle-class Pākehā males, as depicted in mid-twentieth century texts such as Barry Crump's *A Good Keen Man*, and John Mulgan's *Man Alone*. This demographic change includes many "new" New Zealanders, – migrants and their Aotearoa New Zealand-born families whose cultures value physical activities different from what has historically been popular in Aotearoa New Zealand – as well as older New Zealanders, whose outdoor recreation activity preferences may have changed over time according to fitness level, or tolerance for discomfort in the outdoors. Moreover, those New Zealanders arriving at the age of 65 are the healthiest ever to reach this milestone (Spoonley 2020) – a critical factor in understanding the outdoor recreation needs of this growing sector of the population.

Social and demographic change over the last three decades has contributed to investment decisions among providers of outdoor recreation opportunities. New Zealand's Department of Conservation, for instance, has put considerable resources into the development of its Great Walks, in order to accommodate current and anticipated changes in demand for outdoor recreation experiences. The Great Walks product (both guided and unguided) is well-suited to less experienced and more comfort-oriented recreationists, such as international tourists, new New Zealanders and those in the post-retirement phase of life. New technologies such as e-bikes and hand-held safety and communication devices intersect with the needs of this emerging group of outdoor recreationists, affording them access and security in settings previously the domain of the young and fit.

Accommodating an increasingly diverse population may not come without controversy. Attempts to provide for users whose expectations are different can be met with resistance from those concerned about changes to the natural landscape, especially in backcountry settings. For traditional outdoor recreationists, more recreation infrastructure, increased mobile internet coverage, new access roads, amenities, interpretive signage and so on can be the antithesis of the wilderness experience (Wray et al. 2010) and ultimately detract from nature's status as untouched and unencumbered by development. Proponents of equal rights, however, emphasise that equal rights include equal access to recreation and its facilities (IMM 2020). This represents an important challenge for managers, who will be required to reflect carefully on the principles of diversity, ultimately retaining the spectrum of opportunity from "developed" to "remote" inherent in best practice outdoor recreation management frameworks such as the Recreation Opportunities Spectrum (ROS) (Taylor 1993). To enable this, a number of changes may be needed in recreation management, including assessing the affordability, accessibility, facilities, leadership and management structure of recreation opportunities to become more inclusive of the "superdiversity" that is projected to become the norm (NZRA 2018).

Climate change

Another example of a slow-moving but powerful disrupter is climate change. Climate and other environmental change, precipitated by increasing Greenhouse Gas (GHG) emissions, is now well-established as a contributor to increased surface temperature, sea-level rise and growing frequency of adverse weather events (IPCC 2018). These enduring effects, and the accompanying social and political responses, have the potential to cause significant disruption to society, including patterns of recreation consumption (Sport NZ 2020). Aotearoa New Zealand's commitment to the Paris Agreement, and to the United Nations' Sustainable Development Goals (UN SDGs), reflect public perceptions that, without large-scale social and political change, the environment will not sustain life as it is currently lived. There is a growing body of scholarly literature documenting the effects of changing climate conditions on outdoor recreation pursuits including the impact of temperature changes on cycling (Chan & Wichman 2020), fishing (Dundas & von Haefen 2020) and skiing (Hewer & Gough 2018). Less formal/structured outdoor pursuits, such as the use of beaches and coastlines, have also been found to be at risk of climate change related degradation due to shoreline recession (Toimil et al. 2018).

Outdoor recreation is significantly affected by the various social, political and economic responses to climate change. The vast majority of current recreational visits to New Zealand's public conservation lands and waters, for instance, are heavily reliant upon relatively cheap and readily available fossil fuels. Most outdoor recreation is fundamentally linked to the motor car, with recreationists

140 Stephen Espiner et al.

frequently travelling considerable distances from where they live in order to access natural resource settings, especially those in the backcountry and wilderness areas (Brabyn & Sutton 2013).

Similar challenges face the tourism industry – the nature-based element of which is essentially a commercial subset of the outdoor recreation sector. Prior to the COVID-19 pandemic and the consequential closure of New Zealand's border, the number of international arrivals was projected to increase from nearly 4 to 5 million visitors by 2025 (MBIE 2019b). The social and environmental impacts of such growth in international tourism, alongside concerns about the absence of public transport infrastructure linking remote areas of iconic value, have led to important questions about sustainability in the sector (Higham et al. 2019). There is also evidence emerging to suggest that some consumers are seriously considering the emissions associated with air travel when making travel decisions (Higham et al. 2016), with the concept of "flight shaming" (Mkono 2020) signalling changing attitudes towards long haul flights for what is increasingly considered excessive carbon use. Given Aotearoa New Zealand's distance from major tourist markets and the high number of international tourists who participate in nature-based activities (MBIE 2020), the outdoor recreation sector is likely to be significantly impacted if collective attitudes to long-distance air travel change.

Specific national and international governance actions in response to climate change also have the potential to disrupt the outdoor recreation sector. At the global level, for instance, the remit of SDG13 is to "take urgent action to combat climate change and its impacts" (United Nations 2020, p. 18). On New Zealand's part, such actions are contained within the carbon neutrality goals set out in the Climate Change Response (Zero Carbon) Amendment Act 2019, and reflect the government's commitment to the Paris Agreement target to reduce GHG emissions for the purpose of combatting climate change. With individual responses often viewed as an integral part of slowing the rate at which global temperatures rise, outdoor recreationists are likely to face increasing pressure to reduce their personal carbon footprints or order to contribute to this collective goal.

In addition, New Zealand's Department of Conservation has published a *Climate Change Adaptation Action Plan 2020/21–2024/25* (Christie et al. 2020) which illustrates the potential for disruption identified by key government agencies with responsibilities for recreation access to public conservation lands. In the coming decades, alpine tramping, mountaineering and glacier access opportunities will be increasingly altered (Purdie et al. 2020), ski seasons truncated, walking tracks washed out and forest bike trails threatened by fires. More indirectly, shifting habitat ranges and the potential for pest proliferation are likely to make management of New Zealand's conservation lands and waters, upon which so many people rely for outdoor recreation, all the more uncertain.

In future decades, outdoor recreation is likely to undergo considerable transformation, including changes to transport infrastructure, activity duration, travel mode and spatial use patterns as new norms develop around more careful use of scarce resources and awareness of environmental change becomes more imbedded in the collective consciousness. It is possible that some recreationists will be ready

Outdoor recreation in an age of disruption **141**

and willing to adapt to such new practices, and there is already limited evidence that New Zealand's outdoor recreationists operate within a broad ethos of custodianship over the land and as such can reasonably be expected to be early adopters of pro-environmental behaviours (Harbrow 2019). For most outdoor recreationists, however, larger structural (economic, socio-political and physical) changes will be required to effect the scale of behavioural change necessary to mitigate and/or adapt to the anticipated climate conditions in the coming decades.

Conclusion and research agenda

The third millennium is an era in which the effects of change, be they rapid, slow-burning or profound will manifest across society at a variety of scales including the local, national and global level. In this chapter we have showcased four disrupters and outlined the impact they are having, or could have, on outdoor recreation. While they have been treated separately in this chapter, it is important to note that the disrupters coalesce and should be thought of as overlapping and interconnected.

At the time of writing this chapter, the world is in the grip of the COVID-19 pandemic. There is perhaps no better example that illustrates the far-reaching effects that a fast-evolving and highly disruptive event can have at multiple scales. By mid-March 2020, New Zealand had effectively closed its border to all but returning New Zealand citizens. As a consequence, Tourism New Zealand reacted quickly to pivot tourism and recreation experiences towards domestic markets by encouraging those in New Zealand to "do something new, New Zealand" (Tourism New Zealand 2020). The implications of this seismic shift in recreation are only just beginning to be understood, but the effects are likely to be wide ranging and experienced at multiple scales. Economies, communities and environments will change as a result of this new tourism and outdoor recreation landscape. Alongside the significant losses and challenges, there may also be opportunities – not least the possibility for the sector to take stock of the many issues it faced under the previous (pre-pandemic) high-growth environment – perhaps even re-imagining how the phenomenon of tourism might contribute differently to New Zealand in the future. Furthermore, there is some evidence that during the pandemic New Zealanders' use of nature-based settings for outdoor recreation may have deepened (Landcare Research 2020). Periods of great disruption have the potential to prompt innovation and creativity, and, in turn, behaviour change; this poses interesting questions for the future of outdoor recreation as it could provide the context for a re-examination of the terms by which recreation is undertaken and managed.

Research agenda

Research on outdoor recreation in Aotearoa New Zealand has a rich history dating back 50 years, much of it building on themes and ideas initially established by scholars of leisure studies and, more latterly intersecting with the study

FIGURE 12.3 A research agenda for outdoor recreation in Aotearoa New Zealand

Axes: PACE (Fast — Slow); SCALE (Local — Global)

Natural disasters
- Documenting the adaptive capacity of the outdoor recreation sector post-natural disaster (such as fires and earthquakes)
- Developing resilience indicators for the outdoor recreation sector to assist planning to adapt to change

political change
- Exploring the implications for outdoor recreation in response to anticipated changes to key legislation and policy, including to national park management plans and the Resource Management Act
- Understanding the significance of new governance models for public conservation lands subject Treaty Settlement outcomes and associated processes
- Exploring the potential for enhancing outdoor recreation opportunities through harnessing significant potential for partnerships between government, iwi, business and the community

Environmental attitudes
Understanding outdoor recreation in a carbon-conscious future, including changes to transport infrastructure, activity duration, travel mode and spatial use patterns
- Exploring the link between participation in outdoor recreation and pro-environmental behaviour

Socidemographic change
- Exploring the offerings that outdoor recreation can provide to Maori and pasifika communities, that continue to resonate with their culture and which can participation
- Identifying how to engage with sectors of society traditionally least likely to engage in outdoor recreation

Pandemics
- understanding outdoor recreation in the covid-context, including social / travel practices post-Covid to understand how the sector is changing (such as needs of new users)
- Documenting and exploring whether New Zealanders have been motivated to experience the outdoors in new ways post-pandemic; and whether they identify the altered tourism landscape as a new recreation opportunity

Technological innovation
- Responding to and harnessing opportunity and challenge associated with new tecnologies in ways that preserve the character of traditional outdoor recreation (e.g escape /self-reliance/ risk) while fostering the engagement of new users.
- Exploring the future of the car as the centrepiece of mobility in outdoor recreation and the potential of zero-emission alternatives

Economic recession
- Documenting the economic impact of Covid-19 (including re-orientation of the economy) on the outdoor recreation sector

Climate change
- Identifying the impacts of climate-related weather events on outdoor or recreation activities and settings
- Analysis of long-term adaptation to climate change among outdoor recreationists
- understanding the carbon cost of outdoor recreation

Globalisation
- Understanding how 'brand' New zealand and its association with the outdoors, are factoes influenceing outdoor recreation choices
- Exploring how individualisation (the process by which society increasingly adapts to the needs and preference of individuals) is shaping outdoor recreation practices

Urbanisation
- Tracking the importance of peri-urban settins for outdoor recreation

Outdoor recreation in an age of disruption **143**

of tourism. It is now timely to pause and reflect on the areas that require urgent research attention so that we can be appropriately equipped to anticipate change as well as facilitate adaptation for the outdoor recreation sector. Our proposed research agenda attempts to outline some key research objectives under each of the disrupters identified (Figure 12.3).

Against a backdrop of unprecedented environmental and social change, this chapter has traversed the opportunities and challenges for outdoor recreation in an age characterised by disruption. This chapter has provided an analysis of outdoor recreation in Aotearoa New Zealand in the context of the current disruptive age in which the past may not be the best predictor of future patterns. An increasingly carbon-conscious community, natural disasters, environmental change, technological innovation, and the hyper-connected world in which we live have been explored as key disrupters whose effects are set to impact outdoor recreation practices. It remains clear that the nature of outdoor recreation and its management is not immune to the global and local forces that continue to shape society. Through addressing the proposed research agenda, it is envisaged that the outdoor recreation sector in Aotearoa New Zealand will be better positioned to adapt to these changes and ultimately more prepared to convert challenge into opportunity.

References

Climate Change Response (Zero Carbon) Amendment Act, 2019, Part 1B, 5Q, viewed 18 August 2020, http://www.legislation.govt.nz/act/public/2019/0061/latest/LMS183736.html.

AF8. 2020, *Alpine Fault Magnitude 8,* viewed 18 August 2020, https://af8.org.nz/

Barnett, S. & Maclean, C. 2014, *Tramping: A New Zealand history,* Craig Potton Publishing, Nelson, New Zealand.

Brabyn, L. & Sutton, S. 2013, 'A population based assessment of the geographical accessibility of outdoor recreation opportunities in New Zealand', *Applied Geography,* Vol. 41, pp. 124–131.

Chan, N. W. & Wichman, C. J. 2020, 'Climate change and recreation: evidence from North American cycling', *Environmental and Resource Economics*, pp. 1–33.

Christchurch City Council. 2020, *Rockfall and cliff collapse in the Port Hills,* viewed 6 August 2020, https://ccc.govt.nz/environment/land/slope-stability/rockfall-and-cliff-collapse-in-the-port-hills.

Christie, J., Pearce, P., Phifer, P., Parsons, S. & Tait, A. 2020, *Department of Conservation climate change adaptation action plan 2020/21–2024/25,* Department of Conservation, Wellington.

Dépatie, C., Kerr, R., Espiner, S. & Stewart, E. J. 2016, 'Experiencing outdoor recreation in the digital technology age: a case study from the Port Hills of Christchurch, New Zealand', in S. Carnicelli, D. Mcgillivray & G. Mcpherson (eds.), *Digital Leisure Cultures,* Routledge, London & NY, pp. 53–65.

Devlin, P. 1993, 'Outdoor recreation and environment: towards an understanding of the use of the outdoors in New Zealand', in H. Perkins & G. Cushman (eds.), *Leisure, recreation and tourism,* Longman Paul, Auckland, pp. 84–98.

Department Of Conservation. 2020, *Extreme weather event in Fiordland,* viewied 8 August 2020, https://www.doc.govt.nz/news/issues/extreme-weather-event-in-fiordland/.

Dundas, S. J. & Von Haefen, R. H. 2020, 'The effects of weather on recreational fishing demand and adaptation: implications for a changing climate', *Journal of the Association of Environmental and Resource Economists*, Vol. 7, pp. 209–242.

Harbrow, M. 2019, Visitors as advocates: A review of the relationship between participation in outdoor recreation and support for conservation and the environment *Science for conservation series,* Department of Conservation, Wellington.

Harding, E. & Kelly, R. 2020, *Landslide hits Fiordland hut trapping 31 people as heavy rains batter South,* Stuff, viewed 8 August 2020, https://www.stuff.co.nz/national/119250239/landslide-hits-fiordland-hut-trapping-31-people-as-heavy-rains-batter-south

Hewer, M. J. & Gough, W. A. 2018, 'Thirty years of assessing the impacts of climate change on outdoor recreation and tourism in Canada', *Tourism Management Perspectives*, Vol. 26, pp. 179–192.

Higham, J., Cohen, S. A., Cavaliere, C. T., Reis, A. & Finkler, W. 2016, 'Climate change, tourist air travel and radical emissions reduction', *Journal of Cleaner Production*, Vol. 111, pp. 336–347.

Higham, J. E. S., Espiner, S. & Parry, S. 2019, *The environmental impacts of tourism in Aotearoa New Zealand: A spatio-temporal analysis*, Parliamentary Commissioner for the Environment, Wellington.

Independent Monitoring Mechanism. 2020, *Making disability rights real New Zealand*, Independent Monitoring Mechanism and the Office of the Ombudsman, Wellington.

Intergovernmental Panel on Climate Change. 2018. 'Summary for policymakers', in V. Masson-Delmotte, P. Zhai, H.-O. Pörtner, D. Roberts, J. Skea, P. R. Shukla, A. Pirani, W. Moufouma-Okia, C. Péan, R. Pidcock, S. Connors, J. B. R. Matthews, Y. Chen, X. Zhou, M. I. Gomis, E. Lonnoy, T. Maycock, M. Tignor & T. Waterfield (eds.), *Global warming of 1.5°C*, Intergovernmental Panel on Climate Change, Switzerland.

Kerr, R. 2016, *Sport and technology: An actor-network theory perspective*, Manchester University Press, Manchester.

Kilgour, G., Manville, V., Pasqua, F. D., Graettinger, A., Hodgson, K. A. & Jolly, G. E. 2010, The 25 September 2007 eruption of Mount Ruapehu, New Zealand: Directed ballistics, surtseyan jets, and ice-slurry lahars. *Journal of Volcanology and Geothermal Research*, Vol. 191, pp. 1–14.

Landcare Research. 2020, Slowing down enabled connection with nature, viewed 18 October 2020, https://www.landcareresearch.co.nz/news/slowing-down-enabled-connection-with-nature.

Martin, S. 2017,'Real and potential influences of information technology on outdoor recreation and wilderness experiences and management', *Journal of Park and Recreation Administration*, Vol. 35, no. 1, pp. 98–101.

Ministry of Business Innovation and Employment. 2019a, *New Zealand Cycle Trail design guide*, Ministry of Business Innovation and Employment, Wellington.

Ministry of Business Innovation and Employment. 2019b, New Zealand Tourism Forecasts 2019–2025. Ministry of Business Innovation and Employment, Wellington.

Ministry of Business Innovation and Employment. 2020, *International visitor survey data available from Stats NZ*, Statistics NZ, viewed 6 July 2020, https://www.mbie.govt.nz/immigration-and-tourism/tourism-research-and-data/tourism-data-releases/international-visitor-survey-ivs/international-visitor-survey-data-available-from-stats-nz/.

Ministry for the Environment and Statistics New Zealand. 2019, *New Zealand's environmental reporting series: Environment Aoteroa 2019*, Ministry for the Environment and Statistics New Zealand, Wellington.

Mkono, M. 2020, 'Eco-anxiety and the flight shaming movement: implications for tourism', *Journal of Tourism Futures*, Vol. 6, No. 3, pp. 223–226.

Nielsen, T., Palmatier, S. M. & Proffitt, A. 2019, *Recreation conflicts focused on emerging e-bike technology*, Boulder County Parks & Open Space, Boulder, CO.

New Zealand Police 2020, *Death toll Whakaari/White Island eruption rises to 20*, viewed 8 July 2020, https://www.police.govt.nz/news/release/death-toll-whakaariwhite-island-eruption-rises-20.

New Zealand Recreation Association. 2018, Outdoor recreation in a superdiverse New Zealand. New Zealand Recreation Association.

Orchiston, C., Manuel, C., Coomer, M., Becker, J. & Johnston, D. 2013, 'The 2009 New Zealand West Coast shakeout: improving earthquake preparedness in a region of high seismic risk', *Australasian Journal of Disaster and Trauma Studies,* Vol. 2, pp. 56–61.

Potter, S. H., Becker, J. S., Johnston, D. M. & Rossiter, K. P. 2015, 'An overview of the impacts of the 2010–2011 Canterbury earthquakes', *International Journal of Disaster Risk Reduction,* Vol. 14, pp. 6–14.

Purdie, H., Hutton, J. H., Stewart, E. & Espiner, S. 2020, 'Implications of a changing alpine environment for geotourism: A case study from Aoraki/Mount Cook, New Zealand', *Journal of Outdoor Recreation and Tourism*, Vol. 29, p. 100235.

Ross, K. 2008, *Going bush: New Zealanders and nature in the twentieth century*, Auckland University Press, Auckland.

Shultis, J. D. 2015, "Completely empowering": a qualitative study of the impact of technology on the wilderness experience in New Zealand, *USDA Forest Service Proceedings,* RMRS, viewed 10 July 2020, https://www.fs.fed.us/rm/pubs/rmrs_p074/rmrs_p074_195_201.pdf.

Smith, A. 2004, 'A Màori sense of place?-Taranaki Waiata Tangi and feelings for place', *New Zealand Geographer*, Vol. 60, pp. 12–17.

Spoonley, P. 2020, *The New New Zealand: Facing demographic disruption*, Massey University Press, Auckland.

Sport New Zealand. 2015, *Sport and active recreation in the lives of New Zealand adults: 2013/14 active New Zealand survey results*, Sport New Zealand, Wellington.

Sport New Zealand. 2019, *Active NZ 2018 participation report*, Sport New Zealand, Wellington.

Sport New Zealand. 2020, *Ensuring the play, active recreation and sport sector is fit for the future*, Sport New Zealand, Wellington.

Stiegler, B. 2019, *The age of disruption: Technology and madness in computational capitalism,* Polity, Cambridge, UK.

Taylor, P. 1993, *The New Zealand recreation opportunity spectrum: Guidelines for users,* Hillary Commission for Sport, Fitness and Leisure, and the Department of Conservation, Wellington.

Toimil, A., Díaz-Simal, P., Losada, I. J. & Camus, P. 2018, 'Estimating the risk of loss of beach recreation value under climate change', *Tourism Management*, Vol. 68, pp. 387–400.

Tourism New Zealand. 2020, *Do something new, New Zealand*, viewed 8 September 2020, https://www.newzealand.com/nz/campaign/do-something-new/

United Nations. 2020, Sustainable Development Goals Report, United Nations.

Wray, K., Espiner, S. & Perkins, H. C. 2010, 'Cultural clash: interpreting established use and new tourism activities in protected natural areas', *Scandinavian Journal of Hospitality and Tourism*, Vol. 10, pp. 272–290.

13

MASCULINITIES IN ALTERNATIVE SPORTS

Ultimate Frisbee™ and parkour

Hamish Crocket, Richard Pringle and Damien Puddle

Introduction

In this chapter we examine the performance and production of masculinities and gender relations in alternative sports using ultimate Frisbee™ (ultimate) and parkour as case studies. We use alternative sports as an umbrella term for those activities that were, originally at least, held to "either ideologically or practically provide an alternative to mainstream sport or mainstream sports values" (Rinehart 2000, p. 506). Both alternative sports and masculinities are amorphous concepts that defy simple categorisation. Yet, we argue, it is vital to critically examine the production of masculinities across all forms of sport.

Since the popularisation and institutionalisation of Western sport from the late 1800s, sport has been recognised as a distinctly gendered and gendering activity, that was designed by males, for the benefits of males, and has been dominated by males. Critical feminist scholars have correspondingly acknowledged sport as a "fundamentally sexist institution" (Theberge 1981, p. 342) that privileged males over females and promoted a dominant form of masculinity over marginalised and subjugated forms (Messner 1992). Yet with increased female sport participation, changing forms of masculinities and the growth of alternative sports, the notion that sport simplistically reproduces a dominant form of masculinity has been challenged (Pringle & Markula 2005; Ralph & Roberts 2020). The question we accordingly examine in this chapter is whether participation in alternative sports shape masculinities in more inclusive and pro-feminist ways?

We begin this chapter by outlining our understanding of alternative sports and masculinities. We then briefly introduce ultimate and parkour and develop the case studies on ultimate and parkour in New Zealand, focusing on the rapidly evolving nature of these sports and the impact of sportisation within each

DOI: 10.4324/9781003034445-13

Masculinities in alternative sports **147**

subculture. We finish by drawing conclusions about the performances of masculinities by those participating in alternative sports.

Alternative sports

The activities which we refer to as alternative sports have been variously labelled "whiz", "action" and "lifestyle" sports (Midol 1993; Thorpe 2010a; Wheaton 2004a). They tend to have short histories, change rapidly, claim an ethos that de-emphasises competition, have a strong aesthetic element, involve male and female participants and be associated with non-conformative lifestyles. However, since the late 1990s, a rapidly growing body of research has problematised the simplistic portrayal of alternative sports as fundamentally different to established Western sports. Firstly, alternative sports have simultaneously become commodified and co-opted into traditional Western sporting discourses (Atkinson 2010; Rinehart 2000; Wheaton 2004a). In this context, alternative sports, rather than being fundamentally different from modern achievement sport (Guttmann 2004), are simply at an earlier stage of the sportisation process. Maguire (2013) explains, sportisation broadly refers to the processes through which physical cultures transition from being heterogenous, unregulated activities towards becoming "competitive, regularized, rationalized, and gendered " (para. 1).

Secondly, alternative sports have tended to reproduce problematic masculinities that are very similar to those critiqued within traditional Western sports (e.g., Messner 1992). In particular, alternative sports were often initially dominated by young male participants who constituted informal fratriarchies which valued hypermasculine performances such as the sexual objectification of women and excessive consumption of alcohol (Thorpe 2010b; Waitt & Warren 2008). Males have tended to be the dominant participants in most alternative sports and successful performances have typically been understood as masculine. Although many scholars identified sub-groups of men within alternative sports that actively pursued alternative masculine identities to these fratriarchal masculinities (e.g., Thorpe 2010b; Wheaton 2004b), such sub-groups typically sought their own space to participate, rather than operating as "core" participants.

Research in alternative sports specifically located within New Zealand is relatively rare. Moreover, alternative sports have increasingly been conceptualised as transnational subcultures (Thorpe 2010a). The first and second authors of this chapter, Hamish and Damien, have undertaken extensive ethnographic research on ultimate and parkour respectively. The majority of their ethnographic work was located within New Zealand. These ethnographic engagements form the empirical basis of this chapter. In writing this chapter, when drawing specifically on either Hamish's or Damien's ethnographic work we will specifically refer to "Hamish's" or "Damien's" work and provide the reference. For the rest of the chapter, we have opted to write as "we", sharing responsibility for the synthesis of the case studies and overall direction of the chapter.

148 Hamish Crocket et al.

Theorising and examining masculinities

The concept of masculinity, although often used in a matter-of-fact manner by many sociologists, is complex, contested and can be confusing. Kimmel (2010), the founding editor of the academic journal *Men and Masculinities*, revealed this complexity by claiming "we still don't know how to talk about masculinities" (p. 2). More recently, Waling (2019) used the same phrasing to reiterate that "we still do not know how to talk about masculinities in men and masculinity studies" (p. 90). Such contentions seem strange after four decades of productive research on masculinities, yet it reflects the complexity of the topic and the on-going theoretical debates. Contemporary debates, for example, question whether the notion of masculinity: should be tied to male *and* female bodies, refers to something fluid and fractured *rather* than solid and identifiable, affirms *or* rejects the concept of a gender binary, is a performance *rather* than an identity category, and whether theories of masculinities should be underpinned by feminist ideals *or* not (Ralph & Roberts 2020). Researchers draw answers to these debates differently in relation to the various theories that they use. In recognising the "slipperiness" of the concept of masculinity (Donaldson 1993) and the importance of theory, we detail our theoretical understandings of the concept.

Although a contested term, we accept that masculinities change over time and are performed differently in various cultures, and can therefore be considered as multiple, socio-historic constructions. We more specifically understand masculinity as the socially constructed gender *ascribed* to male bodies. In this manner we acknowledge a symbolic link between masculinity and male bodies but reject the notion that biological sex is the *primary factor* in determining gender (Pringle, Kay & Jenkins 2011). We make three points about these seemingly simple premises. First, we critically note that the broad scholarship on masculinities has overwhelmingly linked male bodies to masculinities by almost exclusively focusing on boys and men. Such research, we contend, problematically acts to reify the male body as an exemplar of masculinity and indirectly props up a gender binary (e.g., male bodies and masculinity/female bodies and femininity). We are politically motivated, however, to challenge the binaries that work to divide and create hierarchies between humans (e.g., straight/gay, black/white, masculine/feminine). In this manner, we do not link masculinity exclusively to bodies that are assumed to be male.

Second, although we regard masculinity as a socio-historic construct we accept, via our neo-materialist readings of the body, that physiology, hormones and anatomy should not be eschewed in the examination of masculinities. In this light, we understand that material and discursive forces interact in the assembling and performance of masculinities.

Thirdly, we recognise that a social constructionist stance renders the concept of masculinity as something seemingly nebulous to examine: as masculinity – as a social construct – is not directly observable but has to be *inferred*. This process of inference is not a precise science but is typically associated with how people

Masculinities in alternative sports **149**

theorise and *read* bodies (e.g., with respect to how they look, what they do, who and what objects they interact with). Although there are many useful theorists, we find the work of Derrida and Foucault helpful for "reading" masculinities. Derrida's (1978) concept of *différance* informs that a gendered reading (or deconstructing) of the body occurs through an ongoing process of comparison of differences and an associated deferral of meanings. For example, a manoeuvre in parkour, might be read via a comparison of differences such as whether the action is graceful, athletic or vigorous. This comparison of differences is then connected to a deferral of meanings, for example, the parkour manoeuvre might then be inferred as hypermasculine, masculine, feminine or non-gendered. Importantly, through drawing on Derrida we understand masculinity as a relational concept connected to the concept of femininity and linked to associated workings of power.

Through drawing from a Foucauldian lens we further accept that the readings of masculinities are shaped by the workings of discourse and power relations within material contexts. Foucault (1978) theorised that discourse constrained "the order of things" or how people viewed reality. Accordingly, given the conjunction between discourse and power, we have found the analysis of the complex interplay of discourses useful for understanding particular performances as masculine and the constitution of multiple and fragmented subjectivities (see Pringle & Hickey 2010; Pringle & Markula 2005). In this light, we do not understand masculinity as belonging to a coherent type or typology of masculinity, such as inclusive, hybrid or mosaic masculinities (Waling 2019).

This brief overview of how we theorise and examine masculinities reveals many of the complexities that make gender studies a complicated field of political examination. Yet in summary, we suggest that "masculinities can be understood as *constructed*, *performed* and *read* via complex webs of on-going social interactions in specific relations to the workings of discourse and associated power relations that are allegorically connected to male bodies" (Pringle & Hickey 2010, p. 119).

Introducing ultimate and parkour

Ultimate is a self-refereed team sport played with a flying disc. It originated in the United States in 1968 and gradually spread across the world. Although ultimate has grown rapidly, in particular from the early 2000s onwards, it has not yet grown to the point where it is recognised in popular culture to the extent that larger alternative sports are, such as skateboarding or snowboarding. Although in many respects it appears to be a conventional team sport, it is distinctive for being self-refereed at all levels,[1] with players' actions being governed by the *Spirit of the Game*, an ultimate-specific version of fair play (Crocket 2015a, 2015b; Griggs 2011). Nevertheless, the rapid growth of ultimate has led to increasing evidence of sportisation (Maguire 2013), with competitive tournaments being increasingly distinguished from social tournaments and national governing bodies becoming increasingly restrictive with regards to team uniforms and names (Crocket 2016c) as well as eligibility and rostering requirements.

150 Hamish Crocket et al.

Parkour was developed by nine ethnically diverse young males, the "founders", in the suburbs of Paris in the late 1980s (Marshall 2010); children of first-generation migrant families, who were "neither integrated into the culture of their parents nor their country" (Guss 2011, p. 75). Some historical roots of parkour date back to the 1900s (Atkinson 2009), but the modern activity packaged as parkour has only gained global awareness in the early 2000s. The expansion of parkour from its origins in France has been swift and widespread, particularly amongst young urban populations (Gilchrist & Wheaton 2011). However, even amongst the nine founders of parkour, differing ideological stances quickly emerged, and with its rapid global dissemination via YouTube, parkour exhibits a "great divergence in styles, practice and definition" (Saville 2008, p. 892). Although primarily a non-competitive outdoor activity, the institutionalisation of parkour (see Puddle et al. 2019; Wheaton & O'Loughlin 2017) has resulted in formalised lessons, competitions, commercial indoor spaces, and national and international governing bodies. Thus, in a similar manner to ultimate, the "sport" has undergone forms of institutionalisation.

Much of the literature on ultimate and parkour echoes that on alternative sports more broadly. Thornton (2004), for example, argued the ultimate Frisbee espoused a rhetoric of inclusivity, yet consistently discriminated against women in mixed teams by giving them marginal on-field roles. In men's ultimate, Crocket (2013) noted that poor performance was gendered as feminine, yet highlighted that male-ultimate players typically engaged in a range of masculine, and, at times, feminine performances, rather than adhering to a singular masculine identity. Similarly, the parkour community "perceives itself as having a participatory gender inclusive ideology" (Angel 2011, p. 134). Yet Kidder (2013) found that men's training practices had "unintentional and unfortunate exclusionary results" (p. 6) and Puddle (2019) identified that women's movements tend to be negatively compared against normative athletic male standards now common in online media. Nevertheless, from Damien's (see, Puddle 2019) and Hamish's (see, Crocket 2013, 2016a, 2018) ethnographic research, and ongoing experiences as active participants in these sports within Aotearoa New Zealand, we see the increasing organisation and formalisation of parkour and ultimate as offering new ways of engaging with the ethos of the activities and to potentially offer participants a wider array of masculinities to perform.

Reflections on the "sportisation" of ultimate and parkour within New Zealand

As Crocket (2018) has highlighted, the 2010s were a decade of significant change for ultimate in Aotearoa New Zealand. Prior to this time, ultimate was largely governed by volunteers who were almost exclusively from the most skilled and competitive tier of Aotearoa New Zealand's players. Governance was minimalist and largely focused on completing the bare minimum of tasks to ensure New Zealand held national championships and remained eligible to compete

Masculinities in alternative sports **151**

in international competitions. In contrast to the focus on competition in the national championships of more traditional sports, various states of drunkenness were central to many ultimate players' tournament experiences (Crocket 2016a). During the 2010s, New Zealand Ultimate (NZU), the governing body, engaged with regional organisations and players to consult on a restructuring process, intended to bring governance into line with traditional sports organisations within New Zealand. Ultimate is now primarily run by regional bodies, who are responsible for implementing NZU policies and organising leagues. National level competition, however, is based on clubs who are largely unaffiliated with the regional bodies. At the same time, efforts to develop youth level competition within New Zealand gained significant momentum and regular age-group competitions began to be held at regional, national, trans-Tasman and international levels. These processes led to increasing restrictions on eligibility for national level tournaments, reducing the previous blurred lines between social and competitive forms of the sport. Consumption of alcohol at competitive tournaments became heavily restricted, including being banned on playing fields. National tournaments began to be live-streamed, most notably with NZU signing a deal with Sky Television, New Zealand's dominant pay for view sports broadcaster, in 2019.

Since 2004 parkour has typically been experienced via "jams". Jams are unstructured training sessions involving any number of practitioners, sometimes led by senior community figures but otherwise entirely self-governed with variations in length, location and challenges. However, a significant number of practitioners felt that a national governing body would improve the public perception of parkour and increase the credibility and safety of the developing practice. Thus, Parkour NZ – Tauhōkai Aotearoa[2] was incorporated in 2011. In 2013, members of Parkour NZ, recognising that parkour was having a significantly positive influence on their lives, set a goal for parkour participation to deliver "positive self-development, health and education" (Parkour NZ 2017), rather than participation being a goal in-and-of itself. Simultaneously, despite many communities and practitioners claiming they were resolutely opposed to the commercialisation of parkour, often seeing it as a dilution of the practice and its values (see Clegg & Butryn 2012; De Freitas 2011), the development of indoor parkour grew. The interaction between Parkour NZ, the commercial parkour businesses, and the evolving culture has resulted in annual competitive fixtures since 2017.

These developments within New Zealand occurred in parallel to the global trend towards sportisation for ultimate and parkour and show strong similarilities to the processes of sportisation that other alternative sports have exhibited particularly from the 1990s onwards. For both sports, the increased division between competitive and social forms of participation and the visibility and emphasis on elite performance has the potential to diminish the ethics of inclusion and enjoyment being prioritised over competitive success that had previously been valued, if not consistently lived up to, in these sports.

152 Hamish Crocket et al.

However, the recent history of these sports does not neatly match the "descent" narrative that has typically been linked to the rapid growth and commodification of alternative sports. We offer a focused example here of ultimate and the changes that were evident throughout 2010–2020. The organisational changes in ultimate and increasing separation of competitive and social forms of the game occurred alongside increasing conversations about the role and meaning of spirit of the game globally and within New Zealand. Earlier generations of players had identified patterns linking refusing to party at national tournaments with taking winning too seriously and the rejection of the spirit of the game (Crocket 2016a), which is fundamentally a notion that fair play is more important than winning. Indeed, spirit of the game is now arguably disassociated from the pursuit of determined drunkenness at competitive levels. This shift, we suggest, may reflect a growing concern with wellbeing and process (which can be deferred as feminine values) rather than a focus on competition and winning (i.e., masculine values).

Hence, rather than diminishing the role of spirit of the game, it has been reinvigorated as a central tenet of how competitive ultimate should be played. Increasing emphasis has been placed on knowledge of rules and appropriate ways of interacting with opponents when making calls, with players being required to pass online tests of rules knowledge in order to be eligible to play in competitive tournaments. Relatedly, teams are now required to nominate "spirit captains", whose role is to provide a clear path of communication between teams should disagreements over conduct develop during a game. While these developments have been lead globally by ultimate's international governing body, the World Flying Disc Federation (WFDF), New Zealand players have rapidly and enthusiastically embraced these developments. Notably, at recent world championships, New Zealand teams have regularly won awards for being the "most spirited" team in their division (see, for example, Stewart 2018).

In a similar vein, attempts have been made to encourage more equitable sets of gender relations within ultimate. Ultimate is typically split into three divisions: women's, open (a de facto men's division) and mixed. Many mixed teams have historically assigned key playing roles and more playing minutes to male players (Crocket 2016b; Pringle & Crocket 2013; Thornton 2004). While this pattern is still identifiable, following rules changes being issued by WFDF, NZU has adopted new rules for mixed ultimate which are designed to ensure that playing time is equally shared between male and female players. Following international trends, there has been increased discussion within the community about the need for the mixed division to be more inclusive of female participants. Although a positive shift it, nevertheless, reflects a history of male dominance which is a hallmark of the workings of hegemonic masculinity.

Masculinities and gender relations

In the practice of parkour, the physical landscape provides fundamental opportunities for the practitioner. Parkour movement skills, when not including

Masculinities in alternative sports **153**

acrobatics, are ascribed value based on their practicality. As a result, men embrace physical skills typically associated with women, such as agility and balance (Wheaton 2013) and value this feminine aesthetic. Relatedly, many of Damien's male participants (but not all) revealed their dislike of traditional organised sport, particularly team sports. Not simply because of the requirements for organised team training sessions and playing timetables but also the underpinning masculine values with the focus on face-to-face competition, winning and the associated jockeying for masculine status. In their adoption of parkour these athletes were seemingly attempting to distance themselves from the performative masculinities of traditional NZ sports, particularly in relation to the dominance of rugby (see Pringle 2004) and, in contrast, develop a sporting identity divergent from dominant NZ narratives (see Falcous 2007). A parkour coach noted this trend and commented, "We're slowly getting the boys that are going 'I'm not going to play rugby anymore, I'm just going to do parkour'" (personal communication, July 2017). While this coach's comments appear to suggest a rejection of some of the masculine performances associated with contact sports such as rugby, equally his focus on "boys" highlights the male-dominated nature of both rugby and parkour. Yet the parkour players apparent rejection of Kiwi "bloke" values, was complicated by the reality that during their participation they take physical risks, admire physicality and jockey for a degree of masculine status: thus reflecting the complexity of inferring masculinities via Derrida's ongoing process of deferral of meanings.

However, some of the players observations about masculine performances were very transparent. The importance of the physical landscape, for example, means that parkour is "often measured by the distance or height of something" (personal communication, December 2016). This "measuring" creates the opportunity for the exaltation of physical prowess, and demonstrations of such prowess become a measure of masculine standing. Commenting on the masculinities of such displays of physical prowess, a NZ participant noted that at some parkour gatherings, "the first day and a half is like a dick measuring contest ... to see who can do the gnarliest shit" (personal communication, November 2016). In apparent contrast, Damien (see, Puddle 2019) reported that women with similar body sizes and levels of experience performed many of the same kinds of physical movements. Nevertheless, despite these similarities of physical movement, Damien found that many core movements were gendered as masculine within New Zealand in a similar manner to what has been observed internationally (see, for example, Tran 2008). Hence, the female participants did not necessarily gain the same "masculine" respect thus revealing that a participant's biological sex could influence how their body and their performances were read by other participants.

Despite the virile analogy noted above of parkour performances being competitive "dick measuring", like De Martini Ugolotti (2015) in Italy, Damien (Puddle 2019) did not witness overt macho displays of skill at local parkour community events. Nor did he see the same kinds of masculine displays identified by Kidder (2013) in his Chicago cohort, such as "shirtless o'clock", or Wheaton's

154 Hamish Crocket et al.

(2016) description of English male practitioners purposefully displaying their "chests and pecs". This is an important observation because it demonstrates that the sportisation of parkour in the NZ context has resulted in different expressions of masculinity than in other nations and communities overseas, suggesting no homogenous global representation of masculinity in parkour.

Within ultimate, as noted above, many of the most skilled performances – throws over 40 metres in distance, diving to catch or block the disc, outjumping opponents to catch or block the disc – are gendered as masculine, at least by many male participants (Crocket 2013). However, both male and female players who perform these skills are recognised as elite athletes by other players, and female players within this elite cadre are not regarded as "manly". Similarly, while the masculine trait of playing through some degree of pain and injury is widely considered to be a normal part of ultimate, players who take excessive risks by playing through serious injury, or returning to play without adequate rehabilitation after a serious injury do not gain additional status for prioritising their team and victory over bodily health. Rather, it is players who exhibit care for self and others – by avoiding physical contact, by refraining from playing through serious injury, by checking on the status of their opponent should a collision occur – that are accorded greater status within the ultimate community. In this sense, it is important to acknowledge that a range of both masculine and feminine performances are expected and valued of male and female ultimate players.

Amongst male-ultimate players in particular, it is notable that poorly executed plays and a lack of willingness to endure minor levels of pain and discomfort are gendered as feminine (see Crocket 2013). Yet many of the male players who make these assertions and engage in sexist jokes when playing on male-only teams also dedicate time and effort to supporting women's ultimate. The gendered performances of ultimate players defy reduction into narrow definitions of feminine and masculine, and equally, the gendered performances of any given player can rarely be uniformly interpreted as "problematic" or "unproblematic". These performances are complex and difficult to interpret with any certainty via Derrida's processes of meaning deferral and deconstruction, as such, we regard the gendered performances amongst individual players as multiple, fragmented and seemingly divergent.

Concluding words

In summary, then, processes of sportisation are evident in both ultimate and parkour within Aotearoa New Zealand. Both sports have become increasingly codified and organised, while also significantly growing participation numbers. This process of sportisation can be deemed to reflect masculine values, as it is underpinned by an interest in organisation, hierarchical structures, rules, timetables, training methods and ultimately a focus on winning and finances. Yet, at the same time, this sportisation process has focused on diminishing specific

Masculinities in alternative sports   **155**

problematic "masculine" performances as well as the promotion of gender equity. In ultimate, for example, aspects of the broader lifestyle, namely the centrality of tournament parties featuring determined drunkenness (Crocket 2016a), have been largely removed from high level competition, while in parkour, formal competition is now sanctioned by the national governing body. Moreover, rather than presaging the advent of the harmful, "win-at-all-costs" masculinities that are central to modern achievement sport (Messner 1992), these changes have not (yet) lead to the widespread adoption of these problematic masculine performances. On the contrary, a range of performances that might typically be understood as feminine, such as avoidance of player-to-player contact when making a play on the disc in ultimate and performing movements within one's own limits of ability, skill and risk, are widely valued within each sport.

Equally, neither of these case studies offer a utopian alternative to the gendering effects of modern achievement sport. In both sports, often the most highly valued athletic performances are gendered as masculine and males make up the majority of participants. Additionally, there are many ways in which participating women are subtly positioned as inferior in ways that male participants may inadvertently, or in some cases explicitly, reproduce. For example, in ultimate, many male receivers tend to crowd female throwers, only allowing them to make a short throw to a male receiver who, having caught the disc, will invariably expect their team mates to not crowd around and thus allow a longer throw to be made (Crocket 2016a). Relatedly, in parkour, the vault known as a "cat-pass" is commonly one of the first movements taught to novices. Two of Damien's participants suggested that this move tended to be easier for men to execute due to their higher centre of gravity and that most male participants were unaware that this basic manoeuvre might be more difficult for women to perform.

In light of these observations, we highlight that the influence of processes such as sportisation have not been uniform, and the founding ethics that underpinned ultimate and parkour have been re-interpreted, rather than discarded, in the face of increasing regulation and organisation. Relatedly, our *readings* of the construction and performance of masculinities in these settings, via Derrida and Foucault, support Fitzclarence and Hickey's (2001) conclusion from two decades ago, that sport does not unambiguously produce culturally dominant conceptions of masculinities but that shifts, complexities and contradictions are ongoing. In this sense, it is important to highlight the murkiness of masculinities within alternative sports in Aotearoa New Zealand. While engaging in these sports may be an important aspect of how participants come to identify themselves, there is no singular way of performing masculinities in these sports. Through their participation, we argue, alternative sport athletes are likely to perform a range of masculinities and femininities, rather than adhere to a narrowly defined gender archetype. The ability and legitimacy of performing gender in diverse ways within these sports is, however, a sign of optimism yet progress and activism is still warranted.

156 Hamish Crocket et al.

Notes

1 In the United States, some elite tournaments have "observers", who can be invited by players to make a binding call on a particular play. At world championship level, match officials are available to clarify rules, but are not able to make any binding decisions.
2 Taukōkai means to glide [flow], move quickly, reach. This describes the manner in which parkour practitioners glide fluidly over their terrain.

References

Angel, J. 2011, '*Ciné Parkour: A cinematic and theoretical contribution to the understanding of the practice of parkour'*, PhD thesis, Brunel University, London.

Atkinson, M. 2009, 'Parkour, anarcho-environmentalism, and poiesis', *Journal of Sport & Social Issues*, Vol. 33, no. 2, pp. 169–194. https://doi.org/10.1177/0193723509332582

Atkinson, M. 2010, 'Entering scapeland: yoga, fell and post-sport physical cultures', *Sport in Society*, Vol. 13, no. 7–8, pp. 1249–1267, https://doi.org/10.1080/17430431003780260

Clegg, J. L. & Butryn, T. M. 2012, 'An existential phenomenological examination of parkour and freerunning', *Qualitative Research in Sport, Exercise and Health*, Vol. 4, no. 3, pp. 320–340, https://doi.org/10.1080/2159676X.2012.693527

Crocket, H. 2013, '"This is men's ultimate": (re)creating multiple masculinities in elite open ultimate Frisbee', *International Review for the Sociology of Sport*, Vol. 48, no. 3, pp. 318–333, https://doi.org/10.1177/1012690211435185

Crocket, H. 2015a, 'Foucault, flying discs and calling fouls: ascetic practices of the self in Ultimate Frisbee', *Sociology of Sport Journal*, Vol. 32, no. 1, pp. 89–105, https://doi.org/10.1123/ssj.2013-0039

Crocket, H. 2015b, '"I'm just going to be silly with this person": exploring the ethics of humour and irony in ultimate Frisbee', *Qualitative Research in Sport, Exercise and Health*, Vol. 7, no. 5, pp. 557–572, https://doi.org/10.1080/2159676X.2014.981575

Crocket, H. 2016a, 'An ethic of indulgence? Alcohol, ultimate Frisbee and calculated hedonism', *International Review for Sociology of Sport*, Vol. 51, no. 5, pp. 617–631, https://doi.org/10.1177/1012690214543960

Crocket, H. 2016b, 'The changing face of ultimate Frisbee and the politics of inclusion', in H. Thorpe & R. Olive (eds.), *Women in action sports*, Palgrave Macmillan, London, pp. 259–278.

Crocket, H. 2016c, 'Tie-dye shirts and compression leggings: an examination of cultural tensions within Ultimate Frisbee via dress', *Annals of Leisure Research*, Vol. 19, no. 2, pp. 194–211. https://doi.org/10.1080/11745398.2015.1106326

Crocket, H. 2018, 'Grappling with ambiguity and contradiction: an examination of the role of reflexivity in coach education research', *Sports Coaching Review*, Vol. 7, no. 1, pp. 82–99, https://doi.org/10.1080/21640629.2017.1361167

De Freitas, E. 2011, 'Parkour and the built environment, spatial practices and the plasticity of school buildings', *Journal of Curriculum Theorising*, Vol. 27, no. 3, pp. 209–220.

De Martini Ugolotti, N. 2015, 'Climbing walls, making bridges: children of immigrants' identity negotiations through capoeira and parkour in Turin', *Leisure Studies*, Vol. 34, no. 1, pp. 19–33, https://doi.org/10.1080/02614367.2014.966746

Derrida, J. 1978, *Writing and difference*, Trans. Alan Bass, University of Chicago Press, Chicago, IL.

Donaldson, M. 1993, 'What is hegemonic masculinity?' *Theory & Society*, Vol. 22, no. 5, pp. 643–657.

Falcous, M. 2007, 'Rugby league in the national imaginary of New Zealand Aotearoa', *Sport in History,* Vol. 27, no. 3, pp. 423–446.

Fitzclarence, L. & Hickey, C. 2001, 'Real footballers don't eat quiche: old narratives in new times', *Men and Masculinities,* Vol. 4, no. 2, pp. 118–139.

Gilchrist, P. & Wheaton, B. 2011, 'Lifestyle sport, public policy and youth engagement: examining the emergence of parkour', *International Journal of Sport Policy and Politics,* Vol. 3, no. 1, pp. 109–131. https://doi.org/10.1080/19406940.2010.547866

Griggs, G. 2011, '"This must be the only sport in the world where most of the players don't know the rules": operationalizing self-refereeing and the spirit of the game in UK Ultimate Frisbee', *Sport in Society,* Vol. 14, no. 1, pp. 97–110, https://doi.org/10.1080/17430437.2011.530013

Guss, N. 2011, 'Parkour and the multitude: politics of a dangerous art', *French Cultural Studies,* Vol. 22, no. 1, pp. 73–85, https://doi.org/10.1177/0957155810386675

Guttmann, A. 2004, *Sport: The first five millennia,* University of Massachusetts Press, Amherst, MA.

Kidder, J. L. 2013, 'Parkour, masculinity, and the city', *Sociology of Sport Journal,* Vol. 30, no. 1, pp. 1–23.

Kimmel, M. 2010, *Misframing men: The politics of contemporary masculinities,* Rutgers University Press, Piscataway, NJ.

Maguire, J. 2013, 'Sportization', in G. Ritzer (ed.), *The Blackwell online encyclopedia of sociology,* Wiley-Blackwell, Malden, MA, https://doi.org/10.1002/9781405165518.wbeoss242.pub2

Marshall, B. 2010, 'Running across the rooves of empire: parkour and the postcolonial city', *Modern & Contemporary France,* Vol. 18, no. 2, pp. 157–173. https://doi.org/10.1080/09639481003714872

Messner, M. A. 1992, *Power at play: sports and the problem of masculinity,* Beacon Press, Boston, MA.

Midol, N. 1993, 'Cultural dissents and technical innovations in the "whiz" sports', *International Review for the Sociology of Sport,* Vol. 28, no. 1, pp. 23–32, https://doi.org/10.1177/101269029302800102

Parkour NZ. 2017, 'Who are we', viewed 10 March 2021, http://nzparkour.co.nz/about/#1

Pringle, R. 2004, 'A social-history of the articulations between rugby union and masculinities within Aotearoa/New Zealand', *New Zealand Sociology,* Vol. 19, no. 1, pp. 102–128.

Pringle, R. & Crocket, H. 2013, 'Coaching with Foucault: an examination of applied sports ethics', in P. Potrac, W. Gilbert & J. Denison (eds.), *Routledge handbook of sports coaching,* Routledge, Oxon, pp. 16–26.

Pringle, R. & Hickey, C. 2010, 'Negotiating masculinities via the moral problematization of sport', *Sociology of Sport Journal,* Vol. 27, no. 2, pp. 115–138.

Pringle, R., Kay, T. & Jenkins, J. M. 2011, 'Masculinities, gender relations and leisure studies: are we there yet?', *Annals of Leisure Research,* Vol. 14, no. 2–3, pp. 107–119.

Pringle, R. & Markula, P. 2005, 'No pain is sane after all: a Foucauldian analysis of masculinities and men's rugby experiences of fear, pain, and pleasure', *Sociology of Sport Journal,* Vol. 22, no. 4, pp. 472–497.

Puddle, D. 2019, *Making the jump: Examining the glocalisation of parkour in Aotearoa New Zealand,* PhD thesis, The University of Waikato, Hamilton, New Zealand, https://researchcommons.waikato.ac.nz/handle/10289/12712

Puddle, D., Wheaton, B. & Thorpe, H. 2019, 'The glocalization of parkour: a New Zealand/Aotearoa case study', *Sport in Society,* Vol. 22, no.10, pp. 1724–1741. https://doi.org/10.1080/17430437.2018.1441010

158 Hamish Crocket et al.

Ralph, B. & Roberts, S. 2020, 'Theories of men and masculinity, and their ability to account for positive change', in R. Magrath, J. Cleland & E. Anderson (eds.), *The Palgrave handbook of masculinity and sport*, Palgrave Macmillan, Cham, pp. 19–38.

Rinehart, R. E. 2000, 'Emerging arriving sport: alternatives to formal sports', in J. Coakley & E. Dunning (eds.), *Handbook of sport studies*, Sage, London, pp. 504–519.

Saville, S. J. 2008, 'Playing with fear: parkour and the mobility of emotion', *Social & Cultural Geography*, Vol. 9, no. 8, pp. 891–914. https://doi.org/10.1080/14649360802441440

Stewart, I. 2018, *World junior ultimate championships round up*. Ultimate, viewed 10 March 2021, https://ultimate.org.nz/p/world-junior-ultimate-championships-round-up

Theberge, N. 1981, 'A critique of critiques: radical and feminist writings on sport', *Social Forces*, Vol. 60, pp. 341–353.

Thornton, A. 2004, '"Anyone can play this game": ultimate Frisbee, identity and difference', in B. Wheaton (ed.), *Understanding lifestyle sport: Consumption, identity and difference*, Routledge, Oxon, pp. 175–196.

Thorpe, H. 2010a, '"Have board, will travel": global physical youth cultures and transnational mobility', in J. Maguire & M. Falcous (eds.), *Sport and migration: Borders, boundaries and crossings*, Routledge, Oxon, pp. 112–126.

Thorpe, H. 2010b, 'Bourdieu, gender reflexivity, and physical culture: a case of masculinities in the snowboarding field', *Journal of Sport and Social Issues*, Vol. 34, no 2, pp. 176–214, https://doi.org/10.1177/0193723510367770

Tran, A. 2008, *Parkour: Issues of gender*. Girl Parkour, viewed 10 March 2021, http://www.girlparkour.org/articles/2008/05/parkour-issues-of-gender

Waitt, G. & Warren, A. 2008, '"Talking shit over a brew after a good session with your mates": surfing, space and masculinity', *Australian Geographer*, Vol. 39, no. 3, pp. 353–365, https://doi.org/10.1080/00049180802270549

Waling, A. 2019, 'Rethinking masculinity studies: feminism, masculinity, and poststructural accounts of agency and emotional reflexivity, *The Journal of Men's Studies*, Vol. 27, no. 1, pp. 89–107.

Wheaton, B. 2004a, 'Introduction: mapping the lifestyle sport-scape', in B. Wheaton (ed.), *Understanding lifestyle sports: Consumption, identity and difference*, Routledge, Oxon, pp. 1–28.

Wheaton, B. 2004b, '"New lads"? Competing masculinities in the windsurfing culture', in B. Wheaton (ed.), *Understanding lifestyle sports: Consumption, identity and difference*, Routledge, Oxon, pp. 131–153.

Wheaton, B. 2013, 'Risk-taking and regulation: examining the sportization of parkour', in B. Wheaton (ed.), *The cultural politics of lifestyle sports*, Routledge, Oxon, pp. 71–97.

Wheaton, B. 2016, 'Parkour, gendered power and the politics of identity', in H. Thorpe & R. Olive (eds.), *Women in action sport cultures*, Palgrave Macmillian, London, pp. 111–132.

Wheaton, B. & O'Loughlin, A. 2017, 'Informal sport, institutionalisation, and sport policy: challenging the sportization of parkour in England', *International Journal of Sport Policy and Politics*, Vol. 9, no. 1, pp. 71–88.

14

THE CONTRIBUTION OF POSITIVE RELATIONSHIPS TO GIRLS WELLBEING IN A NEW ZEALAND SCHOOL BASKETBALL TEAM

Ricardo Milheiro Pimenta and Richard L. Light

Introduction

There has long been recognition of the potential benefits that sport offers for children and young people with a traditional focus on moral, ethical, social and personal learning. More recently, there is growing interest in its possible benefits for health, wellbeing and, social and personal development (Kerr & Stirling 2013; Light 2010; Wright et al. 2013). While this is a positive development, it must be considered in relation to decreasing participation in sport from the early teens, as a global development, and recognition that participating in sport does not necessarily lead to these benefits.

We see two important issues here in regard to helping young people realise the range of benefits that sport offers. The first is the challenge of maximising the number of children and young people participating in sport. Research on youth sport consistently identifies the importance of social relationships, meaning and enjoyment as factors that make participation in sport attractive for young people and help keep them in sport (see Harvey & Light 2013). This is an issue of quantity.

The quality of participation in sport is the second issue. As Harvey et al. (2013) suggest with regard to ethical learning, learning is not "caught" by playing sport. It has to be "taught" by the teacher and can be "taught" by the nature of young people's experiences and the socio-cultural context in which it occurs. Learning in and through sport is shaped by the learners' depth of engagement, the meaning it has for them, their sense of competence, sense of achievement and, how much fun it is. The bulk of studies on young people's participation in sport highlight the importance of participation being positive. This is particularly important when considering how sport can make positive contributions to wellbeing.

DOI: 10.4324/9781003034445-14

The study we report on in this chapter inquired into why New Zealand adolescent girls joined and remained in a school basketball team. In our analysis we draw on Seligman (2011) and others' work in Positive Psychology with a strong focus on the PERMA model for happiness and wellbeing. This model draws on over two decades of research to identify six factors that most contribute to happiness and wellbeing in life. One of these six factors is positive relationships, which is the focus of this chapter.

With its roots in humanistic psychology, Positive Psychology focuses on what is good about life and what makes it worth living, as opposed to the focus of mainstream psychology on identifying and treating mental illness. The PERMA model identifies what conditions facilitate and produce happiness and subjective wellbeing in life. The conditions it identifies are: Positive emotions, Engagement, positive Relationships, life having Meaning, and having a sense of Achievement. The PERMA model is focused on life experience but in this chapter, we apply it to sport.

Relationships and happiness in sport

Positive relationships in sport between peers/athletes, coaches and athletes have been identified as being important for enhancing enjoyment and performance at all levels of sport (see, Evans 2014; Riley & Smith 2011; Smoll et al. 2011) and particularly for girls (Light & Kentel 2015; Weiss & Kipp 2018). The importance of peer relationships for young people is particularly evident in paediatric sport psychology studies (Padilla-Walker et al. 2014) and has been identified as making one of the strongest contributions towards enjoyment in sport (Jaakkola et al. 2017).

Young people who experience positive peer relationships have higher levels of enjoyment and commitment to the activity they are involved in (Atkins et al. 2015). The development of positive peer relationships is facilitated by an emotional and supportive environment that builds confidence and in which students/athletes feel valued and have a sense of belonging. In these environments there is an emphasis on collective effort that enhances the participants enjoyment and encourages creativity and reflection (Keegan et al. 2009; Light & Harvey 2019).

Methodology

Focused on six, 13 to 17-year-old girls in a private school basketball team and their coach in New Zealand, this study aimed to find out why the girls chose to play basketball and continued to play it. It adopted a combined ethnographic and grounded theory methodology with the lead author acting as a participant observer. This combination is compatible because ethnographic studies can generate the thick description that provides such valuable data for grounded theory analysis (Glaser & Strauss 1968). Ethnography involves observing and analysing behaviour as it naturally occurs (Belk et al. 1988) and grounded theory is most effective when data are generated in natural settings (Robrecht 1995).

Participants and selection

The study was approved by the University of Canterbury Ethics Committee. The participants were selected through purposive sampling, with the six girls and their coach in the study referred to using pseudonyms.

Data generation

The first author adopted the role of participant observer by working as an assistant coach over the entire season. Data collection was conducted over a six month period, beginning in March 2016. Data were generated through participant observation, field notes, and three rounds of semi-structured interviews that lasted between 30 and 45min for each one.

Data analysis

We analysed the data by using a constructivist grounded theory process (Charmaz 2006). This involved developing substantive theory from data in a continuous process of data generation and analysis. In this process the use of formal theory and literature is delayed until theoretical saturation reached a point at which we could not develop conceptual theories (see, Charmaz 2006; Glaser & Strauss 1968). Substantive themes were developed and then elevated to conceptual theory by drawing on the relevant literature and formal theory.

Findings

The three factors that most contributed to the girls' positive experiences of basketball were: (1) relationships, (2) how the team provided a safe haven from stress outside basketball and, (3) a sense of individual and collective achievement. In this chapter we focus on relationships with peers and between the players and the coach.

Relationships with peers

The girls all felt that support for each other and strong interpersonal bonds most motivated them to continue to play basketball. They all enjoyed interacting with their peers. They valued the relationships they developed through being in the team and were welcoming to new players like Sophie. From her first day in the team, the other girls did their best to develop good relationships with her and help her be part of the team. When asked, "What do you like about the team?"

all the girls responses highlighted the central importance of social interaction and the deep bonds between them:

> I like the girls. They are super fun to hang with and we have a really good time. We've known each other for three or four years now and in the beginning, it wasn't like this, but I believe we became really close. We just laugh with each other. I can say that I genuinely care about every girl here.
>
> *(Jessica, int. 1)*

Sophie was new to the school and had some challenges settling in but she found the transition into a new team easier than she had anticipated:

> It's hard changing schools and get to know people all over again but it's different with these girls... like they made me feel welcomed straight away. I thought it would take me some time to get to know them, but they are super friendly, and it makes it easier to be a part of this team.
>
> *(Sophie, int. 1)*

Any social group typically, experiences some tensions and disagreements but, over the season the first author did not note any major conflict within the team. As the oldest player and team captain, Anna was the social glue that held the team together. She always encouraged her teammates, even when they were "little bit hard" to deal with:

> There are some people that are a little bit hard but still get along with them. There is a couple of girls that I've gone through school with, and I've kinda known them for a while. I try to be supportive of everybody but if I have to call somebody out, I don't have a problem with that.
>
> *(Anna, int. 1)*

As complicated as relationships can be, those in this team developed confidence in each other, provided emotional and moral support, and emphasised collective effort.

Over the season, the first author saw the girls' relationships develop within the team, and noted the formation of smaller relationships within the team. Jessica and Sarah were from the same year group at school, had played basketball together since they were children and were very close friends:

> It's good to have that kind of support. Having someone on the field that understands you and that you can talk to besides the coach is a pretty nice. I can talk with Jessica if I think I'm sucking and she helps me get my spirits back up.
>
> *(Sarah, int. 2)*

The close relationships developed in the team promoted trust and allowed them to be completely open with their coach and teammates. The girls felt so comfortable in the team environment that some described it as a family, and this was the intent of the coach:

> They have to know something about their teammates' lives outside of basketball. I want them to trust each other outside of the court so it transfers that trust into the game. I believe that trust and knowing each other is more important than any type of play or skill I could teach them.
>
> *(Sylvia, int. 1)*

The coach placed great importance on building an environment of trust and care for each other: "With girls I believe if you show you care for them, they will learn and play hard for you, regardless" (Sylvia, int. 1).

Relationships with the coach

As Jowett (2017) suggests, leadership is a shared role that requires meaningful interaction and positive relationships. Sylvia and the girls had a symbiotic relationship. Sylvia's support for the girls made a strong contribution to their being able to play well enough to be elevated to the top league and then place in the top four in the next season. At the same time, without the girls' talent, commitment, and enthusiasm, Sylvia would not have been successful. The collective belief of this group created an enhanced environment within which the girls felt confident in their capabilities as a team to perform tasks in a coordinated, well-organised, and successful fashion (Bandura 1997). Positive relationships and emotions, and success on the court, created an environment in which they flourished.

The girls' skills and performance improved through Sylvia's focus on their social skills and the relationships in the team. Her development of good relationships with the girls did not just develop over time. It was an intended part of her coaching approach, as suggested by her warmth towards new girls in the team from their first day. As a new member of the team, Sophie's view of Sylvia reflects the trust between the players and the coach:

> I never met Sylvia before, but she's great... the coach in my previous school was friendly but I like Sylvia's vibe... I don't know. She seems the type of person I can open up to and she will listen and try to help me.
>
> *(Sophie, int. 2)*

Sylvia adopted a maternal approach to her coaching that she clearly and regularly articulated herself. During long conversations in the car travelling to and from games, she would typically say, "I'm more like a mum to them". Even her own daughter expressed their belief that her mother was like a mother to all the girls in the team: "She is more of a mother figure because we're part of the team and mum treats everyone equally". Sylvia went into more detail on her maternal approach that resonates with the role of a mentor (McKenzie 2019):

> We are here to educate them as well... our job is to teach them how to play basketball, but you know with girls it's just that the emotional side is always present, and you have to be aware of it and really care for them... make them feel important.
>
> *(Sylvia, int. 1)*

Coaches are typically expected to run "quality" training sessions and prepare players for competition (Short & Short 2005) but, for Sylvia and many other coaches, there is more to coaching than just developing technique and tactical knowledge (Stodter & Cushion 2019).

Coaches like Sylvia are also an important source of support for athletes when they experience stressful situations (Jowett & Nezlek 2011). Sylvia was always aware of, and interested in, what was going on outside of practice sessions for the girls. Several times during the season the first author noticed her pulling some of the girls aside to talk to them and asked her about it. Her response was:

> It might be pretentious of me, but I can almost see when somebody is feeling down. I pulled Jessica out of training last night because she didn't look like herself, and I was right. She was feeling a lot of pressure to have good grades from her parents and she just wanted someone to listen to her.
>
> *(Sylvia, int. 1)*

Jessica enjoyed having someone who could instantly pick her up when she was not feeling good and someone who genuinely cared about her:

> I believe there's *(sic)* not a lot of coaches like Sylvia... the way she cares it's something that I never had from my other coaches... it's almost like she can sense when we are not ok or having a bad day, it's crazy sometimes, and every single one of us can open up to her. I feel appreciated and heard.
>
> *(Jessica, int. 2)*

Having someone to confide in and who cared for her was of particular importance for Sophie because she was a boarder at the school. She only saw her parents on the weekends. Towards the end of the year Sophie was having some problems at school and needed someone to talk to. Sylvia was that person. Sophie would talk to Sylvia and seek advice before, or after almost every training session:

> It's been hard with the rowing and boarding, and I don't have as many friends like I wanted to, but Sylvia has been pretty awesome with me and has been helping through this. I like that I have someone that I can open

up with and she always asks me how I'm doing and knows if I'm lying so I know I can open up to her and tell her what is going on.

(Sophie, int. 3)

Relationships in sport teams often reflect a separation of the coach from, and elevation above the athlete or athletes (Light & Harvey 2019), but not with this team. There was less of the power difference between coach and players and more of the equal relationship of power promoted in athlete-centred coaching (see Light & Harvey 2019). In place of the monologue of directive coaching, there was productive dialogue between coach and players that is normally found in athlete-centred coaching such as Teaching Games for Understanding and Game Sense (see Light 2013).

Sylvia saw her players as thinking, feeling people with a life outside the sport. Her approach echoed the humanistic and holistic nature of athlete-centred coaching approaches (Light et al. 2015). It is also evident in the approach adopted by the world renowned, New Zealand All Blacks (Evans 2012, 2014). She acknowledged the importance of the girls' lives outside of basketball and took the time in every session or game to talk to the girls. Despite caring for her players and the positive relationship she had with the team, she was very demanding. Although the environment was supportive, she set standards that she expected the team to meet:

With Sylvia, although she can be a bit scary sometimes, I feel like I've gotten a lot more confident, sometimes I would be nervous to take the shot, but I feel like she releases the pressure "if you miss don't worry about it they can get back". I know that she does like me, and she thinks I'm a good player and stuff, so I don't let anything (negative) that she says about my game worry me I don't take it heart because is just to help me.

(Grace, int. 2)

While Sylvia focused the team on being the best they could be and winning games, it was not win-win at all costs. Her coaching focused on the whole team doing the best it could every week to make the girls better basketball players and better people. All she asked from the girls was to play their best as her daughter suggests:

Yeah, my mum can be intense sometimes in games... she always on my and Mary's case... but we are already used to it, she coached us in almost every sport we've both been on... she even coached us when we started gymnastics when we were young.

(Anna, int. 3)

Anna and Mary had a different relationship with Sylvia on the basketball court, they would always call Sylvia by her name. There were a few moments when

Mary would call her "mum" and she would say "I'm not mum here I'm Sylvia". Sylvia did not want the rest of the team to think she was treating her daughters differently:

> It's a funny thing coaching your daughters, I think I try to be fair to everybody, but I know that I'm harsher on them than the rest of team. I want the team to feel that everybody is on equal footing, that if my daughters screw up they will get the same treatment as the rest of them.
>
> *(Sylvia, int. 1)*

Mary believed that Sylvia was always looking out for the best interests of the team, and it was a plus having her mum coaching the team because she knew her strengths and weaknesses:

> When you give away the ball or you get the ball taken off you, it doesn't really matter, but she yells at you and you don't want to feel like you're letting her down as much as someone else because she related to me. Because she knows my strength and weaknesses she knows I'm not comfortable dribbling, and if I get the ball taken of me she'll know that I tried my best.
>
> *(Mary, int. 2)*

Sylvia's approach was not demanding to a point where she alienated the players. She took a humanistic approach (see, Light & Light, 2021), but this did not necessarily mean being easy or soft on players. She set standards and drove them to do their best over a very successful season. This earned her respect from the girls who also felt her care for them:

> …Our school is not known to be quite high up in basketball. So that helps, but I reckon the coach plays a big part in the team culture. Compared to the other coaches I've had through other sports she's definitely been one of the understanding ones, in terms of your personality wise.
>
> *(Sophie, int. 2)*

Relationships in successful competitive teams provide important support for individuals during intense, stressful events regardless of culture (Light & Yasaki 2017). Close relationships have the ability to aid individuals deal with stressful events, in their personal and sporting life, but "also enable individuals to prevent stressful events" (Pierce et al. 1996, p. 441).

Emotional support was more visible during the close games throughout the year, particularly when the team needed a couple of points to win and fell short. During these games everybody would huddle, interlock their arms and say what was positive about the game and what needed to be improved for the next game. Sylvia would always finish with "I'm proud of you" which appeared to make the girls happy that their effort was recognised.

Discussion

This study suggests the importance of relationships for the development of the positive wellbeing of the girls in the study. At the same time, these relationships also made an important contribution to the performance of the team. Basketball made these girls happy through being in a team with strong positive relationships. As Seligman (2011) suggests, people cannot attain happiness alone because it can only be experienced with others.

Relationships appeared to most contribute to the girls' experiences of fun and enjoyment and to giving basketball meaning in their lives. From the start of the study the team was really tight with the girls all supportive of each other. This extended to new players like Sophie, who felt "a part of the group right from the start" (Int. 1). Research on children's and youth sport consistently identifies the pivotal role that the social dimensions of sport play in attracting and retaining them and reaching peak performance (Light et al. 2013). Of course, the social experiences of young people in sport can work both ways. It can have a positive influence (see Ommundsen et al. 2006) or a negative one (see Santos et al. 2017). In this study the positive social environment and experiences of the girls were built around positive relationships.

While we focused on one team in this study, the positive influence of the coach's approach must be considered within the context of coaching in New Zealand and the use of athlete-centred approaches. At the elite level, this is reflected in the coaching of professional rugby (see Evans 2014), but similar coaching is adopted across a range of sport in New Zealand. For example, the NZ Coach Approach that "promotes athlete learning, and ownership of that learning through creating awareness, responsibility and self-belief" (New Zealand Golf, n. d.).

In this study the girls felt like they belonged. They knew they could count on their friends/teammates for support whenever they needed it and striving to win each game strengthened their relationships. This was also one of the findings in a study on a high-performance team of girls who were a similar age in Australia (Light & Pimenta 2020, Light & Yasaki 2017). The literature suggests that positive peer relationships increase young people's enjoyment and commitment to an activity, such as sport (Atkins et al. 2015) with other research identifying the positive influence of a supportive environment on enjoyment and performance (Keegan et al. 2009).

Drawing on the PERMA model (Seligman 2012) and applying it to this study illuminates how positive emotions, engagement, positive relationships and achievement (of the team) interacted to promote happiness and positive wellbeing. Relationships cannot be separated from the other elements of the PERMA model, but they were central to the creation of a very positive environment. It was also an environment intentionally created and developed by the coach to achieve her aims of facilitating the personal, social and physical learning she valued.

168 Ricardo Milheiro Pimenta and Richard L. Light

This study highlights the importance of relationships for coaching and particularly for contemporary approaches in New Zealand that adopt more athlete-centred approaches where relationships are of prime importance (see Evans 2014). As Jowett (2017) argues, the effectiveness and success of coaching is dependent on the relationship between coach and the athlete(s). It is equally important between the athletes or players in the team or squad as a social group.

References

Atkins, M. R., Johnson, D. M., Force, E. C. & Petrie, T. A. 2015, 'Peers, parents, and coaches, oh my! The relation of the motivational climate to boys' intention to continue in sport', *Psychology of Sport and Exercise*, Vol. 16, pp. 170–180, https://doi.org/10.1016/j.psychsport.2014.10.008

Bandura A. 1997, *Self-efficacy: The exercise of control*, Freeman, New York.

Belk, R. W., J. F. Sherry, and M. Wallendorf, 1988, 'A naturalistic inquiry into buyer and seller behavior at a swap meet', *Journal of Consumer Research*, Vol. 14, no. 4, pp. 449–470. https://doi.org/10.1086/209128

Charmaz, K. 2006, *Constructing grounded theory: A practical guide through qualitative analysis*, Sage, London.

Evans, J. R. 2012, 'Elite rugby coaches' interpretation and use of game sense in New Zealand', *Asian Journal of Exercise and Sport Science*, Vol. 9, no. 1, pp. 85–97.

Evans, J. R. 2014, 'The nature and importance of coach-player relations in the uptake of Game Sense by elite rugby coaches in Australia and New Zealand', in R. L. Light, S. Harvey & A. Mooney (eds.), *Contemporary developments in games teaching*, Routledge, London & New York, pp. 133–146.

Glaser, B. G. & Strauss, A. L. 1968, *The discovery of grounded theory: Strategies for qualitative research*, Weidenfeld & Nicolson, London.

Harvey, S., Kirk, D. & O'Donovan, T. M. 2013, 'Sport Education as pedagogy for promoting sport as ethical practice', in S. Harvey & R. L Light (eds.), *Ethics in youth sport: Policy and pedagogical implications,* Routledge, London & New York, pp. 107–121.

Harvey, S. & Light, R. L. (eds.), 2013, *Ethics in youths port: Policy and pedagogical implications*, Routledge, London & New York.

Jaakkola, T., Yli-Piipari, S., Barkoukis, V. & Liukkonen, J. 2017, 'Relationships among perceived motivational climate, motivational regulations, enjoyment, and PA participation among Finnish physical education students', *International Journal of Sport and Exercise Psychology*, Vol. 15, no. 3, pp. 273–290, https://doi.org/10.1080/1612197X.2015.1100209

Jowett, S. 2017, 'Coaching effectiveness: the coach–athlete relationship at its heart', *Current Opinion in Psychology*, Vol. 16, pp. 154–158, https://doi.org/10.1016/j.copsyc.2017.05.006

Jowett, S. & Nezlek, J. 2011, 'Relationship interdependence and satisfaction with important outcomes in coach-athlete dyads', *Journal of Social and Personal Relationships*, Vol. 29, pp. 287–301, https://doi.org/10.1177/0265407511420980

Keegan, R. J., Harwood, C. G., Spray, C. M. & Lavallee, D. E. 2009, 'A qualitative investigation exploring the motivational climate in early career sports participants: coach, parent and peer influences on sport motivation', *Psychology of Sport and Exercise*, Vol. 10, no. 3, pp. 361–372. https://doi.org/10.1016/j.psychsport.2008.12.003

Kerr, G. & Stirling, A. 2013, 'Putting the child back in children's sport: nurturing young talent in a developmentally appropriate manner', in S. Harvey & R. L Light (eds.), *Ethics in youths port: Policy and pedagogical implications,* Routledge, London & New York, pp. 25–39.

Light, R. L. 2010, 'A cross-cultural study on meaning and the nature of children's experiences in Australian and French swimming clubs', *Asia-Pacific Journal of Health, Sport and Physical Education*, Vol. 1, no. 3–4, pp.37–43, https://doi.org/10.1080/18377122.2010.9730336

Light, R. L. 2013, *Game Sense: Pedagogy for performance, participation and enjoyment*. Routledge, London & New York.

Light, R. L., Evans, J. R., Harvey, S. & Hassanin, R. 2015, *Advances in rugby coaching: An Holistic Approach*, Routledge, London & New York.

Light, R. L. & Harvey, S. 2019, *Positive Pedagogy for coaching*, 2nd edn., Routledge, London & New York.

Light, R. L., Harvey, S. & Memmert, D. 2013, 'Why children join and stay in sports clubs: case studies in Australian, French and German swimming clubs', *Sport Education and Society*, Vol. 18, no. 4, pp. 550–566, https://doi.org/10.1080/13573322.2011.594431

Light, R. L. & Kentel, J. A. 2015, '*Mushin*: learning in technique-intensive sport as uniting mind and body through complex learning theory', *Physical Education and Sport Pedagogy*, Vol. 20, no. 4, pp. 381–396, https://doi.org/10.1080/17408989.2013.868873

Light, R. L. & Light, A. L. (2021), 'Holism and humanism as the philosophical foundations of Game Sense', in R. L. Light & C. Curry (eds.), *Game sense for teaching and coaching: International perspectives*, Routledge, London & New York.

Light, R. L. & Pimenta, R. 2020, 'Why Adolescent girls play basketball in Australia and its meaning for them', *World Journal of Social Science Research*, Vol. 7, no. 2, pp. 52–65. https://doi.org/10.22158/wjssr.v7n2p52

Light, R. L. & Yasaki, W. 2017, 'Adolescent girls' experiences of being in Australian and Japanese basketball clubs', *Asia-Pacific Journal of Health, Sport and Physical Education*, Vol. 8, no. 2, pp. 147–160, https://doi.org/10.1080/18377122.2017.1304156

McKenzie, B. C. 2019, *The circuit of concussion knowledge in youth sport: Regulating guidelines and athlete and maternal framing experiences*, PhD thesis, Graduate Department of Exercise Science University of Toronto, Toronto, Canada.

New Zealand Golf,. n.d., viewed 5 August 5, https://www.golf.co.nz/PlayGolf/CoachingPhilosophy.aspx

Ommundsen, Y., Roberts, G. C., Lemyre, P-N. & Miller, B. W. 2006, 'Parental and coach support or pressure on psychosocial outcomes of pediatric athletes in soccer', *Clinical Journal of Sport Medicine*, Vol. 16, no. 6, pp. 522–526, https://doi.org/10.1097/01.jsm.0000248845.39498.56

Padilla-Walker, L. M., Fraser, A. M., Black, B. B. & Bean, R. A. 2014, 'Associations between friendship, sympathy, and prosocial behavior toward friends', *Journal of Research on Adolescence*, Vol. 25, no. 1, pp. 28–35, https://doi.org/10.1111/jora.12108

Pierce, R. G., Sarason, I. G. & Sarason, B. R. 1996, 'Coping and social support', in M. Zeidner & N. S. Endler (eds.), *Handbook of coping*, Wiley, New York, pp. 434–451.

Riley, A. & Smith, A. L. 2011, 'Perceived coach-athlete and peer relationships of young athletes and self-determined motivation for sport', *International Journal of Sport Psychology*, Vol. 42, no. 1, pp. 115–133. https://www.researchgate.net/publication/235760209_Perceived_coach-athlete_and_peer_relationships_of_young_athletes_and_self-determined_motivation_for_sport

Robrecht L. C. 1995, 'Grounded theory: evolving methods', *Qualitative Health Research*, Vol. 5, no. 2, pp. 169–177.

Santos, F., Corte-Real, N., Regueiras, L., Dias, C. & Fonseca, A. 2017, 'Personal and social responsibility development: exploring the perceptions of Portuguese youth football coaches within competitive youth sport', *Sports Coaching Review*, Vol. 6, no. 1, pp. 108–125. https://doi.org/10.1080/21640629.2016.1249643

Seligman, M. E. 2011, *Flourish: A visionary new understanding of happiness and well-being*, Ransom House, Sydney, Australia.

Short, S. E. & Short, M. W. 2005, 'Role of the coach in the coach–athlete relationship', *The Lancet*, Vol. 366, S29–S30. https://doi.org/10.1016/S0140-6736(05)67836-1

Smoll, F. L., Cumming, S. P. & Smith, R. E. 2011, 'Enhancing coach-parent relationships in youth sports: increasing harmony and minimizing hassle', *International Journal of Sports Science and Coaching*, Vol. 6, no. 1, pp. 13–26. https://doi.org/10.1260/1747-9541.6.1.45

Stodter, A. & Cushion, C. J. 2019, 'Evidencing the impact of coaches' learning: changes in coaching knowledge and practice over time', *Journal of Sports Sciences*, Vol. 37, no. 18, pp. 2086–2093. https://doi.org/10.1080/02640414.2019.1621045

Weiss, M. R. & Kipp, L. E. 2018, Social relationships rock! How parents, coaches, and peers can optimize girls' psychological development through sport and physical activity, in *The 2018 Tucker Center Research Report, Developing physically active girls: An evidence-based multidisciplinary approach*. Tucker Center for Research on Girls and Women in Sports, Minneapolis, pp. 37–54.

Wright, P. M., Burroughs, M. D. & Tollefsen, D. 2013, 'Doing moral philosophy with youth in urban programs: strategies from the teaching personal and social responsibility model and the philosophy for children movement', in S. Harvey & R. L Light (eds.), *Ethics in youths sport: Policy and pedagogical implications*, Routledge, London & New York, pp. 174–189.

15

THE HEALTH AND WELLBEING BENEFITS OF ACTIVE AGEING THROUGH PARTICIPATION IN AN ANNUAL SPORTS EVENT

Marching out of the margins

Trudie Walters and Richard Keith Wright

Introduction

The World Health Organisation (WHO 2013) recommends that older adults engage in at least 30 minutes of moderate intensity aerobic activity a day, five days a week and two muscle-strengthening activities and three sessions of balance and flexibility activities per week. Recommended aerobic activities include cycling, golf and walking, whilst tai chi, aqua aerobics and weight training are listed as effective resistance activities. Gardening, pilates and yoga are suggested as activities that can assist with flexibility, whereas bowls and social dancing are presented as activities that help with balance (WHO 2013). To date, however, there has been little focus on the benefits of participant-driven sport event experiences on the mental health of older adults.

In Aotearoa New Zealand, 80 percent of adults (aged 15 years or older) have had direct or indirect experience of mental distress, and data shows this is often linked to feelings of isolation and disconnection (Kvalsvig 2018). While adolescents (those aged 15–19 years) and older adults (those aged 60 and over) are the worst affected members of the community, females are more likely to experience a common mental disorder than males, regardless of age (Community & Public Health 2020; Kvalsvig 2018).

Established in 1977, Aotearoa New Zealand's Mental Health Foundation is a charity that works towards creating a society where all people enjoy positive mental health and wellbeing (Mental Health Foundation 2018). In partnership with the Health Promotion Agency, they launched the *Five Ways to Wellbeing* toolkit in 2018, consisting of five actions adapted from those first created by the UK's New Economic Foundation. These actions are designed to improve physical, psychological and sociological wellbeing: Give; Be Active; Keep Learning;

DOI: 10.4324/9781003034445-15

172 Trudie Walters and Richard Keith Wright

Take Notice; and Connect (Mental Health Foundation 2018; New Economic Foundation 2008).

While the Aotearoa New Zealand toolkit was developed for use in the workplace, it applies equally to life more generally. Here we apply it to a case study analysis of the 2019 New Zealand Leisure Marching Nationals, an annual Aotearoa New Zealand sports event, and offer a rare insight into the clear contribution that even a single annual event can make to the achievement of the *Five Ways to Wellbeing*. In this chapter, we argue that such events may act as a vehicle for active ageing through their contribution to health and wellbeing for an arguably overlooked segment of society: actively ageing "mature ladies".[1]

Leisure marching: A distinctly Aotearoa New Zealand sport

Marching, a competitive team sport for girls and young women, was created in Aotearoa New Zealand in the late 1930s and remained popular as an outdoor summer sport until the late 20th century. It draws on military precision and pageantry, having been described as a "performance of order and highly orchestrated synchronicity" which highlights the girls' bodies by virtue of the fitted uniforms with short skirts that "[draw] attention to the legs and rigid torso" (Macdonald 2011, p. 88). In parts of Australia, marching was used to enact the national policy of indigenous "assimilation" in the mid-20th century; however, this was not the case in Aotearoa New Zealand (Olive et al. 2021). Such was the popularity of marching in Aotearoa New Zealand by the late 1940s that central government had resourced the formation of a national association, and the prime minister, governor general and other leading political and public figures attended the national championships (Macdonald 2011). In 1952, the leading senior team travelled to the UK and Australia to promote the sport: while there was uptake for a period of time, it never flourished as it did in its birthplace (Williams et al. 1993).

Leisure marching, a non-competitive form of the sport, began in 1991 with a group of six women over the age of 50 who decided to form a marching team called "The Marching Grans" for "exercise, fun and friendship" rather than competition (Leisure Marching New Zealand 2017b). Founder Audrey Rodgers recalls:

> I used to see these girls jogging round the streets and keeping fit – everybody was looking for something to do, sports-wise, and I said to my husband Alan, I'd like to start a marching team [...] We'll have to advertise and have a meeting and see how we get on – well, the place was packed out! We formed five teams that night!
>
> *(Sweet Pie Media 2018)*

The team were interviewed on a national primetime television lifestyle show, inspiring a further dozen teams to form around Aotearoa New Zealand within a year. The first New Zealand Open Day for Leisure Marchers was held in Rotorua in 1993, with 22 teams from around the North Island taking part.

Active ageing in marching **173**

TABLE 15.1 Location of leisure marching teams in Aotearoa New Zealand (Leisure Marching New Zealand 2017a; Stats NZ 2017)

Location	Number of teams	Percentage
Major and large urban areas (>30,000 residents)	58	54.7
Medium urban areas (10,000–29,999 residents)	20	18.9
Small urban areas (1,000–9,999 residents)	24	22.6
Rural settlements (200–1,000 residents)	3	2.8
Rural	1	0.9
Totals	**106**	**99.9**

The informal "over 50s" requirement was relaxed over the years, and in 2017 there were 110 leisure marching teams comprised of more than 1,000 "mature ladies" in Aotearoa New Zealand (Leisure Marching New Zealand 2017a). The Leisure Marching Nationals event is held annually, alternating locations between the North and South Islands.

Analysing the location of these teams reveals valuable insights into the structure and reach of the sport in Aotearoa New Zealand, and perhaps some of the reasons for its significance to its mature women participants. In 2006 (the most recent figures available) 72 percent of the Aotearoa New Zealand population lived in main urban areas with more than 30,000 people (Environmental Health Indicators New Zealand 2018). However, the location of the leisure marching teams (Table 15.1) indicates just under 55 percent of teams came from these areas, with a higher percentage living in smaller urban and rural areas.

Active ageing and mental wellbeing

Boudiny (2013) highlights a lack of agreement on what constitutes active ageing, especially when compared with the similar yet subtly different notions of healthy ageing and productive ageing. But in sum, active ageing aims to optimise participation in the range of political, social, cultural, economic and leisure (and other) activities that constitute a full life, and in so doing enhances overall wellbeing (Bowling 2005; Clarke & Warren 2007; Mayhew 2005). Physical activity is one of the "health" pillars of active ageing, with benefits including reduced risk of disease, disability and chronic illness, improved mental wellbeing, maintaining independence and fostering social connection (Fox et al. 2007; WHO 2002). Unfortunately, however, ageist discrimination "is widespread, generally accepted, and largely ignored" (Angus & Reeve 2006, p. 138) and has been found across a range of sectors including within the workplace and in medicine (North and Fiske 2012; Roscigno et al. 2007; Ranzijn 2010; WHO 2002).

Women in particular feel this discrimination, with many noting they feel "invisible" in the eyes of society when they reach their late 40s (Clarke & Griffin 2008). This type of devaluation and stigmatisation may impact their self-esteem and social behaviour (Chrisler 2011). Older women and those living in rural areas face additional challenges such as social isolation, loneliness and less access to health services, which in turn may lead to poor physical and mental health (Keating et al. 2011; North & Fiske 2012; WHO 2002). Indeed, as noted in the introduction, mental health issues disproportionately affect older people and women (Community & Public Health 2020; Kvalsvig 2018). The concept of active ageing then, with its focus on physical, mental and social wellbeing, may therefore be especially beneficial for women, who are more likely than men to live longer (WHO 2002).

The UK's Foresight Mental Capital and Wellbeing Project (FMCWP) defines mental wellbeing as "a dynamic state, in which the individual is able to develop their potential, work productively and creatively, build strong and positive relationships with others, and contribute to their community" and suggests that this form of wellbeing can be enhanced "when an individual is able to fulfil their personal and social goals and achieve a sense of purpose in society" (FMCWP 2008, p. 10). The outcome of the project was the Five Ways to Wellbeing, which was

TABLE 15.2 The Aotearoa New Zealand *Five Ways to Wellbeing* toolkit (Mental Health Foundation 2018)

Five Ways	*Five Ways in action*	*Why the Five Ways work*
Connect/Me whakawhanaunga – be there for others, build strong relationships	Connect with the people around you. With family, friends, colleagues and neighbours.	Strengthening relationships with others and feeling close to and valued by others, including at work, is critical to boosting wellbeing.
Be Active/Me kori tonu – do regular physical activity that you enjoy	Go for a walk or run. Step outside. Garden. Play a game.	Being physically active, including at work, improves physical health and can improve mood and wellbeing and decrease stress, depression and anxiety.
Keep Learning/Me ako tonu – be curious and seek out new experiences	Try something new. Rediscover an old interest. Take on a new responsibility at work.	Being curious and seeking out new experiences at work and in life more generally positively stimulates the brain.
Give/Tukua – carry out acts of kindness, whether small or large	Do something nice for a teammate. Thank someone. Volunteer your time.	Carrying out acts of kindness, whether small or large, can increase happiness, life satisfaction and general sense of wellbeing.
Take Notice/Me aro tonu – appreciate the world around you	Remark on the unusual. Notice the changing seasons. Savour the moment.	Paying more attention to the present moment, to thoughts and feelings and to the world around boosts our wellbeing.

Active ageing in marching **175**

adopted and adapted by the Aotearoa New Zealand Mental Health Foundation a decade later as a toolkit for the workplace (Mental Health Foundation 2018; New Economic Foundation 2008). The Aotearoa New Zealand *Five Ways to Wellbeing* toolkit provides examples of how to achieve each of these actions, and why they work (Table 15.2).

The social connection element of active ageing (i.e., the "Connect" action in the Five Ways to Wellbeing framework) is a significant contributor to mental health. The concept of social capital offers a way to understand this contribution. Putnam (1995, p. 67) refers to it as "networks, norms, and social trust that facilitate coordination and cooperation for mutual benefit". He offers two ways in which an individual could find themselves belonging to a larger collective, having argued that social solidarity and cohesion is a consequence of social connectedness. "Bonding" can occur in situations where deep-rooted ties and strong/ lasting connections are established by likeminded, inward-looking, individual group members. "Bridging" occurs between individuals who find themselves occupying a space within a more inclusive and open network (Putnam 2000). Both types of social capital have been identified in events and sports settings and have been found to be positively associated with wellbeing (see, for example, Hassanli et al. 2020; Misener & Mason 2006; Wright 2019).

Methods

The 2019 Leisure Marching National Championships were held in Hamilton on 8–10 March, with a structured format consisting of a formal march past parade during the opening on the first day, followed by the main attraction: individual teams performing five-minute routines. The event finished late in the afternoon of the second day with a "maze march" with all teams on the stadium floor. At the completion of the event on the second night there was a highly anticipated dinner and dance where tradition dictates each team dons fancy dress according to the theme.

Participant observation and short semi-structured in-the-moment interviews were used to collect empirical material for this research. A total of 29 such conversations (individually or in groups of up to four) were conducted with participants. In order to minimise participants' disruption of the event, these informal in-the-moment interviews ranged from 2 to 15 minutes and were not recorded. Instead, immediately after the conversation, the researcher took detailed field notes about the thoughts and experiences the participants had shared, and as many quotes as possible were captured (Quinn & Wilks 2013).

A qualitative approach was the most appropriate methodological fit to address the research objective, and thematic analysis was chosen for its ability to reflect the richness of data in the findings (Braun & Clarke 2006). The fieldnotes from both the in-the-moment interviews and the participant observation were subjected to two phases of thematic analysis, using the *Five Ways to Wellbeing* framework to code the material. The notes were initially read to get a sense of the participants' response to the Leisure Marching Nationals, and the researcher's observations of the event. Repeated readings were carried out to deductively code the material according to the framework, and then inductively to develop themes within it. The two researchers worked both independently and collaboratively at different points during the analysis to ensure the credibility, dependability and confirmability of the study through investigator triangulation (Decrop 2004).

Findings and discussion

The most important benefits for the women were connection and activity, which align with the Leisure Marching creed of "Fun, Fitness and Friendship", along with learning. Each of the *Five Ways to Wellbeing* framework themes and their subthemes will now be unpacked in turn.

Connect

Two subthemes of connection were evident. First, the connection *between* the teams was important to most participants, who noted the Nationals event allowed them to connect with teams from afar who they would only see once a year:

> I know lots of people now, we don't see the South Island teams any other time of the year, so it's great to see them at Nationals. We have a great time, it's so social.
>
> *(Porirua)*

> It's such fun, catching up with friends from other teams that we hardly ever see.
>
> *(Invercargill)*

The teams' travelling uniforms (worn when not competing) also helped with this connection between teams (Olive et al. 2021), serving as a form of bridging capital (Putnam 2000). They allowed teams to recognise each other in the street or at places outside the event thus establishing a sense of membership and belonging. However, the connections that were created and maintained *within* the teams were even more significant for the women's wellbeing:

> I've never been in a team before – well, I have at work, but that's different. Here, I've got 14 girls who really care, who support me, who want to know how things are going.
>
> *(Manawatu)*

> It's a great opportunity for people who don't have a family or whatever, you know, there are a lot of lonely women out there, and this event gets them out.
>
> *(Dunedin)*

It helps us to get to know each other on a deeper level, you know, we're sharing rooms and we're up half the night yapping away. Sometimes you really just need to download stuff, and you can't talk to anyone else, but you can talk to the girls – what goes on tour stays on tour.

(Gore)

Almost all participants mentioned the importance of "the girls" and being able to really connect on a different level as a result of training for and travelling to the Nationals event. Some were able to open up and discuss things in a way they could not do with others, and this enabled them to cope better with challenges or issues in their lives – an example of deep connection that speaks of Putnam's (2000) bonding capital. Olive et al. (2021) noted the importance of this relationality in their work with indigenous marching girls in Australia. For example, the girls in the team formed strong bonds with each other and found pleasure in the collective nature of marching. For them, this also included creating the uniforms, which the women in the indigenous community engaged in as a collective practice. Indeed, Olive et al. (2021) conclude that the sisterhood that was formed as a result of marching allowed the girls to challenge colonial structures and deflect racism.

Others in our study recognised the loneliness often experienced by older women, who may be widowed and without regular contact with others, reflecting the research discussed earlier regarding older women's issues with social isolation and mental wellbeing (Community & Public Health 2020; Kvalsvig 2018; Phoenix & Orr 2013). Our participants viewed the Leisure Marching Nationals as a vehicle for overcoming that social isolation. The little-researched "invisible woman" phenomenon is the elephant in the room here: the deep connection shows women they are visible, valued and validated, which contrasts to a sense of "not existing" in the eyes of society when their hair greys, and their skin wrinkles and sags (Clarke & Griffin 2008, p. 661).

Be Active

Certainly, the participants had found an activity that they enjoyed; however, this enjoyment was more nuanced than simply "having fun". For example, although fun was mentioned, the emphasis was squarely on the benefit of the Leisure Marching Nationals in allowing the women to be active in the body they had:

They're out there with their gammy hips, wonky shoulders, crutches, and it's ok, they're having fun!

(Auckland)

There are also health benefits in the "fitness" aspect of the motto, especially after surgery or heart attacks.

(Invercargill)

178 Trudie Walters and Richard Keith Wright

These women, in their mature bodies which did not always function as well as they used to, were able to be active in a meaningful way. Being active also extended beyond the marching to the dance floor of the dinner on the final evening:

> The dance floor [at the dinner on the final night] is full right from the very first song to the last, and no-one cares what you look like!
>
> *(Gore)*

Participating in this sporting event therefore allowed the women to be active in a way they enjoyed (Phoenix & Orr 2013) and in a way that took into account both the abilities and constraints of their actively ageing bodies. Through careful choreography that still adhered to the regimented precision demanded by the very nature of marching, the Leisure Marching Nationals functioned as a liminal and liberating space, providing a safe place for the women to move in whatever way they liked or whatever way they could, without fear of judgement by others but in an atmosphere of acceptance – implying that was not the case in their everyday lives. This resonates with other studies which have identified negative stereotypes of people over the age of 50, including common aphorisms such as being "over the hill" and perceiving older people as frail and incapable of living independently (Angus & Reeve 2006; Roscigno et al. 2007). To that end, there is an element of pride evident in the above comments from these physically active participants that suggests they are happily challenging stereotypes of ageing and what is possible (Phoenix & Orr 2013).

It is important to mention here that, as noted in the introduction, leisure marching participants are less likely to live in larger urban areas than the general Aotearoa New Zealand populace. We therefore argue that the Leisure Marching Nationals event provides a valuable focal point for sustained activity for mature women, especially in regional areas where there may be fewer opportunities for active ageing.

Keep Learning

For some women leisure marching was a new sport, but many were rediscovering a sport they had participated in as children and teenagers. Learning was a large part of the benefit, with a number of women noting that learning a new routine for the Nationals event was important for keeping their brains active as well as their bodies. This finding echoes the work of Narushima et al. (2018) who found that engaging in an informal lifelong learning programme had significant benefits for the mental wellbeing of older people. These benefits were greater when the social element of participation was taken into account, and we argue that when combined with the physical element, as is the case here, participants gain further wellbeing advantages.

Additionally, although leisure marching is a non-competitive sport, each team was learning and trying to improve on their previous performance:

> It doesn't matter if you get a move wrong, no-one cares, they clap anyway! It's about being better than last time.
>
> *(Auckland)*

> Being able to come to the Nationals is the "be all and end all" – it means a lot. You practice all year for it and get to march in front of everyone else.
>
> *(Christchurch)*

Again, the benefits of attending the Nationals extended beyond the event itself:

> It's nice being able to travel to new places too, see other parts of the country.
>
> *(Gore)*

> Sometimes my husband will come, if it's somewhere we've not been before, and we'll get a car and spend a few days afterwards travelling around.
>
> *(Dunedin)*

There was a sense of learning inherent in being able to travel to new places to participate in the event, and the importance of this travel was also evident in the "Give" theme.

Give

This theme was less well demonstrated than Connection, Being Active and Learning; however, there was some evidence to suggest that giving was facilitated. For example, attendees gave of themselves while watching other teams perform – they clapped and cheered to show appreciation and acknowledgement when a team executed a move well. In addition, the Nationals are hosted by a different team each year who volunteer their time to organise the event. But perhaps the most surprising way in which the event contributed to the "Give" action of the *Five Ways to Wellbeing* framework was through travel. One team were very open about having some members who were on a fixed income (superannuation) and could not afford a holiday. The team made travelling to the event itself into a holiday by adding on a few days before/after the event each year to explore the area. Rather than highlighting the disparities, the team fundraised so that no-one was disadvantaged; those who had the financial means gave of their time, money and energy to those who did not, in an act of kindness and compassion. Without the strongly integrative social capital of companionship and community that this leisure event engenders, we argue such giving would be less likely (Rojek 2000).

Take Notice

The final theme in the *Five Ways to Wellbeing* framework was the least well supported, although there were still some ways in which it was achieved. For example, during the opening ceremony, a minute's silence was held for marchers who had passed away, thereby helping participants stop, reflect and savour the moment. Also, the Master of Ceremonies introduced each team before they began their marching display. She gave anecdotes about the teams, coaches or mentors (some obviously provided by the teams themselves but others from her own observations), and in remarking on the unusual, she enabled others to take notice.

Conclusions and recommendations

Participant-driven sports events such as the one presented within this chapter offer an opportunity for new and old friends to not only come together and establish/articulate social capital, but to also showcase the many tangible and intangible benefits of active ageing. In this chapter we explored the notion that the systematic pursuit of a distinctly Aotearoa New Zealand sport can yield positive psychosocial health and wellbeing benefits for a cohort of New Zealanders at risk of feeling isolated or disconnected as they get older. The findings reveal that some of the actively ageing "girls" who engage in the team sport of leisure marching in Aotearoa New Zealand are consciously aware of the benefits attached to their efforts. The *Five Ways to Wellbeing* provides a practical, equally pragmatic framework that focuses on the importance of engaging in regular physical activity. What differentiates this holistic framework from others available to health practitioners, however, is the emphasis on maintaining social connections, taking notice of one's surroundings, learning new skills and finding ways to give back to one's local community.

Although we are unable to offer any generalisations within this exploratory case study, we can offer some recommendations. The first focuses on the need for further research into the development and delivery of the *Five Ways* framework, including a more comprehensive and critical evaluation of potential to make a positive difference to those most at risk of feeling isolated and/or disconnected. Although there is no shortage of academic literature on the benefits of active ageing, there is still a surprising disconnect between sports and leisure scholars and the practitioners out in the "real world" (Boudiny 2013; Ranzijn 2010). With the knowledge available on leisure and social capital, there needs to be more collaboration between active ageing researchers and those operating within the public health and recreational sport sectors. The second recommendation is for advocates of the *Five Ways to Wellbeing* to further showcase and celebrate the personal stories of those actively ageing mothers and grandmothers who have chosen to give back to their local community through either volunteering at or actively participating within team-based sports competitions. In sum, there is a clear need

Active ageing in marching **181**

for more people, of all ages and any gender, to "take notice" of and, even better, "to learn" from those already actively ageing in Aotearoa New Zealand.

Note

1 This is the term that Leisure Marching New Zealand uses to refer to the women who participate in their sport (Leisure Marching New Zealand 2017a).

References

Angus, J. & Reeve, P. 2006, 'Ageism: a threat to "aging well" in the 21st century', *Journal of Applied Gerontology,* Vol. 25, no. 2, pp. 137–152, https://doi.org/10.1177/0733464805285745

Braun, V. & Clarke, V. 2006, 'Using thematic analysis in psychology', *Qualitative Research in Psychology,* Vol. 3, no. 2, pp. 77–101, https://doi.org/10.1191/1478088706qp063oa

Boudiny, K. 2013, '"Active ageing": from empty rhetoric to effective policy tool', *Ageing and Society,* Vol. 33, no. 6, pp. 1077–1098, https://doi.org/10.1017/S0144686X1200030X

Bowling, A. 2005, *Ageing well: Quality of life in old age,* Open University Press, Maidenhead.

Chrisler, J. C. 2011, 'Leaks, lumps, and lines: stigma and women's bodies', *Psychology of Women Quarterly,* Vol. 35, no. 2, pp. 202–214, https://doi.org/10.1177/0361684310397698

Clarke, L. H. & Griffin, M. 2008, 'Visible and invisible ageing: beauty work a response to ageism', *Ageing and Society,* Vol. 28, no. 5, pp. 653–674.

Clarke, A. & Warren, L. 2007, 'Hopes, fears and expectations about the future: what do older people's stories tell us about active ageing?' *Ageing & Society,* Vol. 27, no. 4, pp. 465–488.

Community and Public Health. 2020, *Mental health and illness,* viewed 10 April 2020, https://www.cph.co.nz/your-health/mental-illness/

Decrop, A. 2004, 'Trustworthiness in qualitative tourism research', in J. Phillimore & L. Goodson (eds.), *Qualitative Research in Tourism,* Routledge, London, pp. 156–169.

Environmental Health Indicators New Zealand. 2018, *Urban-rural profile,* viewed 3 February 2020, https://www.ehinz.ac.nz/indicators/population-vulnerability/urbanrural-profile/

Foresight Mental Capital and Wellbeing Project. 2008, *Final project report,* viewed 10 April 2019, https://www.gov.uk/government/publications/mental-capital-and-wellbeing-making-the-most-of-ourselves-in-the-21st-century

Fox, K. R., Stathi, A., McKenna, J. & Davis, M. G. 2007, 'Physical activity and mental well-being in older people participating in the better ageing project', *European Journal of Applied Physiology,* Vol. 100, pp. 591–602.

Hassanli, N., Walters, T. & Williamson, J. 2020, '"You feel you're not alone": how cultural festivals foster social sustainability through multiple psychological sense of community', *Journal of Sustainable Tourism,* https://doi.org/10.1080/09669582.2020.1797756

Keating, N., Swindle, J. & Fletcher, S. 2011, 'Aging in rural Canada: a retrospective and review', *Canadian Journal on Aging,* Vol. 30, no. 3, pp. 323–338.

Kvalsvig, A. 2018, *Wellbeing and mental distress in Aotearoa New Zealand: Snapshot 2016,* Health Promotion Agency, Wellington.

Leisure Marching New Zealand. 2017a, *Helping to spread the word about Leisure Marching in New Zealand,* viewed 3 February 2020, http://www.leisuremarching.org.nz/

182 Trudie Walters and Richard Keith Wright

Leisure Marching New Zealand. 2017b, *History record,* viewed 3 February 2020, http://www.leisuremarching.org.nz/history-record/

Macdonald, C. 2011, *Strong, beautiful and modern: National fitness in Britain, New Zealand, Australia and Canada, 1935–1960,* Bridget Williams Books, Wellington.

Mayhew, L. 2005, 'Active ageing in the UK – issues, barriers, policy directions', *Innovation: The European Journal of Social Science Research,* Vol. 18, no. 4, pp. 455–477.

Mental Health Foundation. 2018, *Five Ways to Wellbeing at Work Toolkit,* viewed 12 May 2020, https://www.mentalhealth.org.nz/home/our-work/items/4/

Misener, L. & Mason, D. S. 2006, 'Creating community networks: can sporting events offer meaningful sources of social capital?', *Managing Leisure,* Vol. 11, no. 1, pp. 39–56.

Narushima, M., Liu, J. & Diestelkamp, N. 2018, 'Lifelong learning in active ageing discourse: its conserving effect on wellbeing, health and vulnerability', *Ageing and Society,* Vol. 38, pp. 651–675.

New Economic Foundation. 2008, *Five ways to well-being: The evidence,* viewed 10 April 2019, https://www.gov.uk/government/publications/five-ways-to-mental-wellbeing

North, M. S. & Fiske, S. T. 2012, 'An inconvenienced youth? Ageism and its potential intergenerational roots', *Psychological Bulletin,* Vol. 138, no. 5, pp. 982–997.

Olive, R., Osmond, G. & Phillips, M. G. 2021, 'Sisterhood, pleasure and marching: indigenous women and leisure', *Annals of Leisure Research,* Vol. 24, no. 1, pp. 13–28, https://doi.org/10.1080/11745398.2019.1624181

Phoenix, C. & Orr, N. 2013, *Moving stories: Understanding the impact of physical activity on experiences and perceptions of (self) ageing,* University of Exeter Medical School, Exeter.

Putnam, R. 1995, 'Bowling alone: America's declining social capital', *Journal of Democracy,* Vol. 6, pp. 65–78.

Putnam, R. 2000, *Bowling alone: The collapse and revival of American community,* Simon & Schuster, New York.

Quinn, B. & Wilks, L. 2013, 'Festival connections: people, place and social capital', in G. Richards, M. P. de Brito & L. Wilks (eds.), *Exploring the social impacts of events,* Abingdon, Routledge, pp. 15–30.

Ranzijn, R. 2010, 'Active ageing – another way to oppress marginalized and disadvantaged elders? Aboriginal elders as a case study', *Journal of Health Psychology,* Vol. 15, no. 5, pp. 716–723.

Rojek, C. 2000, *Leisure and culture,* Macmillan Press, Basingstoke.

Roscigno, V. J., Mong, S., Byron, R. & Tester, G. 2007, 'Age discrimination, social closure and employment', *Social Forces,* Vol. 86, no. 1, pp. 313–334.

Statistics NZ. 2017, *Statistical standard for geographic areas 2018,* viewed 3 February 2020, http://archive.stats.govt.nz/methods/classifications-and-standards/classification-related-stats-standards/geographic-areas.aspx

Sweet Pie Media. 2018, *NZ Leisure Marching: Friends not trophies,* viewed 3 February 2020, https://www.youtube.com/watch?v=t3WrAw17e7s

Williams, J., Browning, V. & Macdonald, C. 1993, 'New Zealand Marching Association', in A. Else (ed.), *Women together: A history of women's organisations in New Zealand,* Department of Internal Affairs, Wellington, pp. 437–439.

World Health Organisation (WHO). 2002, *Active ageing: a policy framework,* viewed 13 May 2020, https://www.who.int/ageing/publications/active_ageing/en/

World Health Organisation (WHO). 2013, *Physical activity and older adults,* viewed 2 March 2020, https://www.who.int/dietphysicalactivity/factsheet_olderadults/en/

Wright, R. K. 2019, '"All the lonely people": embracing autoethnographic creative analytical practice at the 2017 World Masters Games', *Annals of Leisure Research,* Vol. 22, no. 3, pp. 342–361.

INDEX

Note: **Bold** page numbers refer to tables and page number followed by "n" refer to end notes.

"accessible community facilities" 11
Accident Compensation Corporation (ACC) 60
accountability 13, 26, 56, 72, 73, 75, 84
active ageing, participation: be active 177–178; findings and discussion 176–177; gave of themselves 179; keep learning 178–179; leisure marching 172–173; and mental wellbeing 173–175; methodological fit 175–176; take notice 180
Adams, Valerie 116
Adidas 21; AIG, American insurance company 25; All Black jersey 22; "Black" advertisement 23; challenges 21; corporate nationalism 22; global advertising campaign 23; long-standing relationship 22; Louis-Dreyfus, Robert 21; promotional culture 25; rugby sport 21; strategic decision 21
Adidas All Blacks 21–23
adult Māori cricket 34
African boycott 110
Afrikaner nationalism 111
age 2; ageist discrimination 173; age of disruption 134, 135; "age plus stage" rules 35
A Good Keen Man (Crump) 138
AIG (American insurance company) 25; "Diversity is Strength" 26, 27; 2005

financial fraud scandal 27; integrity and politics 27
Alderson, A. 125, 128
All Blacks 4, 7, 10, 19; AIG sponsor 25–26; corporate nationalism 21, 25–27; cultural and economic value 21, 23; emergence and transformation 19; global rugby professionalisation 19; international success 10; jersey, AIG logo placement 25; jersey sponsorship 21, 22; South Africa tour 108; *see also* Adidas
1907–1908 All Golds 112–114
alternative sports 147; concept of 148; and gender relations 152–154; and male bodies 148; sportisation of ultimate 150–152; theorising and examining 148–149; traditional Western sports 147; ultimate and parkour 149–150
amateurism 8–10, 114, 115
amateur-professional split 113
AMI stadium 14
Andrew, G. 42
Andrews, D. 121
anti-racist tolerance 110–112
anti-tour campaign 110–112
ANZ Premiership (netball) 11
Aotearoa New Zealand: bicultural foundation 53; femininity, historical overview 43–44; *Five Ways to Wellbeing* toolkit 175; government reports 87;

184 Index

"hegemonic femininity" 50; inter-racial harmony 122; mainstream sport in 61; Mental Health Foundation 171; netball and femininity 50; netball dominance 42; players and leaders in 53; rural femininity 49; women's game in 46; *see also individual entries*

artificial intelligence (AI) 138

athlete-centred coaching approaches 5, 165, 167

athlete-centred philosophy 98–99

Athlete Development Pathway 100

athletes: broader sports integrity issues 73; coach relationships 165; development 99; maltreatment 70; welfare and integrity 70, 73, 74, 76, 77

Athletes Commission in 1995 62, 74

Auckland Cricket 36; *see also* New Zealand Cricket (NZC)

Auckland Warriors 34; *see also* New Zealand Rugby (NZR)

augmented reality (AR) 138

Australia 35, 61; age plus stage rules 35; Big Bash League 34; expressions of interest 27; 2023 FIFA Women's World Cup 13; hotel toilet tryst 124; indigenous marching girls 177; professional event 127; rugby unions 9; women's game development 37

Australian Big Bash League (BBL) 34

Australian Rugby League 20

Avanti Bikes 11

balance and flexibility activities 171

"Balance is Better" philosophy 2, 100, 101

Balyi, I. 99

"Barbarian" games 28

Barker, L. 42

Barron, Jackie 26

Barrow, G. 111

Barthes, Roland 107

Baskerville, Albert 113

Bates, Suzie 38

Bayi, Flibert 109, 110

be active 177–178

Beckham, David 121

Beck, Kathryn 26

Bell, D. S. 108, 115

benchmark/targets 72, 77, 78

better people 26, 165

bicultural foundation 53

Black advertisement 23, 24

Black jerseys 22

#BlackLives-Matter 26

blame culture 75

Bless Them All song 22

"bloomers" 46

board diversity 86

Boock, Richard 31

Botham, Ian 125

Boudiny, K. 173

Boult, Trent 35, 36

brand protection 75

Brazen hero 125–127

Brighton Declaration 83

Britain: New Zealand sporting culture 8

British sporting traditions 5

broader dominant paradigm 73

business capability team 72

Canterbury brand 21

Captains television advertisement 22, 24

"carded athletes" analysis 32

Carrington, Lisa 26, 116

Cassidy, T. 2, 97

Castle, Raelene 1

Chang, I. 128

Chapple, G. 110

Chester, R. H. 111

Child Poverty Monitor 102

child protection 70

1974 Christchurch Commonwealth Games 109

Christchurch economy 14

Christchurch Sun 45

Christian faith 43

cinema industry 119

climate change 139–141

Coach Development Framework (CDF) 97, 98

coach education: in Aotearoa New Zealand 97; athletes, relationships with 163–166; coach development 97, 98; coaching programme 97; learning opportunities 98; strategic documents 97–98; talent development 98–99

Coaching Association of New Zealand (CANZ) 97

"coaching communities" concept 98

Coaching New Zealand (CNZ) 97

Coakley, J. 3, 107

Cockburn, Robyn 26

"code-hopping" propensity 122

collective configurations 121

colonial pioneer spirit 9

commercialisation 2, 4, 23, 151

commodification 14, 20–21, 28, 123, 126, 152

Index

communications 26
Community Trust of Southland 11
competitive team sport 172
complex socio-spatial relationship 44
compulsory Afrikaans tuition 108
Connell, R. 82, 84
Connew, B. 111
Consedine, R. 107
conspicuous consumption 120
constructivist grounded theory process 161
consumer demand 23
Contra these myths 107
conventional feminine dress 46
Cook Islands heritage 36
corporate: nationalism 21, 24, 25–27, 26;
    sponsorship 11, 19, 21, 74
Côté, J. 99
Cottrell, S. 74–77
COVID-19 pandemic 13, 14, 15, 28, 85, 95,
    103–104; New Zealand rugby 27–28;
    tourism industry 140
cricket: cricket league 1; and football
    organisations 86; Māori and Pasifika
    cricket 33; Māori population 32; in New
    Zealand 32; Pacific Cup 33; Pasifika
    peoples 33; whiteness domination 4; see
    also New Zealand Cricket (NZC)
Cricket Players Association (CPA) 36
Cricket World Cup 13, 126
criticism 76, 101
Crocket, H. 3, 150
Crowe, Martin 31
Crown agency 71, 96
Crump, Barry 138
culture: identity 21; misappropriation 59;
    resistance 23–25; value 120
customary rituals (Mana Māori) 55
cycling 70, 76

Daly, Kate 26
data analysis 161
data generation 161
Davis, Heath 33
Dawbin, Timothy M. 5
Dawson, Liz 26
decision-making process 58, 82, 83, 85
deliberate practice concepts 100
De Martini Ugolotti, N. 153
Derrida, J. 149, 153–155
Developmental Model of Sport
    Participation (DMSP) 99, 100
Devoy, Susan 116
différance concept 149
digital technology 137

"Diversity is Strength" advertisement 26, 27
domesticity 44, 49
dominant femininity 44, 47, 48
Douglas, Roger 8
dysfunctional system 75–76

earthquake damage 135
economic prosperity 14
effective resistance activities 171
egalitarianism 110
electric vehicles (EVs) 137
elite athletes 75, 100; rights and welf 70
Elite Athletes' Rights and Welfare (Cottrell) 74
elite netball players 48
elite sport 11, 69
emotional relations 82, 83, 89, 166
e-mountain bikes (e-MTBs) 137
English Rugby Football Union (RFU) 9,
    113
equity (Mana tangata) 55
Erueti, B. 3, 5
ethical learning 159
ethnic composition 38, 138
ethnicity 2, 81, 86, 120, 121
ethnography 160–161
European Economic Union 8
"exceptional" amateur rugby system 9

Falcous, M. 3, 107, 108, 112, 114
"Farah Palmer" Cup 28
Federation Internationale de Football
    Association (FIFA) 70, 86
"feel-good" mentality 15
female-centred sporting culture 42, 43
female leadership 5
female players 26, 37, 38, 47, 48, 152, 154
femininity 44; in Aotearoa New Zealand
    44; conventional feminine dress 46;
    heteronormativity 43; historical
    overview of 43–44; (re)producing
    femininities 45–50
2023 FIFA Women's World Cup 13
FIFA World Cup 14
2005 financial fraud scandal 27
Fisher and Paykel brand 49
FitzSimons, Peter 20
Five Ways to Wellbeing toolkit 171, **174,** 179,
    180
"flight shaming" concept 140
football 13, 15, 42, 70, 75, 84, 123
Ford, P. 99
foreign concept 43
Foucault, Michel 149, 155
"freedom" rhetorics 8

186 Index

free markets 8; ethos 7; financial
    deregulation 10; New Zealand rugby 10
"fundamentally sexist institution" 146
Future Shock (Toffler) 134

Gallaher, Dave 113
"gaming" behaviours 73
Ganga, Jean-Claude 109
gave of themselves 179
gender 2; complex reality 82; discrimination
    83; distribution 82; diversity 83, 84,
    90, 91; equality 26, 81, 91; inequity
    83, 84; policies 5; relations 152–154;
    representation 85; roles reorganisation 43;
    and (hetero)sexuality 47; sociocultural
    norms 42
Giardina, M. 121
"girl next door" appeal 49
girls: competitive team sport 172;
    emotional and moral support 162;
    high-performance team 167; maternal
    approach 163; positive experiences
    161; skills and performance 163; social
    interaction 162; symbiotic relationship
    163
girls wellbeing: coach, relationships
    with 163–166; data analysis 161;
    data generation 161; findings 161;
    methodology 160–161; participants and
    selection 161; peers, relationships with
    161–163; relationships and happiness
    160
1977 Gleneagles Agreement 110
global advertising campaign 23
global corporate brand 19
2008 Global Financial Crisis 27
globalisation 20
global/local celebrity 121, 122
global-local dilemma 20
global-local fluidity 119–122
global sporting commodity 21
global visibility 120
"glue of masculine culture in New
    Zealand" 50
Gordon, B. 46
Grainger, A. D. 121
great sport myth 3, 107
Great Walks development 138
Greenhouse Gas (GHG) emissions 139
Greive, Howard 23, 24

"haka" advertisement 22
Hancock, D. J. 99
harassment 70

Harvey, S. 159
hauora 54, 56, 57
Hawes, P. 42
"hegemonic femininity" 50
hegemonic professional model 8–11
He Oranga Poutama (Stairway to Wellbeing)
    programme 54
heteronormativity 43
heterosexuality 44
high-performance funding 73, 76
High Performance Sport New Zealand
    (HPSNZ) 37, 71, 72, 74
Hillary Commission (HC) 71, 86, 87, 91;
    multi-level coach education 97; *New
    Zealand Coaching Strategy* 97
Hingis, Martina 121
hockey 70, 85
Hockley, Debbie 37
Hokowhitu, B. 32
Hooked on Cricket programme 36
Howman, David 26
humanistic approach 166
humanistic psychology 160
human rights laws 81

ICC East Asia-Pacific region 37
"ideal" game 45
ignorance 111
inclusive leadership 26
inclusivity rhetoric 150
independence 26
Indian Premier League in 2008 126
indigenous "assimilation" 172
indigenous empowerment 53
indigenous people 43
individual engagement 134
individualism 120
informal "over 50s" requirement 173
institutional theory 70, 77, 146
international competition 107
International Netball Federation 51n2
International Olympic Committee (IOC)
    25, 70, 83, 108–109
International Rugby Football Board
    (IRFB) 9
International Society for Sport Psychology
    (ISSP) 99
International Working Group (IWG) 83
internet of things (IoT) 138
inter-racial harmony 122
"interventionist" approach 7
intolerance 111
Invercargill City Council 11
Invercargill Licensing Trust 11

Index **187**

Jackson, L. 61
Jackson, S. J. 2, 4, 121
jersey sponsorship 21, 22
Jones, Michael Sir. 26
Jordan, Michael 121
Jowett, S. 163, 168

kaitiakitanga 55, 133
"Ka mate Attribution Bill" 24
Ka Mate haka 23–25
Kavanagh, Thomas 3
Keelty, D. 97
keep learning 178–179
Kellner, D. 121
Kendall, Barbara 116
Kent, P. 123
Key, John 11
Keynesian social infrastructure 7
Keynes, John Maynard 7
key performance indicators (KPIs) 77
Kidder, J. L. 150
Kidman, L. 97
Kim, Christina 128
Kimmel, M. 148
Kirikiti tournaments 33
"kiwi bloke" masculine ideal 126
Kobayashi, Koji 3
Ko, Lydia 119, 127–129; global golf
    circuit 127; global sport media industry
    127; inclusion of immigrants 128;
    multiculturalism 128; multicultural
    narratives 128; postfeminist sensibility 127
Kopua, Casey 49
Kournikova, Anna 121

labour: gender division of 82; labour market
    33
Ladies Professional Golf Association
    (LPGA) 127
Laidlaw, Chris 20, 25
Lange, David 8
Lange expressing regret 8
Larner, W. 128
leadership 163; women in sport 87, **90**
Lefebvre, H. 44, 45
leisure marching 172–173, **173**
Lewis, Maia 33, 38
lifestyle sports 3
Light, Richard L. 2
liquid and agential celebrity 122–124
local/national sensibility 121
Lomu, Johan 121
Long Term Athlete Development (LTAD)
    model 99

Los Angeles Summer Olympic Games in
    1932 61
Louis-Dreyfus, Robert 21

manaakitanga 56, 57
mana Māori (customary rituals) 55, 56, 59,
    60, 63, 64, 65
mana motuhake (self-determination) 55, 56,
    57, 59, 60, 62, 65
mana tangata (equity) 55, 56, 58, 60, 61,
    64, 65
mana whakahāere (stewardship) 55, 58, 60,
    61, 62, 64, 65
Māori: athletes 62; cricket team 34;
    empowerment 58; girls and women 37,
    43; involvement 31; Kirikiti tournaments
    33; liberation 110; participation 58; and
    Pasifika engagement 31; philosophies
    5; provincial representative cricket
    33; rugby camps 59; rugby teams 60;
    schoolgirls' team 38; secondary school
    boys' team 36; urbanisation 33; warrior
    culture 24
Māori All Blacks (MABs) team 60
Māori clubs 32
Māori Cricket Scholarship 35
Māori Rugby 58–61
Māori Sports Awards 35
Māori wellbeing: and English versions
    53; indigenous empowerment 53;
    Māori athletes experience 63; Māori
    participation in sport 53; philosophy 57;
    Whakamaua model 59, 61
Macdonald, F. 111
MacDonald, John Hoani 61
MacLean, M. 111
Macris, L. I. 74
major female sporting code 42
male bodies 148
male rugby culture 111
Mallard, Trevor 95, 96
mana concepts 55
Man Alone (Mulgan) 138
Mana Māori 60
marae-based physical activity 54
MaraeFit Aotearoa 54
"The Marching Grans" for "exercise, fun
    and friendship" 172
Marfell, Amy 2
market *vs.* network *vs.* federation 70
Martin, A. 46
"masculine" behaviour 45
masculinities, alternative sports: alternative
    sports 147; concept of 148; and gender

188 Index

relations 152–154; and male bodies 148; "sportisation" of ultimate 150–152; theorising and examining 148–149; traditional Western sports 147; ultimate and parkour 149–150
material wealth 120
maternal approach 163
maverick individualism 125
maze march 175
McCarthy, W. 114
McCullum, Brendon 119, 125–127; 2015 Cricket World Cup 126; "extraordinary" achievements 126; fluid transnational performances 126; Indian Premier League 126; "kiwi bloke" masculine ideal 126; longevity and stability 126; maverick individualism 125; T20 cricket 126; white masculinity 125
McCully, Murray 11, 104n1
McDonald, Fiona 22
McMillan, N. A. C. 111
Mealamu, Keven 26
"mega-events" 7, 12
membership 176
Men and Masculinities journal 148
mens and womens: cricket administration 37; cricket and football organisations 86; hockey organisations 85; national bowls organisations 85; national golf organisations 85; national sports bodies 85; provincial representative cricket 33
mental and physical spaces 47
Mental Health Foundation 171, 174, 175
mental wellbeing 173–175
mercenary 123, 124
Metcalfe, Amigene 49
methodological fit 175–176
#MeToo 26
Miskimmin, Peter 76
Mitre 10 Cup (rugby) 11
moderate intensity aerobic activity 171
modernisation: integrity movement 73–76; new public management 71–73
mono-cultural environment 58
1976 Montreal Olympic Boycott 108–110
Moran, Bill 1
Mulgan, John 138
multiculturalism 128
multilateral boycott movement 109
multi-level coach education 97, 98
multi-social media campaign 27
Murdoch, Rupert 9, 20, 21
muscle-strengthening activities 171
mythscapes 3; 1907–1908 All Golds 112–114; anti-racist tolerance 110–112;

definition of 108; 1976 Montreal Olympic Boycott 108–110; rugby league suppression 112–114

Narushima, M. 178
national game 32
national golf organisations 85
National Rugby League (NRL) 123, 124
national sport organisations (NSOs) 71–74, 98; blame culture 75; dysfunctional system 75–76; female and male merging 85–86; gender inequity 81; independent reviews 83–85; leadership and administration 87; performance funding regime 75; Women and Girls strategy 91; women's programme 74
natural disasters 135–136
neoliberalism, New Zealand 3; economic model 15; groundwork for 7–8; hegemonic professional model 8–11; neoliberal mechanism 14; pro-market values 14; public–private synergies 11–12; sporting mega-events 12–15
neo-liberal policy culture 10
Nepia, George 114, 115
netball: female participation 42; and femininity 44, 50; "ideal" game 45; mental and physical spaces 47; method and theory 44–45; netball league 1; participant knowledge 44; (re)producing femininities 45–50; *vs.* rugby players 47; social acceptance 50; socio-spatial analysis 45–50; uniform 48; by women for women 42; women's participation 45
Newman, J. 108
new public management (NPM) 71–73
NewsCorp 10
News Corporation: broadcasting rights 9
New Zealand Academy of Sport 32
New Zealand All Blacks 165
New Zealand Amateur Athletics Association 110
New Zealand Association of National Sports Coaches 97
New Zealand Coaching Strategy 97, 98
New Zealand Cricket (NZC) 125; ethnic and gender diversity 31; female players 37, 38; finances and global profile 31; India, international leagues in 34; Māori involvement 31; men's domestic twenty20 competition 34; "One Cricket" project 35; twenty20 format 31; women's cricket 37; 2015 World Cup 35
New Zealand Cycle Trail 136
New Zealand Football 76

Index **189**

New Zealand Māori Rugby Board (NZMRB) 60, 65
New Zealand Olympic Committee (NZOC) 62, 65, 83, 109
New Zealand Open Day 172
New Zealand Rugby (NZR) 26, 54, 65, 121; Adidas All Blacks 21–23; AIG (American insurance company) 25; commodification 20–21; corporate nationalism 25–27; COVID-19 challenges 27–28; cultural resistance 23–25; "exceptional" amateur rugby system 9; with foreign teams 26; free market outcomes 10; hegemonic professional model 8; Ka Mate haka 23–25; middle-class southern clubs 8; professionalisation 20–21; racism and cultural misappropriation 59; sponsorship deals 20
New Zealand Rugby Football Union (NZRFU) 110, 111, 114
New Zealand Rugby League (NZRL) 112
New Zealand Rugby Union (NZRU) 9, 10, 20, 21
New Zealand's Department of Conservation 140
New Zealand Sport Foundation 71
New Zealand Sports Hall of Fame in 1995 113, 114
New Zealand Super Rugby 10, 33
New Zealand Treasury 8
New Zealand Ultimate (NZU) 151
New Zealand Woman's Weekly 49
Ngāti Toaiwi 24
non-aesthetic sport 47
non-government organisations 83
northern hemisphere clubs 10
North Harbour Rugby Union 101
NZC Strategic Plan 36
NZ Māori Rugby Board 65
NZOC Māori Advisory Committee 63
NZ Rugby Board 60
NZ Soccer board 86
NZ Women's Golf Open 86

Olive, R. 177
Olympic and Commonwealth games 12, 13, 54, 61–64
2016 Olympic Games in Rio 61
O'Meara, D. 108
"One Cricket" project 35, 36
opportunity 13, 14, 85, 99
Orangetheory stadium 14
Ordia, Abraham 109

organisational cultures 70
Origin cricket tournaments 37
Osaka stadium 26
Otago Daily Times 45
The Otago Witness 45
outdoor recreation: change and disruption 134; climate change 139–141; natural disasters 135–136; research agenda 141–142; socio-demographic change 138–139; technological innovation 136–138
outdoor summer sport 172

Pākehā education system 32
Pacific Cup 33
Packer, Kerry 9, 20
Pakeha psyche 107
Palenski, R. 109–111
Parkour NZ – Tauhōkai Aotearoa 151, 156n2
Parore, Adam 33
participants: knowledge 44; and selection 161
participation 2, 107, 120; women in sport 87, **88**
Pasifika: girls and women 37; Kirikiti tournaments 33; provincial representative cricket 33; sporting participation 33
Pasifika team 28
peers, relationships with 161–163
performance-based funding model 72, 73, 74
performance measurement systems 71, 73
PERMA model 160, 167
Petone borough council 114
physical activity 173
physical fitness 45
physical landscape 152
Pimenta, Ricardo Milheiro 2
Play, Active Recreation and Sport system 101
political accountability 13
popularisation 146
population profile 31
positive development 159
Positive Psychology 160
positive relationships 2
post-COVID-19 era 28
postfeminist sensibility 127
Potgieter, Sebastian 3
power relations 44, 82, 83, 89
Pragnell, Andrew 13
pre-game war challenge 23
Pringle, R. 3
private sector 7, 71

190 Index

"probability of success" 74
(re)producing femininities 45–50; dominant femininity 48; female body and feminine identity 46; netball mental and physical spaces 47; netball uniform 48; socio-spatial analysis 45; traditional femininity 47
production 82
professional coaching systems 9
professionalisation 4, 9, 19, 20–21
public-private enterprise 11–12, 15
public relations campaign 27
public sympathy 34
public welfare services 7
Puddle, D. 3, 150, 153
Putnam, R. 177

qualitative approach 175
quality: of participation 159; standard 72; training sessions 164
"quasi-markets" 72
Quinn, K. 114

racism 59, 110, 111
radio broadcasts introduction 9
Randell, Taine 22
Reagan, Ronald 7, 10
Recreation Opportunities Spectrum (ROS) 139
Redmond, S. 120
regional identity 9
regional sports trusts (RSTs) 71–73, 87, 101
relationships 165, 166, 167; and happiness 160
Respect and Responsibility Review (RRR) 26
Richards, T. 110
Rinehart, Robert E. 3
Robertson, Grant 13, 104n2
Robinson, Deb Dr. 26
Roche, M. 12
Rodgers, Audrey 172
Rogernomics model 3, 10, 33
Romanos, J. 109, 110
Rowe, D. 120
Rugby Championship 27–28
Rugby Institute in Palmerston North 22
rugby union 3, 8, 42; amateurism 9; broadcasting rights 10; as global media commodity 20; ideology 9; league suppression 112–114; vs. netball players 47; New Zealand television 10; professional coaching systems 9; rugby league 1, 130n1; and Rugby League 130n1

Rugby War 20
Rugby World Cup (RWC) 13, 19, 23; in 1995 20; in 2019 26; in 2021 28
rugged individualist model 8
rural femininity 49
Ryan, G. 2, 125

Salesa, Damon 34
Sam, M. P. 5, 74
Scherer, J. 2
School Sport NZ 36
selective funding model 72
self-determination (Mana motuhake) 55
Seligman, M. E. 160, 167
semiotic regime 120
Sevilla Football Club in Spain 100
sexist and homophobic behaviour 26
Shanks, Alida 2, 5
shape community investment 134
She Loves Golf programme 104
Shin-Ae Ahn 128
Shultis, J. D. 137
Silver Ferns 49
SIT Zero Fees Velodrome in Invercargill 11
skill development 36, 163
SKY network 10, 21, 49
Smith, George W. 113
Snedden, Martin 35
social-based models 7
social media platforms 137
social movements 26
social space 45
social "two degrees of separation" 70
societal values 120
socio-cultural context 159
socio-demographic change 138–139
socio-economic scale 8
socio-spatial analysis 42
Sonny Bill Williams (SBW) 122
South Africa 108–109, 110
southern hemisphere competition 10
Southern Institute of Technology 11
Southland District Council 11
Soweto uprising 108
space production 44
Spanish sports organisations 91
spatial framework 45
Spirit of the Game 149
sponsorship 22, 25
Sport and Recreation New Zealand (SPARC) 71, 72, 86, 96, 97, 99
sport celebrity: Brazen hero 125–127; Brendon McCullum 125–127; global-local fluidity 119–122; liquid and

agential celebrity 122–124; Lydia Ko 127–129; Sonny Bill Williams 122–124
sporting mega-events 12–15
sport integrity: athlete welfare 70, 73, 74, 76, 77; contemporary governance issue 70; integrity governance 77; integrity movement 73–76; NPM and modernisation 71–73; targets and modernisation 73–76
Sport Integrity Review 74, 77
"sportisation" of ultimate 150–152
Sport New Zealand (SNZ) 1, 2, 34, 35, 70, 73, 83; annual report 54; Athlete Development Pathway 100; athlete welfare 74; capable organisations 73; Diversity and Inclusion team 95; evidence-based decisions 99; high-performance sport 74; Māori wellbeing 53; neoliberalism and 8; participation and skill development 36; performance-based results 73; professionalism 11; public–private synergies 11; quality standard 72; sport development team 101; Strategic Direction 2020–2032 101, 102; Strategic Plan 2015–2020 99; *Talent Plan* 2016–2020 100; Te Tiriti principles 54; Women and Girls strategy 91
SportNZ 65
Sport on the Move report 87
sport participation 11
sport policy 2, 70, 71
sport psychology community 99
Sport Recovery Package 14
1981 Springbok tour 110
stewardship (Mana whakahāere) 55
Stewart, Graeme 35
Stock Market Crash 8
Strategic Direction 2020–2032 101, 102
Strategic Plan 2015–2020 99
Sturm, Damion 3, 4
Su'a, Murphy 33
substantive theory 161
1908 Summer Olympic Games in London 61
Summer/Winter Olympic and Paralympic Games 61, 62
Sunday News 24
Super League 9
Super rugby 28
susceptibility 70
sustainability 74
Swimming New Zealand 75
Sydney-based Canterbury Bulldogs in 2008 123
symbiotic relationship 163

symbolic equality 81, 82; Connell's four-dimensional framework 82–83; female and male merging 85–86; government reports 86–91; international context 83; national sports organisations 83–85
symbolism 82, 83, 89
"symbol of female emancipation" 50
systematic analytical framework 45
systematic professionalisation 15

Tahuhu, Lea 38
take notice 180
Talent Development Pathway (TDF) 98, 99, 100, 101
Taylor, Ross 31, 36
team environment 163
team performance 60
"*Te Ara Ranga Tira-The Rugby Way*" 58
technological innovation 136–138
television broadcast rights: Australian Rugby League 20
Te Rauparaha 24
Te Tiritio waitangi principles 54, 55, 66n3
Thatcher, Margaret 7, 10
theorising and examining 148–149
Thompson, S. M. 46
Thornton, A. 150
Thorpe, Ian 121
tikanga 55, 57, 59, 60, 62, 63, 64, 133
tipping point 71
Title IX amendment 83
Todd, Lance 113
Toffler, Alvin 134
tourism and economic benefits 13, 15, 140
traditional mass media 120
traditional Western sports 147
training deployment 71
transformational power 82, 136
transnational sport celebrity 121
transparency 73
travelling uniforms 176
Tri-Nations series 9
Turner, G. 120
twenty20 cricket 31, 36, 38
Twyford, Phil 13

UK's Foresight Mental Capital and Wellbeing Project (FMCWP) 174
UK's New Economic Foundation 171
Ulmer, Sarah 116
ultimate and parkour 149–150
unemployment 33
United Kingdom 77
United Nations 108

192 Index

United Nations' Sustainable Development Goals (UN SDGs) 139
United States 8, 45, 83, 156n1

value, women in sport 87, **89**
virtual reality (VR) 138
visibility, women in sport 87, **89**

Waka ama (canoe vessels) 55–58
Waling, A. 148
Walker, John 109, 110
Walmsley, Kerry 36
Walters, Trudie 2
Warne, Shane 125
Web 2.0 development 137
Wellbeing Budget 26, 96, 102
Wellington's Westpac Stadium 11
Whakaari/White Island eruption 135
Whakamaua framework 54, 55
Whakamaua: Māori Health Action Plan 2020–2025 54
Whakamaua model 64, 65
whakapapa (genealogy) 55
Whannel, G. 125–127
"white elephant" stadiums 13
whiteness domination 4
Wie, Michelle 128
Williams, Sonny Bill 119, 122–124
Williams, Venus 121

Williams, Yvette 116
Winning Women programme in 2002 91
women: behaviours in sport 46; cricket 37, 38; cricket administration 37; discrimination 173; feminine physical features 48; football administration 86; golf 86; gym clothes 46; "ideal" game 45; involvement in sport 87; leadership 87, **90**; leisure marching 178; netball performances 48; participation 45, 87, **88**; unambiguously 42; value 87, **89**; visibility 87, **89**
Women's Big Bash League (WBBL) 34
Women's Rugby World Cup 13
Women's World Cup in 2021 38
2015 World Cup 35
World Cup campaigns 123
World Cup victory in 2019 49
World Flying Disc Federation (WFDF) 152
World Health Organisation (WHO) 171
World Rugby Corporation (WRC) 9, 20, 26
Wright, Richard Keith 2

yoga 171
YouTube 150

Zero Fees Velodrome in Invercargill 11

Printed in the United States
by Baker & Taylor Publisher Services